What Do We Mean By Local?

Grass-Roots Journalism – Its Death And Rebirth

EDITED BY
JOHN MAIR,
NEIL FOWLER and IAN REEVES

Published 2012 by Abramis academic publishing

www.abramis.co.uk

ISBN 978 1 84549 540 4

Printed and bound in the United Kingdom

Typeset in Garamond 11pt

Abramis is an imprint of arima publishing.

arima publishing
ASK House, Northgate Avenue
Bury St Edmunds, Suffolk IP32 6BB
t: (+44) 01284 700321

www.arimapublishing.com

Contents

Acknowledgements

This is the eighth in the Arima 'hackademic' series of books started by Professor Richard Keeble and me in 2008. Most have flowed out of Coventry Conversations/BBC College of Journalism conferences. This one did, too, from an event in November 2011.

Thanks for that and this volume go to:

Professor Madeleine Atkins, the Vice Chancellor of Coventry University, who has been unstinting in her support of the Coventry Conversations over six, sometimes tough, years.

Richard Franklin of Abramis, who supports and publishes the series with great aplomb and little fuss.

David Hayward and his small team from the BBC College of Journalism.

Kevin Marsh who chairs the conferences with inimitable style.

Professor Martin Woolley of Coventry School of Art and Design for a modicum of financial support

The authors and contributors to the conference who have been unstinting in creating their work and who gave their work pro-bono (as did the editors).

My co-editors Neil Fowler and Ian Reeves have both been unstinting in the cauldron of sub-editing. Many thanks to them.

Lastly, our families who have lived the project too long.

John Mair, Oxford, March, 2012

The editors

John Mair is a senior lecturer in broadcasting at Coventry University, a visiting professor at ZUMC university in China and the University of Guyana. In a previous life he was an award winning BBC, ITV and Channel Four producer and director over thirty years. This is his tenth book. He has co-edited with Richard Lance Keeble the seven previous 'hackademic' volumes:
The Phone Hacking Scandal; Journalism on Trial (Feb 2012)
Mirage in the Desert; Reporting the Arab Spring (2nd Edition Nov 2011)
Investigative Journalism: Dead Or Alive (September 2011)
Face the Future; Tools for the Modern Media Age (April 2011.)
Afghanistan, War and Terror; Deadlines and Frontlines (September 2010)
Playing Footsie with the FTSE: The Great Crash/Financial Journalism (2009)
Do We Trust TV? (Abramis 2008)

Neil Fowler is Director of Creative and Content at Headlines Corporate News Ltd and an Associate Member of Nuffield College, Oxford, where he had been Guardian Research Fellow in 2010-11 when he researched the decline and future of regional newspapers in the UK. He began his career as a trainee reporter on the *Leicester Mercury* before becoming editor of the *Lincolnshire Echo* at the age of 29. He then edited the *Derby Evening Telegraph*, *The Journal*, Newcastle upon Tyne, and *The Western Mail*, the national newspaper of Wales, where he was also joint acting managing director for a year. He then became Publisher and Chief Executive Officer of the *Toronto Sun* in Canada before returning to the UK to edit *Which?*, the UK's biggest selling consumer magazine. He is a trustee of the Northamptonshire Theatres Trust and a member of the audit committee of Nuffield College. He was President of the Society of Editors in 1999-2000. Regional Newspaper Editor of the Year in 1994 and BT Welsh Journalist of the Year in 1999. He has contributed chapters to three books – *Face the Future: Internet Tools for the Modern Media Age* (Abramis), *Investigative Journalism: Dead or Alive?* (Abramis) and *Is There a Better Structure for News Providers? The Potential in Charitable and Trust Ownership* (Reuters Institute for the Study of Journalism).

Ian Reeves is director of learning and teaching at the University of Kent's Centre for Journalism. He is a former editor of *Press Gazette*, the weekly magazine covering news and developments throughout the journalism industry. He oversaw the magazine's move into web publishing and was responsible for developing the Student Journalism Awards, the Magazine Design and Journalism Awards, and the innovative Press Cadets project. He was also instrumental in establishing the National and Regional Newspaper Halls of Fame. He was weekly business writer of the year in 2003's Periodical Publishers Association awards, an award for which he has been nominated on three other occasions. He was nominated as weekly editor of the year in 2006 by the British Society of Magazine Editors.

In the 1990s he was editor of Central Press Features, which syndicated copy all over the world. A former engineer, he began his journalism career on magazines including *The Engineer* and *Electronics Times*. He continues to write about business and media issues for titles including the *Guardian* and *The Independent*, and has a particular interest in digital media publishing. He designed and built the Centre for Journalism's live publishing web site at www.centreforjournalism.co.uk and the Centre's unique iPad app, available from the App Store.

Preface

The future is local

Sir Ray Tindle outlines his hopes.

Many of us in local newspapers will be pleased that John Mair, Neil Fowler, and Ian Reeves are publishing this book. Perhaps such a book is long overdue. For there are about eleven hundred local newspapers in the United Kingdom but, with a few excellent exceptions, little has been written about them and little attention has been paid to them – until now.

Local newspapers carry out a vital role in this country, and many have been doing so for a hundred years or more. I have thirty papers of more than one hundred and fifty years of age and there are certainly many others around of this age and older. Of course, there are many excellent new ones as well. New and old local weeklies currently have a combined circulation of more than 17m copies with perhaps a readership of double that with new titles being launched all the time. Together with the local dailies they have a weekly circulation of more than 46m copies.

All of these numerous local newspapers are facing the same problems as every other business in this recession. Perhaps local weekly papers are, in this context, better placed than most as a direct result of being local.

Local residents will always want to take their local paper as they know that matters of concern to them and their children in their own towns or villages will be dealt with and pursued in detail. Local traders know that their customers in almost all cases live in the immediate area. Their potential sales can only be to local people in nine cases out of ten. So the local paper continues to play, and will always play, a major part in the life and trade of its town and immediate area.

The more local a newspaper is, the better paper it is for that locality, both for residents and traders. Its community news in great detail, with many names, faces and places, sets it aside from, and above, all other media for the residents of that town.

With page changing, each area within the town can regard the newspaper as its own. An edition with a front-page change for every street would be read by everyone living there. Of course we can't have that (not yet anyway!) but the nearer we get to it the better.

As this excellent book is being published, the local paper stands supreme in each locality as the prime means of communication both to residents and to potential customers of the local traders who are our advertisers.

I joined my first local weekly newspaper when I left the Army at the end of the Second World War sixty-four years ago, and I've been in local papers ever since. So I could perhaps be just a little biased! I am, however, totally convinced that the future for local papers in rosy – and the more local the paper the better that future will be.

Note on the author
Sir Ray Tindle is chairman of Tindle Newspapers, the publisher of some 200 local and very local newspapers.

Section A. Reports from the front line – the reality of life on the local

Neil Fowler

When I was interviewed for the position of Guardian Research Fellow at Nuffield College, Oxford, I asked the panel sitting in front of me how it would judge the success of my time in those illustrious surroundings. Various answers were given – but towards the end of my year I began asking the same question of myself. How would I judge the success of my time there? And it's a question I thought more about as I witnessed the ramifications of the phone hacking scandal unfold over the summer of 2011.

As a large and influential number of people who should really have known better than to make unsubstantiated comments jumped on the bandwagon, I became increasingly depressed about that was happening.

The Milly Dowler affair was a new low in journalism in this country and one that horrified all those with links to any part of the news industry – but all this act of criminality has done is to divert time, money and, most importantly, policy thinking away from the real issue facing journalism in this country – and this is the current and future funding of the provision of general news. And that is an issue that is magnified in the regional daily news sector, one of the principal areas of my research.

Of course the ethics of how we work are fundamental in any open society like ours, and is a vitally important issue, but if there isn't a news industry to be ethical about, we are somewhat missing the point.

So gradually I worked out how I would answer myself. I would judge my success of my time as Guardian Research Fellow is whether, at the end of all this, I have been able to raise the profile of this crisis in the regional sector – as crisis it is – sufficiently up the business and public policy agenda across the country to give it some meaningful hope for the future.

At the time I was not too hopeful. The political hierarchy in this country find it more fun to pontificate about Rupert Murdoch and his businesses; and as an industry the media has always found it more interesting to discuss the *Manchester Guardian* rather than the *Winsford and Middlewich Guardian*.

I'd lost count of the number of different judicial and parliamentary inquiries that were taking place in 2011 and 2012 in to phone hacking and its first cousins of privacy and injunctions, but who were looking at the real issue – not journalism itself, but the business of journalism? Precious few, I'm sorry to say.

What good is shared frustration?

A classic example of this occurred in the autumn of 2011 when the Office of Fair Trading turned down the request of the Kent Messenger Group (KMG) to be allowed to take over seven titles in its county from Northcliffe Newspapers.

The OFT maintained that the sale of the titles could mean that advertisers might end up paying higher rates if there was a newspaper monopoly in the areas of the seven publications and that therefore there ought to be a referral to the Competition Commission.

KMG, a £20m company that has seen its turnover fall by more than 45% in the last four years, felt this was somewhat expensive at an estimated cost of £750,000 – so it withdrew the offer.

The Prime Minister may well have said that he shared KMG's frustration as the deal fell apart, but that's not of much use to the industry, all those who work in it – and those in society who rely on regional and local news businesses to provide scrutiny of councils and courts where they live.

It's another example of how this government and the previous government – along with bodies such as the OFT – have completely ignored what has been happening in the industry over recent years. Worse still, the OFT appears to hold the naïve view that life for the regional sector may yet go back to where it once was.

This is typified by the Secretary of State for Culture, Music and Sport Jeremy Hunt continuing to press the case for local television – even as a way of helping struggling regional and local newspapers to survive.

Local television is a nice-to-have idea – and would have been brilliant if it had been introduced when ITV was set up in the mid 1950s – but it is just 57 years too late. Not one senior executive I spoke to over the last year saw it in any ways as a move that would genuinely help them. Another distraction in the bad times.

So how has the industry got to where it is?

Over the year at Nuffield I spoke to and received written answers to questions from many current and former executives in the industry. Analysis of the comments received shows that, sadly, this position has been coming for a long time, over many decades, with some factors being outside the control of the industry, others issues having been very much self-inflicted.

What is equally sad is that few people seemed to see what was coming along, or if they did, they chose to ignore it, perhaps feeling that nothing could knock them off their business perches.

On the edge of a precipice

I do not put myself forward as any kind of sage or prophet – but it was on December 12, 2005 that I first applied for this fellowship. Then as now that project was whether the regional press was in terminal decline and whether it had a future.

In the end I withdrew my application when I received an offer to edit Which? magazine – but a look back at my letter to the college makes for interesting reading.

In that letter I wrote that the regional press was "on the edge of a precipice." Classified advertising was haemorrhaging to the Internet, I said, and readers were going the same way.

It may have been that I was still bloodied by my experience in Canada where I had been publisher of a daily newspaper in Toronto. There, as in the rest of North America, havoc had been wreaked on the classified business by the free Internet listings site Craigslist. Great newspapers in San Francisco in particular, but also in other parts of the continent, had been brought to their knees by this start-up and no one had any idea how to deal with it.

Yet, seven days after I wrote that letter it was announced that Johnston Press, one of the country's leading regional groups that had been on a ten-year spending spree of expanding from its small family-owned Scottish base, had bought *The Scotsman* and its associated titles from the Barclay Brothers for £160m.

That made a total spend of £500m for the year, most of it funded by institutions and brokers in the City which clearly felt that the Johnston magic of producing margins in excess of 30% would carry on for years to come. The City and Johnston's senior team clearly did not see even a slight dip in the road ahead, let alone any form of precipice. They believed that what had been a most successful policy up until then – borrow, buy and pay back quickly – would be maintained.

So why could I say that the sector was on the edge of a precipice yet the City and its highly qualified analysts couldn't see it? Johnston then made record profits in the following year – so perhaps the City was right. Sadly that illusion was to be proved wrong very quickly. Earnings were maintained for a year or so – and then began dropping rapidly. Its share price at the end of 2005 was then at its all time high of £4.50. It now hovers around the six pence level.

An essential influence

Three years later, at the end of 2008, I again put in an application for the fellowship; by then, my concerns for the industry had deepened from my precipitous prediction. I said then that the UK regional newspaper industry was in crisis. It was in the jaws of an extraordinary pincer movement of structural change and economic downturn resulting in an increasing number of publications being closed and journalism jobs being lost, with potentially alarming ramifications for local democracy and the generation of news. That was the case at the end of 2008 and remains the case now.

But what hasn't changed is this sector's role in British society. It is the forerunner of all current media in the United Kingdom and whether it prospers or falls could fundamentally alter the free flow of information in this country. Its influence has been, and remains, immense. It is essential that that influence continues.

But sadly it is a business where too few people have been willing to speak out. Too little honest debate has taken place and the industry has been much for worse for it. In the industry there has been substantial internal debate about the how the business operates but little about the ethics and practice of journalism. In academia the reverse has been true.

I believe that gap has been to the detriment of both sides. Academia – and I appreciate these are very broad brush strokes – generally likes to tell the industry what life ought to be like; the industry in return generally likes to tell academia what life is really like. And the two have rarely met – especially in discussions about the business of journalism.

So over the twelve months in college I tried to see myself as a kind of bridge between the two – and hopefully Lord Nuffield, who endowed the eponymous college with the aim of bringing industry and academia closer together would approve.

I started with the assumption that society wants a thriving local press – and that if one exists then civic engagement is promoted and scrutiny of local institutions is maintained for the betterment of all. I was fortunate enough to interview both former and current leaders in the industry. Later on in this book (this introduction and my chapter are together a slightly shortened version of my Guardian Lecture that I presented at Nuffield in November 2011) is an assessment of what they have told me – some on the record, some off – and has given me the ability to take hopefully an objective view of what has happened in the past three decades or so and then come to some conclusions.

And in this section we attempt an overview from both technical and practical standpoints with both external and internal observers giving us their views of what really is happening on the playing fields of local and regional newspapers.

Jim Chisholm, one of the world's leading newspaper analysts, goes through, in his own unique style, all the figures to show exactly the state of financial play, where the industry is compared to other players in the media – and what publishers might be able to do to see their way through. His views are not all pessimistic.

Conversely Paul Marsden surveyed journalists, former journalists and aspiring journalists from the regional press and found a cocktail of anger, despair and passion – but little hope for the future of the industry.

Agnes Gulyas has looked at potential new business models while both Kevin Rafter and Tom Felle take us through the very gloomy and indebted world that is the Irish regional newspaper industry.

Those who made it happen

We then move on to those who have actually made it happen – or, indeed, are continuing to make it happen. Chris Oakley was one of the leading evening editors of his generation before helping to engineer two of the biggest regional deals of the latter years of the last century. He bet his house – but now has strong views of what has gone wrong since.

Ian Turner, editorial director of the Kent Messenger Group, talks us through the challenges of a medium sized family business while Ian Wood describes how the Manchester Evening News has gone in to continuous change and innovation in recent years as it fights to find the right formula to win the hearts, minds and revenue of its patch.

Andrew Adamson talks of how there is still room for newspaper launches in these downtrodden times – and how these new products can be successful working the Tindle way.

And finally Simon Pipe, in a Brysonesque way, brings us news from a small isle – and how even in the remotest part of what remains of the British Empire, strange media rules and laws can still cause concern.

So here is life as it really is for some. Let the story unfold.

The industry in context – and how we can rediscover it

Jim Chisholm looks behind the figures to show the true state of printed news in the UK and how it compares to the rest of the world. Along the way he ponders on where publishers have gone wrong – and where they might go right again.

If you've picked up this book, you are probably, like all of its contributors, passionate about newspapers, and British newspapers in particular. One day someone is going to remind us of what a great business we are in. We only have to rediscover it. It's interesting that among Warren Buffett's most recent acquisitions, were his largest ever acquisition, of a railroad company, and of his local paper.

In this chapter I hope to put the UK regional newspaper industry in context, provide some objective assessment of where we are, how we got here, and where the opportunities lie, before laying out a loose roadmap of where we might travel in the future. In this I adopt the script of the oncologist. First I will outline the diagnosis – not good – then the cause, then a range of prognoses.

The UK in context
Which adjective would you choose when describing the British newspaper industry? Now don't be negative or depressive. Traditional? Exciting? Progressive? Frustrated? Different? Unusual? Unique comes to mind.

We are different. So first some statistical reality

For a start, three-quarters of UK daily newspaper circulation is national as opposed to regional, compared with 38% across Western Europe. Such a large national press only exists in Japan, Austria, and South Korea. In Germany only 8% of sales are national, in France 28%, and in the USA 6%. In the UK the average daily newspaper circulation is one hundred and forty nine thousand, double the European average, five times the level in the USA, and eight times the global average. Around the world newspapers are largely about local community.

Table 1. Key newspaper trends.

	United Kingdom	Western Europe
National variance in sale over last five years	-16%	-13%
Regional variance in sale over last five years	-32%	-12%
Regional share of total daily sale	25%	61%
% of population reading a regional daily	13%	24%
Advertising revenue per copy (regional and national)	£203	$268

I know this won't help my popularity among UK publishers, but internationally there are two well known facts about UK newspaper publishers.

The first is that British newspaper circulations are among the worst performers in Europe with a decline of 20% over the last five years, compared with an average of 12%. Only Denmark with a decline of 21% is worse, caused by the most extraordinary, and failed free newspaper war. During this time UK nationals declined by 16% against a European norm of 13%, while regionals declined by 29% against a norm of 12%. So in circulation we are not doing well.

The second is that across the international news media organisations it is well known that the British are among the lowest level of attendees. Take from that what you will.

Advertising off-take

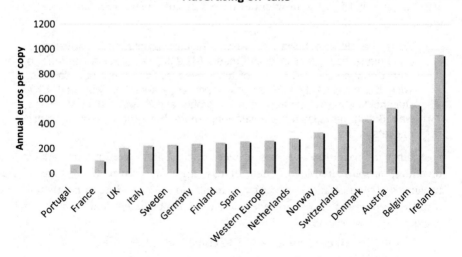

The next issue is that our revenue off-take per copy – a recognised measure of the amount of revenue generated for every copy distributed – are also low. Cover prices have suffered from the price wars of the 1990s and 2000s. In addition UK newspaper advertising revenues per copy are 26% below the European average.[1]

Having looked at dailies, it is vital also to look at regional weekly newspapers, and here the UK is extremely rich. There are more than one thousand regional non-daily titles, against one hundred and four dailies delivering 20m copies per issue, against 3m per issue for the dailies.

Of all newspaper advertising in the UK, 42% is in national press, 21% in regional dailies, and 37% in regional weeklies.

Table 2. Split of newspaper advertising revenue.

	2006	**2010**
National dailies	31%	42%
Regional dailies	28%	21%
Regional non-dailies	41%	37%

On the digital front, international comparisons are harder, given that we operate within the English-speaking world, which has advantages and disadvantages.

But here again, with notable exceptions, the picture is not encouraging. British newspapers share a global challenge in that they may attract high numbers of unique visitors, but those visitors return only occasionally, and view very few pages. There is little research as to why this is, but without increased intensity, it is hard to see how either access or advertising revenues are going to grow.

> While the UK can boast the world's highest proportion of advertising expenditure now spent in digital media (31.2%), newspapers continue to attract only around 6% to 8% of total revenues from these new sources. Take these relatively low revenues per copy together with the UK's shareholders' voracious appetites for profits and it is not difficult to see why British newspapers are suffering more than their peers in other markets.

Against a backdrop of low cover prices, and plummeting advertising revenues, accountants have been demanding large cover price hikes. But because a 10% increase in cover price results in a 4% decline in circulation, the result is an overall increase in revenue. And a 4% decline circulation results in a 3% decline in advertising.

- Of £100 of circulation only £30 come back after costs.
- Of £100 of advertising £85 come back after costs.[3]

So in fact the decision to raise cover prices results in a net decline in gross margin after costs of sales.

Taking the impact of newsprint consumption into account the figures in year one look good, but the cumulative effect of such a strategy over time, means that margin of the price-rising model very rapidly deteriorates.

Comparison of circulation variance and advertising variance

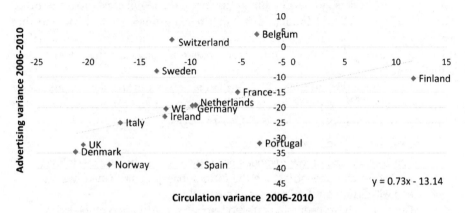

Circulation variance 2006-2010

In the UK only 18% of the total population read a local daily newspaper compared with 53% in Germany, 21% in France and nearly 70% in Norway and Switzerland.

> One casualty of our revenue to profit dichotomy is that publishers have forgotten their brands. Coke spends 17% of turnover on marketing their sugary liquid. Unilever spends 16% on promoting their ubiquitous products. Newspapers spend virtually nothing on above the line or point of sale promotion.

1 Discussion

While the British still connect with their newspapers – according to the Newspaper Society over 70% of the population read their local newspaper – regular readership is low.[5] Only 18% of the population read a regional daily on an average day. Weekly newspapers are relatively more popular, but even here readership is low compared with other markets, and three quarters of non-daily distribution is free newspapers. Of course people are increasingly turning to digital media, and this together with newspapers' ability to target highly focused pockets of communication through leafleting, means that newspapers remain a highly influential medium for society, advertisers and so many other stakeholders, in reach if not in frequency – a continuing theme.

Our challenge is not readership, but reading frequency and intensity, and digital consumption is an exaggerated version of what has happened in print.

As I've written widely, and been widely ridiculed for saying, newspapers are not losing circulation because of the Internet; sales were declining long before the Internet came along. We compete with, rather than be compatible with other aspects of people's lives. The golf course and restaurant are just as big enemies as digital media.

The big loser against the digital cacophony has been radio. Relatively speaking our cup is more than half full.

Digital media options are improving, with the advent of smartphones and tablets. Initial feedback regarding newspaper readership on tablets is that news consumers on tablets are every bit as intense and regular as those in print. Research in the USA and France shows that reading times are as high, and that prospects offered a tablet subscription are more likely to take a tablet subscription than print and retain it. A German study suggests that older people actually read faster on an iPad than on print!

A second interesting pointer is that Britain is unusual in the relative juxtapose of its national and local press, but is no different from any other country in that its people live local lives. London is a city of villages.

> The key strategic messages seem to be:
> - The combination of low revenues per copy and high profit expectations relative to other countries, are the factors that got us to where we are and will dictate our future unless we rethink;
> - Our brands have been emasculated through a cancellation of intelligent marketing;
> - News is under-represented at a local level. Among major markets our lack of local readership is extremely unusual;
> - In the digital world newspapers can have a major impact but there needs to be more scientific attention paid to audience behaviour in terms of loyalty, frequency and intensity;
>
> Much of this is that, digital news media lack the serendipity that print enjoys.

2 Solutions

So within all this where do the opportunities lie?

2.1 Daily to weekly

Many publishers are now looking at the option of converting daily titles to weekly. Of course it is easy to consider such a move a sign of weakness or resignation. However a comparison with other markets, and an examination of changing audience and advertiser behaviour suggests that a move could be a very positive strategy. Consider the following truths about newspaper customers:

- Typically a daily newspaper reader reads less than three days a week;
- While daily advertising is spread across the week, in regional press, frequent advertising is low, and a high proportion is corralled onto a particular supplement on a particular day;
- Weekly newspapers enjoy as high levels of online engagement as daily newspapers;

- There is some evidence to say that when newspapers reduce print publishing frequency online access goes up.

Couple this with some basic financial and operating points:

- Circulation on the one-day of publication goes up, so average readership of an advertisement is, in theory, higher;
- The newspaper package is larger, which can justify a higher cover-price. OK this does not make up for six days' revenues, but the net revenue per copy distributed increases dramatically;
- Operating costs in terms newsprint and distribution plummet;
- There may be a small reduction in editorial production costs, but editorial creative costs will remain the same, since the digital offering has to be improved.

The financial implications vary, both in terms of specific local circumstances and the nature of the implementation. But analyses, together with recent experience suggest both the marketing and media-term financial scenarios look very compelling.[6]

A major factor in all this has been the collapse of public sector advertising, which in some cases is thought to have accounted for up to 50% of the loss in revenues. As a media owner this must be regarded as a major loss. From a citizen's perspective, however, it can be argued that today there are more effective ways for councils, and government to communicate their messages, and some would say, propaganda. Here again a collaborative approach, where the industry comes up with joined up solutions, could regenerate revenue provide a social service, and attract reader attention, and possible digital advertising inventory.

2.2 Localness – is Britain missing out?

The first issue is that of localness, and why historically British society has so little regular local news consumption. As said above this has to be a major opportunity in terms of mobilising public opinion and social participation.

FMCG companies are desperately seeking new strategies that create a seamless linkage between their global brand market, and direct consumer contact, taking distribution, national and local retailing and increasingly digital channels, with a direct relationship, and knowledge of individual customers.

2.3 The hyperlocal opportunity

Publishers have shied away from local television without fully investigating either the strategic opportunities, or the operational capabilities that now exist. Where a camera once cost £50,000 today it costs around £2,000. Studios can be operated remotely.[7] Cloud based production systems can bring programming and scheduling costs to trivial amounts.

Mention collaboration to many publishers and sense of dread combined with a deathly silence enters the conversation. Major players in our industry have taken me aside to tell me that the competition police are out there plotting to throw us into the Tower of London, if even a mention of a joint venture or collaboration is made.

Trinity Mirror and DMGT in particular hold a unique and potent marketing ability, in that they can address global brands' needs at a national level and translate these through a range of media channels to regional, store-level, and personalised communications.

Developing a layering strategy has to be the number one point of uniqueness and opportunity in marketing today.

Such initiatives not only offer a lot of commercial opportunity in the medium term but can also be very attractive to government organisations in the immediate term, in that they may be persuaded to fund such initiatives, through either grants or returning advertising spend.

Research from the Newspaper Society shows:
- 93% of people spend over half their lives with ten miles of their home
- 92% spend more than half their expenditure within ten miles
- People welcome national advertising in their local paper believing it is more relevant.

Localness was the *fad du jour* a couple of years, ago, but undoubtedly is worth a second look. The increasing levels of granularity by interest topic, genre and location will be driving opportunities in localness.

An ever increasing emphasis on devolved power, into Britain's regions, and a realisation that in areas such as health, education and social services responsibility, must be devolved is a trend that publishers can seize, exploit and grow from. In addition there is a growing sense among wealthy entrepreneurs that they can improve their own status by giving back to the communities that made them. This also leads to some interesting opportunities, in terms of creating local digital malls, involving merchants across all the global to local spectra.

2.4 Multiple media

Local media owners must revisit their multiple media offering. But as outlined above, a number of factors bring together a major change in the market, operational and financial dynamics of multiple media publishing.
- The operating costs have plummeted;
- The concept of rotating content and video on demand, both in broadcast on in digital media are well established dramatically affecting the range of choice, cost-per-hour of production viewed or heard, and the variety of channels across which media can be distributed;
- There is a colossal demand for citizen contributions, which are just as high at a local level as they are on a global basis;
- Advertisers will support such concepts as part of their global to personal marketing strategies.

14

2.5 Returning ownership to its roots

Such initiatives may encourage local entrepreneurs to reconsider the opportunity of owning their local news medium, as Warren Buffett has done. Shareholders in major media corporates are never going to sell to one of their peers to realise the value they think they deserve – there are few further synergies to be realised and the potential for innovation is limited by obsession with immediate profitability – but they could realise more than they are likely to on their current paths by offering their local media properties back to local business people with a loyalty and empathy with the markets they know, at a realistic market price.

2.6 Collaboration

A critical industry issue is that of collaboration. Newspapers in the USA have demonstrated that by working together with operations such as Classified Ventures, they can fight back successfully and profitably against the digital pure-plays such as Monster. We must accept that print classified is dying, and that its likely future home will be on one major UK brand per category. Look at the valuations and balance sheets of US newspapers and you will see that much of their value is tied up in their collaborations.

> **Newspapers in the communications mix**
> Newspapers today account for less than 9% of media consumption time and 11% of total marketing expenditure.[8] Yet for some reason publishers are blaming a mythical competitive framework from stopping them working together. Google has around 44% of on-line advertising. Newspapers together have 7% of the digital space. Given the geographical siloing of regional publishers there is little stifling of competition but a great need to have single investments in content delivery, technology, and national sales.
> There is three times as much spent on PR – commercial and political propaganda – than is spent on journalistic reporting.

A similar argument regards pay-walls. As long as *The Times* tries to develop its paywall, and *The Guardian* refuses no one makes any money. As digital consumption shifts from fixed Internet to mobile and tablet – and this rate is only going to accelerate, so the opportunity for charging, and importantly increasing consumption intensity will increase.

It will either be owned by a new entrant or by a partnership of all major UK regional publishers.

In France publishers have been experimenting with a combined newsstand concept where all publishers offer their content through a shared portal.

Such moves here are not only essential in terms of marketing, and revenue generation, but also in terms of cost-saving through technology development.

A simple solution – in theory – is that newspapers collaborate in creating a newsstand where all papers are available, and only available through a newsstand. Within this a competitive framework is established, so one paper choose to charge nothing, while another may charge by the page, or through tiered access, or a fixed monthly fee. This way the industry has value, and the competitive framework decides winners and losers. It could also be possible for people to buy content only about say Manchester City, or the state of RBS, but from a wide range of sources, again with publishers defining their own rates.

This doesn't just protect newspapers' content, but also greatly improves the audience experience.

Such collaboration would also serve to reassert the value of newspapers in British society as well as enabling companies to rebuild their brands outside of Google News' sterile presentation.

> The players in the newspaper industry, with a shared turnover of £4bn are too small to compete with the communications behemoths such as Google, Vodafone, and Sky. Today total UK newspaper advertising is only 73% of Internet advertising. Only France has a lower ratio. Google's revenues are more than half those of the UK newspaper industry.

2.7 Better management information

I never cease to be amazed by not only how poor the level of management knowledge of how their business and market conditions are, by how executives convince themselves that everything is good.

This is not just a UK problem, but certainly UK publishers can learn a lot from best reporting practice in the following areas:

- Econometrics as part of financial planning – the classic example is how cover price increases ultimately impact on advertising revenues so much that profitability is effected, slightly initially and enormously long term.
- Another is the lack of tracking of advertiser count and behaviour. Because most publishers are content to measure revenue, yield and pagination, they fail to understand the drivers behind their revenue variances and respond to them positively.
- A third relates to tracking digital audience behaviour. Averages are very dangerous. Newspapers need to develop a far better understanding of their digital audiences visit behaviour if they are going to overcome our digital conundrum of high numbers of visitors but very low levels of engagement.

3 In conclusion

From within the UK regional newspaper industry things look particularly challenging. Comparison with countries provides a small consolation in that others are experiencing similar structural and economic challenges.

But further comparison also shows that the UK newspaper industry is unusual in its structure, and also that is a very lean industry still managing to suck good profits out unusually low revenues.

The total UK marketing and communications scene is flourishing and diversifying, particularly into digital faster than any other major market in Europe.

As is outlined above there are a number of unique opportunities to which newspapers can apply their considerable market and operational advantage.

It would not a great deal of investment in resources as intelligence for the newspaper industry's already half-full cup beginning to refill itself.

> One observes that one area of the industry that has seen significant cuts lies in the provision of marketing information and research.
>
> Not only does this harm the company's ability to prepare strong, competitive sales arguments, but it has a significant impact strategic development.

Notes

[1] UK ABC, World Press Trends

[2] Zenith Optimedia, Chisholm analysis

[3] Chisholm benchmark analyses

[4] Company annual reports

[5] UK Newspaper Society

[6] Chisholm analysis of newspaper price elasticity, and model impact on advertising

[7] Workflowers

[8] ZenithOptimedia, UK DMA

Note on the author

Based in Scotland, Jim Chisholm advises many of the world's leading news media organisations on strategy and development in business and practice. His clients include publishers, broadcasters, governments, trade associations and suppliers. He can be contacted at jim@jimchisholm.net.

Autumn leaves: the sad and fast decline of the British regional press

Paul Marsden's survey of journalists, former journalists and aspiring journalists from the regional press found a cocktail of anger, despair and passion – but little hope for the future of the industry.

The allure of working in journalism is as strong as ever. In the face of all the warnings of job insecurity, falling circulations and poor working conditions, it seems contradictory that journalism remains so popular as a choice of career. This despite sobering warnings from professionals like BBC radio presenter Andrew Edwards[1], who tells graduates that "there are more people graduating from media related courses this year than there are jobs in the whole of the British media."

The difficulty facing aspiring journalists is that employers not only want them to develop journalistic skills but add on specialist abilities on top. Bosses at Reuters and the Financial Times named the ability to speak exotic languages like Chinese, Persian, Arabic, Russian and Mandarin as key for employability[2]. There is a real possibility that the coalition government's plan to increase student fees will thin down the numbers applying for training in an increasingly insecure and low paying sector. According to data on the UCAS website, 13 out of the 28 straight Journalism BA courses being offered are charging £9,000. This provoked a storm of anger from existing journalism students who branded new expensive courses a "waste of money" and paying to study journalism at that price "reckless".

Other figures in the print industry have called for a uniformity of qualifications to avoid students choosing between taking courses accredited between the National Council for the Training of Journalists (NCTJ), Broadcast Journalism Training Council (BJTC) and Periodicals Training Council (PTC). Ponsford (2007) argues that "Both trainers and employers must find the seas of acronyms in the world of journalism training baffling…[set standards] could help minimise the sort of mistakes which bring the whole profession into disrepute."

18

However it appears having a blizzard of courses and qualifications is a situation some training bodies prefer. In the NCTJ 2009-2010 annual report the body announced plans to "diversify into new areas of journalism including the broadcast sector" (traditionally the BJTC's domain) with their new Diploma in Journalism despite Chief Executive Joanne Butcher admitting "We're conscious that we have moved from an under-supply to an over-supply of qualified new entrants."

All this evidence seems to support the viewpoint that students themselves will have to regulate journalism education throughout the next decade and beyond. For those graduates lucky enough to gain a first job, starting salaries on weekly papers were typically £10,000 at the time of the Journalism Training Forum survey, and do not appear to have risen significantly since. "Too many graduate trainees are giving up after a year or two…Teachers, nurses, policeman all have significantly higher starting salaries" (Cole, 2003: 58-59).

For those graduates unable to gain full time employment or reporters made redundant, the prognosis is potentially even worse. Freelance or short-term contracts are becoming increasingly prevalent. Research into the impact of this unstable environment indicates "an elevated risk of poor subjective health…irregular earnings force many freelancers to work long hours, to postpone vacations or even to disregard episodes of illness" (Ertel et al, 2005).

Despite 'suffering' from the same desire as the new class journalists working within the print media find the allure of the industry from beyond a bizarre spectacle. Caesar (2010) observes "just as belts are being tightened and we are attempting to map our future in the internet age, the legions of graduates keep coming…[Are they] making what the hero of Joseph O'Neill's *Netherland* calls 'a historic mistake'?"

It is clear that with such a large, willing talent pool to pick from, the corporate owners seeking to maximise profits hold all the aces. Under-pressure newspapers no longer merely keep hours long and wages low, but employ 'interns' – unpaid, often well-trained journalists to work alongside senior colleagues. "It has become a fact of life," says the deputy editor of a national broadsheet. "Interns are being used to fill the paper. If you're struggling to have enough money to fill the pages, to have a stream of bright people who are willing to work for free because they want to learn something…it has become quid pro quo." (Caesar, 2010).

All this is also making advancement to nationals doubly difficult for the hard working regional hack. Faced with competition from an increasingly 'higher class' of intern who can afford to work for national and prominent daily newspapers for free advancement is becoming extremely difficult. "Typically, what people do is they go to London and work for free, or for very little, until they get something. A very talented journalist from Newcastle who hasn't got somewhere to stay in London is not going to be able to do that." (Caesar, 2010).

Despite the gloom Jay Rosen (2011), professor of Journalism at New York University and creator of the *PressThink* blog, believes the graduates of today who succeed will have a unique opportunity to become the leaders of tomorrow as the press continues to evolve. "You have to be coming out with skills news organisations don't know they need yet. We want students to teach their employers what they don't know. One of the strange situations is that journalists previously going for a job interview were being asked about skills they already had themselves. Now it's quite likely that employers are asking for skills they don't have themselves."

My study of regional reporters

In order to further investigate the reality of working within the regional newspaper industry I conducted my own study into the views of those who have worked and continue to work within the sector.

To gain perspective on how opinions can shift over time - as evidenced by the Journalism Training Forum (2002), Williams and Franklin (2007) and Nel (2010) – I surveyed 63 existing and former regional newspaper reporters, BA Journalism graduates from 2005 and BA Journalism graduates from summer 2011 via social media and e-mail. The response rate was nearly a third (28.6%). The aim of this approach was to gain a rounded picture of the reality of being in a regional newsroom.

The view from the regional newsrooms

By far the most critical feedback came from those journalists who had solely worked in regional newspapers.

All but two of the respondents were experienced journalists who had worked in the regional newspaper industry for five years or more. One had been a reporter for between 1-3 years and another between 3-5 years. All of the respondents felt that newspapers were the most stressful media sector to work in over online, radio and television. They all also believed the regional newspaper sector had changed 'for the worse' or 'definitely for the worse' in the past five years.

"*[The] quality is getting worse and worse. Conditions for employees are getting worse and worse. This is bad for society and the industry as a whole in terms of a lack of reporting of current affairs / politics etc. The shocking level of inaccuracy also gives an inaccurate perception of events to society.*"
Respondent A, Male daily senior reporter

"*Lack of investment... means newspapers are understaffed, staff are underpaid, under trained and morale is low. Goodwill and youthful enthusiasm only last so long and do not constitute a business strategy.*"
Respondent C, Female daily senior reporter

The reasons for this were laid clear. Every reporter with daily regional experience answered they worked 'more than two hours per day' in excess of their contracted hours, staff had decreased by 'ten people or more' at their title during the last five years and that they had a 'negative' or 'very negative' view of the regional sector.

"Most newspapers are losing staff, readers and profits with no ideas about how to rectify the situation. The current economic situation is making things worse and there are few signs that things will improve in this regard. Hence decline will doubtless continue."
Respondent B, Male daily senior reporter

"Local newspapers need to major on their strengths – community engagement, campaigns, being in touch with what readers need – but don't. Papers are run by accountants who don't see the real inherent worth of the product and the people and the communities...There is no investment in people, just cutting back, and it shows in the product, the morale of those involved and the sales."
Respondent D, Female daily senior reporter

It was clear from the survey that daily reporters feel that making them produce content for a variety of platforms has led to an increasing workload due to low editorial headcounts. However it appears a pragmatic approach towards the realities of multi-platform content may be establishing itself. As Respondent B observes "[It] initially resulted in an increased workload for no more pay, but latterly the newspaper has abandoned most of the contributions made to website by reporters so the workload has gone back down again."

Respondents were also heavily critical of the attempts to resolve industrial disputes that occur between staff and management at regional newspapers. There was heavy criticism for the NUJ, with only one reporter feeling they resolve problems well 'but not often enough'.

"They were talking about securing better pay for trainees when I was reporter in 2005 and I doubt very much they've succeeded. Also they seem to have done little to protect job after job loss and newspaper closure after newspaper closure."
Andrew Price, Former weekly trainee reporter

"The NUJ is as out of touch as the management...[They] should have never let Johnston Press get away with claiming to not employ journalists – arguing local centres did that...thereby winning the battle against a proposed strike on the grounds it was effectively illegal."
Respondent D

Those surveyed who have left the industry within the last five years to pursue careers elsewhere cite low pay, long hours, cutbacks in staffing levels, excessive pressure to deliver, becoming 'disillusioned with the industry' and the promise of a promotional structure in their new job as their motivation.

Interestingly those who have left have retained a clear passion for journalism, reflecting the findings of the Journalism Training Forum (2002), Williams and Franklin (2007) and Nel (2010). All said they would 'definitely' or 'possibly' consider returning to newspaper journalism at some point. Reasons given for this include a lifelong passion for journalism, the excitement and enjoyment, the kudos of being a journalist, the opportunity to work freelance and the opportunity to be a better journalist than before.

"[I would return] if I won the lottery and could work any job I chose, without having to earn a living wage"
Respondent C

2005 BA Journalism graduates – How are they fairing?

I contacted single and joint BA Journalism 2005 graduates from the University of Central Lancashire, an NCTJ-accredited course, to investigate how their careers in journalism have developed since leaving the course.

Five out of nine respondents still considered themselves journalists, with four employed full-time in the industry. Those employed within the industry felt either 'positive' or 'very positive' about their career. Six of the respondents believed newspapers to be the most stressful journalistic sector to work in, with the remaining three selecting online.

Only one still worked in the regional newspaper sector, with three leaving it during the last six years. The overwhelming majority felt the regional newspaper sector had changed 'for the worse' or 'definitely for the worse' in the last five years. Reasons given for this were the prevalence of 'churnalism', shifting production away from local communities, the increase in free media, less staff/more redundancies and falling readership.

"The industry needs to find a reliable model for the modernisation of online platforms…the current practice of giving away the entire shop for free online, while expecting audiences to pay for print equivalents seems unsustainable."
Andy Walker, Daily newspaper reporter

"[I] saw a very promising young journo covering a council meeting. He was doing shorthand, taking pictures and filming it on his phone. A few weeks later he asked me how to get into PR."
Respondent E, Former weekly reporter turned PR consultant

From those who had worked within regional journalism there were both positive and negative reactions to being asked about how training as a multi-platform journalist had affected their role. All of them reported working 'up to two hours a day' more than their contracted hours in fulfilling their roles.

"Once my employers knew I could turn my hand to a number of tasks I was always assigned everything associated with my skills sets – therefore it was hard to manage my workload at times as expectations of me were often too high."
Gemma Stead, Former weekly reporter

"I have no complaints about my workload. For example, if I am working on a video, this is my tour of duty for that day; the print workload is relieved for that period of time. I often find myself tweeting news snippets in my spare time, but this is through instinct, rather than pressure from above to get a certain number of hits."
Andy Walker

When those who have left the regional newspaper sector were asked their motivation, their answers closely collated to those above. The main motivations were better pay, more opportunities to progress, seeking a more creative role and working conditions. It was also clear some had considerable concern about the direction corporate owners were moving the industry in and had lost faith in the NUJ's ability to affect this.

"[My] journalism role did not provide the challenges I needed, and the pay wasn't satisfactory. In fact, it was offensive."
Gemma Stead

"The NUJ is pretty useless. They don't seem to be able to do anything about the changing landscape and when push comes to shove, they don't save jobs."
Jon Phipps, Former daily journalist and sub-editor

Noticeably amongst this group of graduates there was much less of an appetite for returning to full-time journalism than those who had purely worked in regional journalism. Reasons for not considering a return included a "poor roles to applicant ratio", "no longer having the drive or desire", and more freedom in current jobs – however these were countered by respondents stating they still had the passion for the industry, believed in journalistic ideals and wanted to improve ethical standards post-Leveson. This group had more of an opinion about the number of journalists being trained than their regional counterparts but opinions were split. Some worried about a lack of jobs, falling standards and too many 'cheap trainees' but others felt there "would always be a demand" despite too many journalists being trained.

"Many untrained 'journalists' are now operating online damaging the industry's reputation. Overworked/underpaid journalists are adopting a cut and paste culture."
Respondent E

"I feel sorry for people who have trained as journalists but cannot find work in the industry, however I know a number of people who did journalism training and have gone onto other successful career paths."
Andy Walker

2011 BA Journalism graduates – What is it like as a newbie?
In order to compare these experiences with those just leaving journalism training I surveyed BA Sports Journalism graduates from the University of Huddersfield to assess how they felt about a future in journalism. From this I was able to pinpoint four respondents who could offer an insight into the journalism landscape in 2011.

Five months after graduating, three of the four graduates still considered themselves active journalists and had found some work in the industry. The two students who had been unable to secure full-time roles were understandably 'unsure' about their career fearing they were inexperienced, had unsecured roles and were struggling to find companies prepared to pay for content. Those who rated themselves as 'positive' or 'very positive' about their career had been able to find full-time employment and felt they were doing their 'dream job'.

"My degree/interest is in Sports Journalism where you will always be behind retired sportstars moving in and getting jobs"

Simon Mahon, graduate seeking full-time employment in radio

"Having learnt skills in print, internet and broadcast journalism throughout university I feel I'm in a position to combat anything thrown at me with some ability."
Daniel Samme, Newspaper reporter

Surprisingly the respondents had no overall viewpoint on the numbers of journalists being trained. It was even more surprising that one citing fears over job stability and progression was in a full-time position whereas one seeking work was more philosophical stating 'there will always be more trained journalists than jobs'.

All of the graduates considered newspapers the most stressful journalistic sector to work in. Three out of the four consider themselves 'very unlikely' to peruse a career in the industry with the one student 'very likely' to move into the industry already working for a newspaper. Reasons for not pursuing a future in regional newspapers include cutting journalists, getting 'more for less', fears over a dying brand of journalism and pressure being at an 'all time high'.

"[Regionals are] dying out, [there is] not enough money [and] not enough interest in them anymore."
Shamoon Hafez, Online journalist

"[It is] good experience on a smaller scale, builds you up for the future. [You] gain good rapport with local people [which is] useful in future."
Daniel Samme, Newspaper journalist

Is there still hope?
Before undertaking this research it was already abundantly clear to me as a former regional reporter the local newspaper sector was in huge trouble. Anyone with basic journalistic knowledge who has picked up a regional during recent years will have noticed the tell-tale signs of an industry under enormous pressure – longer articles, fewer stories, poorer picture quality, more subbing errors, fewer pages and the same bylines appearing.

I had hoped investigating viewpoints from industry experts, academics, students and most importantly the under-pressure hacks at the centre of it all may have provided some solace and light for the future. However it has sadly confirmed what I suspected when I left my full-time post in 2008 – that in their current form hundreds of regional newspapers will simply not survive the next decade.

That is not to say regional news will not survive. The reporters I have surveyed and those spoken to by Nel (2010), the Journalism Training Forum (2002) and Williams and Franklin (2007) show a clear desire to protect journalism's 'fourth estate' role and bring the latest information to the public's attention. But it is clear many of the historic regional brands will not survive the fall.

Like regional titles in the 1990s, Premiership sides have been snapped up in inflated multi-million pound deals by investors in recent years – many seeking to make capital out of fans. Ticket prices and TV rights have soared but despite this interest in football has gone from strength to strength. During the same period readers' devotion to their local newspaper has fallen away dramatically.

As Cole and Harcup (2010) establish Trinity, Johnston and Gannett invested hundreds of millions of pounds in an industry already in 'irreversible decline'. Thanks to the internet, regionals were already losing their fanbase. Corporate owners chasing their losses as advertising revenue and readership began falling off a cliff at the start of the Credit Crunch appears to have only hastened their newspapers' demise.

Long hours, the ever-present threat of redundancy, matching high output with increasingly fewer staff and 'offensive pay' are unfortunately the lot of the regional reporter. Despite retaining an enormous passion for the industry it is unsurprising that many young trained journalists quickly seek pastures new to avoid running the clock down on failing titles. As someone who aspired to deliver the news to communities it is painful to see the sector becoming reduced to a training ground for Public Relations and other better paying careers.

The disdainful attitude to regionals is also clearly filtering through to graduating students. As my study shows, those who left university in 2005 were badly burnt by the industry. These negative experiences have filtered down to such an extent that in 2011 even graduates seeking work view their local rag as the bottom of the media pile due to the huge pressures and low rewards on offer.

Unless the orderly default suggested by Fowler (2011) can be arranged it is clear we must now look to an alternative future, which hopefully may lay in print in some guise. As corporate regionals disappear there will be space for entrepreneurial projects – such as *Litchfield Live*, the community blog run by journalist and lecturer Ross Hawkes[3] – to thrive or independent owners appearing in the stead of shareholders to run regionals at more realistic profit margins.

If they do one thing is clear - there will always be a team of passionate hacks ready and waiting to run them.

References

Caeser, E (2010) *Hold the front page I want to be on it* Sunday Times, 15th May 2010.

Cole, P (2003) *Escaping from the Timewarp* British Journalism Review (Vol 14, No 1) London, Sage

Cole, P and Harcup, T (2010) *Newspaper Journalism* London, Sage

Ertel, M. Pech, E, Ullsperger, P. Von Dem Knesebeck, O and Siegrist, J (2005) *Adverse psychosocial working conditions and subjective health in freelance media workers* Work & Stress 19 (3), London, Taylor & Francis

Fowler, N (2011) *Have they got news for you? The rise, the fall and the future of regional and local newspapers in the United Kingdom* The Guardian lecture at Nuffield College. 9th November 2011.

Journalism Training Forum (2002) *Journalists at Work*. Journalism Training Forum, Publishing NTO and Skillset, London.

Nel, F. (2010). *Laid Off: What do UK Journalists Do Next?* Report published in collaboration with Journalism.co.uk, September 2010. [http://www.scribd.com/doc/37088778/Laid-Off-What-Do-Journalists-Do-Next] Accessed 20th December, 2011

Ponsford, D (2007) *Can journalism training be unified?* Press Gazette, 19th July 2007. Available at http://blogs.pressgazette.co.uk/editor/2007/07/19/can-journalism-training-be-unified/, Accessed 5th April 2011.

Rosen, Jay (2011) *Just what do we mean by local?* Coventry University conference, 9th November.

Williams, A and Franklin, B (2007) *Turning Around the Tanker. Implementing Trinity Mirror's multimedia strategy*, report for the NUJ

Notes
[1] Wake, (2010) *More media graduates than jobs in entire industry, warns BBC radio presenter* Journalism.co.uk, 24th February. Available at http://blogs.journalism.co.uk/tag/bbc-radio/, Accessed: 12th March 2011.

[2] Pg. J6-7, Press Gazette (2009) *So you want to be a Journalist? Journalism Training Supplement 2009* Press Gazette: London

[3] www.litchfieldlive.co.uk

Note on the author
Paul Marsden is a former regional newspaper reporter who currently teaches Journalism and Media students at Coventry University. Prior to this he taught at Huddersfield New College and the Grimsby Institute of Further and Higher Education. He has experience of working at several regional newspapers, primarily in Yorkshire, Lancashire and Staffordshire. His most prominent role was as South Fylde reporter at the Blackpool Gazette where he covered the capsizing of HMS Riverdance, several murder trials, helped save a swimming pool from council cutbacks and quizzed Nick Griffin at the BNP Summer conference. This chapter forms part of his MA dissertation entitled *Where did all the staff go? – A study of Journalists in the UK Regional Print Media.*

Changing business models and adaptation strategies of local newspapers

The crisis in local newspapers is a revenue problem, not a readership problem, says Dr Agnes Gulyas. She examines the strategies being adopted by publishers as they search for a way out of the darkness.

"In lots of ways when we were producing a newspaper the business was much simpler... now you're thinking about newspapers, you're thinking about websites, you're thinking about the different ways in which information can be displayed on the web. Around the corner you've got mobile...and with each one of those come a greater complexity, greater requirement to tailor the content to its environment and to make sure that you're actually delivering a service in the right way without necessarily being able to afford to put more people in to do it." (Interview, a managing director)

Despite local newspapers having a distinguished history that places them as one of the pillars of local democracies, their future has recently been questioned due to declining revenues and the collapse of traditional business models. Optimistic views describe the changes as a fundamental transformation (see, for instance, Chisholm, 2009) with a more complex business emerging.

More pessimistic opinions herald the end of local newspapers (see, for instance, Engel, 2009) with widespread title closures and entire regions being left without local newspapers. The aims of this chapter are to examine the economic crisis the local newspaper sector is currently facing and to explore what strategies and new business models companies have developed. The article uses primary data from a small scale empirical study which involved ten interviews with managing directors and editors of local media companies and two focus groups with readers.

The local newspaper sector in Britain has faced an economic crisis in recent years. Turnover of the sector as a whole dropped from £3.87 billion in 2006 to £3.1 billion in 2009 (Newspaper Society, 2010), and further declined to about £2.75 billion in 2011. The main reason for the decline was falling advertising

27

revenues which account for 70-75% of the total income. Local press advertising expenditure decreased from nearly £3 billion in 2004 to around £1.5 billion in 2011 (Newspaper Society, 2012). In 2009 alone advertising revenues dropped by 14.1% and in 2010 by 6% (Advertising Association, 2010), though the decline has recently slowed, there are no signs of recovery. The bleak financial picture means that general outlook for many local newspaper firms is unfavourable. Share prices of listed local press firms have declined steadily. 101 local papers closed down in 2009 (Fenton, 2010) and 32 went out of business in 2011 (Greenslade, 2012).

Acceleration of structural change

There are several reasons for the downward trend: economic recession, rise of online advertising and increased competition for advertising revenues from the Internet as well as changing marketing practices of advertisers. Advertising revenues of local newspapers have always been cyclical falling sharply at times of recessions. For instance, advertising expenditures in local newspapers declined by 22% during the 1974-1976 recession and by about 17% during the 1979-1981 recession (OFT, 2009). The recent recession is proving to be enduring and it has coincided with structural changes and technological developments in the sector. These changes and the recession combined intensified the impacts on organisations. As a Managing Director pointed out: "where the economic crisis has probably done us a disservice is that it has accelerated some of the structural change that would otherwise have taken place on a much more incremental basis." (Interview, a Managing Director)

The most notable feature of the structural changes, from the point of view of economics of local newspapers, has been a shift in advertising and migration of advertising revenues to the Internet. Online advertising has expanded rapidly since 2005, indeed Britain has one of the highest levels of online advertising revenues. The share of Internet in the total advertising pie increased significantly from 4 to 25% between 2004 and 2011 (IAB, 2012). The share of local newspapers in total advertising have been particularly hard hit decreasing from 20 to 11.6% between 2004 and 2009, and further declined since. The Internet has been particularly effective at capturing classified advertising spending, which accounts for over two thirds of local newspapers' advertising revenues (Oliver & Ohlbaum, 2009). In addition to the increased competition from online, marketing practices of business organisations have been changing too adding pressure on finances of local newspaper firms. The proportion of marketing expenditure spent on advertising has fallen from 70% to 30% during the last 20 years (Chisholm, 2009), while more money is spent on market research, PR, events and sales promotion. The share of local newspapers in all marketing spending in Britain has declined from 15.7% in 1988 to 6.1% in 2009 (Chisholm, 2009).

The crisis of local newspapers is seen as a *revenue* problem and not a *readership* problem. Indeed, audience demand for local news is strong (albeit declining in the long term). 70.7% of all British adults (32.9 million people) read a local newspaper every week and local media websites attract 42 million unique users each month (Newspaper Society, 2012). The underlying problem of the economic crisis is that the traditional business model of local newspapers has been undermined. The model, which had been in place since the abolition of taxes on knowledge in the mid 19th Century, relied solely on advertising revenues as the key source of income for local newspapers. The traditional business model did not only determine how companies were financed but were a deciding factor in many aspects of their operations[1]. Hence, the problems of local newspapers companies in the current economic crisis are not only financial but also deep-rooted, affecting the foundations of their business. In the midst of complex set of challenges, from the economic crisis through technological developments and changes in the relationships with their audience, local newspaper companies have had to address the basic premise of their venture and identify a new business model to adapt to the new market environment.

Local newspaper companies have responded to the demise of their traditional business model in different ways, influenced by the particular internal and external features of their organisations. However, in the interviews for this study some common elements emerged. Managing directors identified four adaptation strategies which have been applied by most firms: changes in operations, changes in organisational culture, changes in product portfolio and changes in financial models.

Changes in operations

Faced with significant decline in advertising revenues, most companies introduced cost cutting strategies including staff redundancies and restructuring. It is estimated that the local newspaper sector has lost around one in five of its estimated 12,000 journalists since the mid 2000s (Press Gazette, 2010). Companies with more than one title often introduced centralised production facilities to cut cost down and maximise advertising revenues. Managers thought that with centralised hubs their organisations could deliver efficiencies, have greater flexibility in portfolio delivery, share relevant content more easily across different products and introduce uniform standards. Strategies have also included modifications of job specifications of existing staff, new skills requirements and changes in working practices. Historically, many local titles have been weekly publications with corresponding production cycles, which had to change dramatically with online activities to a 24/7 production culture.

Restructuring has also involved outsourcing and changing operational practices of non-core business activities in response to changing value chains. Many companies now do not have printing facilities, instead they outsource printing. Another common response has been changing distribution patterns. Distribution of local newspapers is expensive due to the fragmented nature of distribution outlets. As a response to the external challenges, many local press firms have cut distribution of their titles and have developed more targeted practices. For instance, free titles are not put through people's doors any more in some places, especially in rural and semi rural areas, instead they are distributed in supermarkets or on high streets.

Changes in organisational culture

Changes in organisational culture were cited in the interviews as high on the agenda of adaptation strategies. Most local newspaper companies are incumbent and their organizational culture had been underpinned by core values such as 'focus on tradition', 'solid and reliable' (Interviews, managing directors). However, there has been a general trend to move away from these types of traditional values towards a more flexible and adaptable outlook. "We have to be fast, flexible … so that we can spot an opportunity, try it, and if it works carry on and if it doesn't then stop ... So it's a state of mind. … magazine publishers have been very good at this for a while, they'll try something and they'll launch it and they'll make money and then when it stops working they kill it. The regional press in particular has been very bad at closing things that don't work over their history. We have to learn how to do that. That's a culture shock." (Interview, a managing director) Culture shock was also mentioned in other interviews: "… a big culture shock. We are starting to move from being an oil tanker to being a speed boat, and that's the best analogy I can give you. We all have to change our traditional attitudes and we have been seen as cumbersome, inflexible, and that's not how we will survive and thrive." (Interview, a managing director)

Changes in product portfolio

A common response to the external challenges has been revisiting the companies' product portfolio, which often resulted both discontinuing some products and introducing new ones. Some local press companies have experimented with new type of print products, often specialist magazines targeted to niche audiences in their region/locality, such as regional sports, arts and events magazines. In some cases these titles are published in partnership with local businesses or community bodies, which illustrates the increased importance of alliances and strategic relationships in the new market environment.

However, it was the introduction of multi-platform approach with multimedia content that provided the greatest opportunities for widening portfolios. There has been a significant increase in the quantity of content offered online. Cross-media activities, exploiting content assets across as many platforms as possible, but especially offline and online (Kung et al, 2008: 132), provided advantages. Some firms have applied segmentation strategies, providing content and services for hyperlocal fragments. However, organisations have faced a number of problems in monetizing hyperlocal provisions because of the relatively small audience base and lack of economies of scale.

Focusing on online content as a commercial product appears to have been unsuccessful so far in turning around the economic fortunes of local newspapers. One of the central problems facing local online sites is that their audiences are small, local content is a small niche in the broader Web. The other main problem is competition. There is little evidence that the internet has expanded the number of local news outlets (Hidman, 2011) but online competition is fierce and comes from different sectors and platforms. The growing complex nature of competition is illustrated in the following quote: "We're competing with every other information and consumer choice that is out there, and that means that we're competing with Google when it comes to finding a local plumber or a local electrician, we're competing with the BBC when it comes to online journalism, we're competing with eBay when it comes to buying and selling items. That's where technology if you like in its broader sense has made the business so much more complicated." (Interview, a managing director)

Another challenge for local newspaper organisations is that local news and information is difficult to monetise online, partly because there are often issues with originality and distinctiveness of these types of content and partly because of strong resistance from audiences to pay for online content. Although there have been attempts to erect paywalls on local news sites, these were not successful and publishers such as Johnston and the Express & Star abandoned their experiments (Greenslade, 2012). The use of smart phones and tablets, however, brings new opportunities, as consumers have a greater propensity to pay for content via a mobile device. Several local press groups have introduced or are introducing apps – some free and advertising-supported, and some paid for - albeit it is too early to assess their performance and use. For most local press organizations, digital revenues have been increasing in the last years, although not at the same rate as traditional advertising revenues have been falling and digital revenues still amount to a small percentage of total revenues (Interviews, managing directors).

Changes in financial models[2]

Strategies in relation to finding new finance models vary between local press organizations, but there is a general trend towards greater diversification of revenue streams. One strategy to compensate lost revenues has been to increase prices (Interviews, managing directors). While circulations have been falling most local press firms have increased their cover prices and advertising rates. Advertising rates for local newspapers increased by 55% between 2000 and 2009 which was the largest growth for any medium in the UK during the period compared, for instance, with an 18% drop in advertising rates in television (Chisholm, 2009). Some companies have introduced hybrid financial model to maximise revenues and minimise costs for their titles (Interviews, managing directors). This means that newspapers are part-paid and part-free, the title is freely distributed in targeted – often urban – areas and paid for elsewhere. This strategy is sometimes reversed where sales are particularly strong in urban areas.

Another strategy for diversification of revenue stream has been an increased emphasis on third revenue streams (after advertising and copy sales). These new streams of revenues often play on strengths of traditional local newspapers: the power of their brand and their relationship with their audience. Examples include merchandising activities, events, travel and insurance services, education and training, or affiliate marketing where publishers get paid a commission for linking a vendor with their audience. However, a problem local newspapers have in this respect is that often they do not have enough information about their readers, which makes monetizing customers difficult (Interviews, managing directors). The UK newspaper market has a peculiar feature that only a very small number of people subscribe local newspapers from the publisher, most people buy the papers from a newsstand or get it delivered by the newsagent. This means it is difficult for local newspaper companies to collect hard consumer data of their readers, which then could be used for third revenue streams.

Conclusion

This article examined the current challenges in the local newspaper sector and explored what strategies companies have developed to adapt to the new market environment.[3] The article argued that the crisis of local newspapers is a *revenue* problem and not a *readership* problem and that the biggest challenge for local newspaper firms has been to find a new business model. Companies have introduced a number of different adaptation strategies. Many local news firms have streamlined their operations, moved towards to become more flexible organisations, diversified their portfolios putting more emphasis on online content and are attempting to diversify their financial models including third revenue streams. However, although the traditional business model has been modified, a new business model remains elusive and with that the economic future of local newspaper organisations remains uncertain.

References

Advertising Association (2010) Expenditure Report, Retrieved January 2011 from http://expenditurereport.warc.com/StandardTables.aspx

Chisholm, J. (2009) UK Newspapers the Road Forward, A discussion document on the future of the regional press, Imedia, Society of Editors Annual Conference, November 2009.

Department for Culture, Media and Sport and Department for Business, Innovation and Skills (2009) Digital Britain, Final Report. Retrieved November 2009, from http://www.culture.gov.uk/what_we_do/broadcasting/5631.aspx

Engel, M. (2009) Local papers: an obituary, British Journalism Review, 20(2): pp 55-62.

Fenton, N./Goldsmith Leverhume Research Centre (2010) Meeting the News Needs of Local Communities, Research commissioned by the Media Trust, Retrieved January 2011 from http://www.mediatrust.org/uploads/128255497549240/original.pdf

Greenslade, R. (2011) 32nd regional weekly closure of the year, The Guardian website, Greenslade Blog, Retrieved 17th January, 2012 from http://www.guardian.co.uk/media/greenslade/2011/dec/24/newspaper-closures-downturn

Greenslade, Roy (2012) Regional publisher removes paywall, The Guardian website, Greenslade Blog, retrieved 17th January, 2012 from http://www.guardian.co.uk/media/greenslade/2012/jan/19/paywalls-local-newspapers

Hidman, M. (2011) Less of the Same: The Lack of Local News on the Internet, Federal Communication Commission study, FCC PUR11000027, Retrieved 6th January 2012 from http://www.fcc.gov/document/media-ownership-study-6-revised-study

Internet Advertising Bureau (IAB) (2012) Online advertising grew..., Retrieved 25 January 2012 from: http://www.iabuk.net/news/online-advertising-grew-in-final-quarter-of-2011

Kung, L. (2008) Strategic Management in the Media, London, Sage.

Newspaper Society (2012) Local Media Facts & Figures, Retrieved January 2012, from http://www.newspapersoc.org.uk/

Office of Fair Trading (2009) Review of the local and regional media merger regime, Office of Fair Trading Report 1091, June 2009.

Oliver & Ohlbaum (2009) A macro-economic review of the UK local media sector, Report prepared for Ofcom, Retrieved June 2010 from http://stakeholders.ofcom.org.uk/binaries/research/tv-research/macroecon.pdf

Press Gazette (2010) Editor's Blog, Retrieved January 2011 from http://blogs.pressgazette.co.uk/editor/category/regional-newspapers/

Notes

[1] The exact geographical coverage of local newspapers, for instance, had been often determined on the basis of the needs of advertisers and not necessarily on the basis of interests of the audiences. As a result local newspapers tended to cover larger areas than the immediate locality of their readers because "the majority of businesses will want to reach people within a reasonable drive distance who could become customers of theirs" (Interview, a managing director).

[2] Financial model here is used as a narrower term than business model. Indeed the former is an integral element of the latter. Business model is a broader concept which "represent the relationship between the processes by which products are produced and distributed to consumers and the way in which financial returns are generated and distributed between participants in the sector" (Kung, 2008: 25).

[3] Further research needed about what influence adaptation strategies, and specifically to what extent internal organisational factors, such as organisational culture, resources and financial health determine the success of a company in an uncertain and unstable market environment.

Note on the author

Dr Agnes Gulyas is a Principal Lecturer at the Department of Media, Canterbury Christ Church University. Her general research interests are media organisations, media economics and management, local media, communities and new technologies. Her most recent research projects include neighbours online: local communities and use of Web 2.0 technologies; local media organisations and structural changes in the media industries; social media and journalism in the UK and in other European countries. For further information please see her Academia page at
http://canterbury.academia.edu/AgnesGulyas

When the "Wild West" came to the local newspaper market

The recent history of regional and local newspapers in Ireland is not a happy one, says Kevin Rafter. The future challenges are immense, he argues.

"You'd want to be an idiot not to be making money if you owned any class of regional paper" – this quote was included in an *Irish Times* analysis article on the local newspaper sector in June 1999. The individual is not named but described as an "industry source".

At that time and for some years that followed, local newspaper owners in Ireland – who were willing to sell – were offered high multiples on the earnings of their businesses. Anthony Dinan, managing director of Thomas Crosbie Holdings in June 1999 estimated that the multiples were in some cases as high as fifteen to sixteen times earnings. "In my opinion it's a good time to sell out," Dinan declared.[1] And many did. The 1990s was the "wild west" in terms of mergers and acquisitions for the Irish media sector - in particular at local level and specifically for local newspapers. This chapter traces this acquisition phase – fuelled in part by British publishers – and assesses the impact on the sector against a very changed economic situation.

Historical origins
The local – regional or provincial are substitute terms – press in Ireland grew from the mid-nineteenth century onwards on the back of increased urbanization and improved transport links. This expansion was helped by the abolition of the so-called "taxes on knowledge". Between 1853 and 1861 taxes on advertisements and on paper were repealed while stamp duty obligations were removed.

Many of these publications had their roots in the nineteenth century debates about Ireland's relationship within the United Kingdom. Historian Maire Louise Legg has pointed out that the names of many local newspapers were statements of their stance on the constitutional debate (Legg, 1999: 23). The names also signaled their local attachment. So, for example, publications with the word "constitution" in their title were primarily located in the north east of the island where there was loyalty to the existing political arrangement within the United Kingdom. These newspapers were published alongside those whose editorial stance favoured the nationalist cause with titles featuring the words "People" and "Independent". Moreover, by the end of the 1880s forty five of the one hundred and fort four local newspapers in print were openly nationalist in their editorial stance.

Whatever about their political orientation these local newspapers were businesses. But, it has been observed that the involvement of these individuals in the newspaper industry was not simply about profit: "There was a genuine recognition that ownership of the local newspaper was more likely to grant power and influence than money. By and large that influence was used benevolently, frequently to champion local causes (Dooley, 2011).

Many of these local newspapers operated as family-run enterprises passing through several generations from the late nineteenth century to the latter stages of the twentieth century. The beginnings of change was first signaled in the late 1960s when Independent Newspapers – publisher of national titles such as the *Irish Independent* and the *Evening Herald* – made its first local acquisition when purchasing the *Drogheda Independent* for some IR£40,000. The Murphy family – then in control of the company – subsequently opened talks with proprietors of several local newspapers along the Irish east coast. The *Wexford People* was acquired for €140,000 while €378,000 was required to purchase the *Kerryman*.[2] Individually these titles were small businesses but when combined they became the first blocks in the media empire Tony O'Reilly developed in subsequent decades following his purchase of Independent Newspapers in 1973.

Seamus Dooley of the National Union of Journalists has argued that a new imperative to make money replaced the relatively modest ambitions of the original owners (Dooley, 2011). But change was inevitable for many of these family-owned newspapers. A lack of ongoing investment and high cost bases left them exposed. The Commission on the Newspaper Industry back in 1996 signaled the reality of consolidation in the Irish newspaper market. The Commission's report noted that many local newspapers were vulnerable to competition from better-resourced entrants. Many of these entrants ultimately came from across the Irish Sea with ambitious debt-funded plans to cut inefficiencies and extract high profits in a rapidly expanding Irish economy.

The "Wild West"

The economic boom in Ireland from the mid-nineties onwards fueled a radical shake-up of the local newspaper sector. At this time advertising revenue was buoyant while loyal local readers underpinned strong circulation. Newspaper advertising increased from €351m in 2000 to €928m in 2004 - an increase of 164%.[3] No breakdown is available between local and national newspapers but we can be certain that local newspapers got a fair share of this advertising growth. With regard to circulation, sales were stable, and in some cases growing throughout the 1990s. There was an industry expectation of a similar circulation pattern into the future as strong national economic growth continued. This potent combination of healthy circulation figures, buoyant advertising revenues – and in some cases lucrative printing contacts – combined to catch the eye of leading suitors. And suitors, it has to be noted, who obviously believed higher profits would be taken from these local Irish newspapers through strong cost controls.

Big prices were paid by established media firms in securing – or increasing – a presence in the local newspaper market in Ireland. As mentioned the local market had previously been dominated by family owned-newspapers and the main corporate player was the former Independent Newspapers, rebranded as Independent News and Media. But now the acquisitions trail was also being burnt by the likes of Thomas Crosbie Holdings (TCH) – publisher of the *Cork Examiner* newspaper – and United Kingdom-based publishers Scottish Radio Holdings, Trinity Mirror and Johnston Press, among others.

In one of the first deals of this 'wild west' era Trinity Mirror paid £18.2m for the *Derry Journal* and its titles in Co Donegal in 1998. One report noted: "Despite its dominance of the market in the north-west, there was astonishment at the time at the price paid by (Trinity) Mirror – more than twenty times earnings."[4] Scottish Radio Holdings bought the *Leitrim Observer* – circulation 10,000 – for IR£1m in 1998 as part of an expansion strategy at local and national level and in radio and newspapers. Richard Finlay, the chief executive Scottish Radio Holdings, did not see the amount involved as excessive: "We've never knowingly overpaid for anything."[5] Some time later Finlay spoke about "sensible acquisitions". In 2000 SRH, which by then had interests in the national radio station Today FM and weekly tabloid, *Ireland on Sunday*, had a IR£1.9 bid for the Co Offaly titles, the *Midland Tribune* and the *Tullamore Tribune* rejected.

But through its purchase of the Kilkenny People group for €35.6m in mid-2000, SRH emerged as the second largest regional newspaper purchaser in the Irish Republic. The Kilkenny People group published titles including the *Kilkenny People*, the *Tipperary Star* and the *Nationalist & Munster Advertiser*. Circulation at the three papers was 43,000 copies per week. Operating margins were estimated to be 27%, showing in the words of one commentator that, "clearly there is an awful lot of money locked away in regional papers...".[6]

The leading Irish media groups and new entrants from the United Kingdom did battle over many of these titles. A 2002 report noted that, "both SRH and the Examiner [Thomas Crosbie Holdings] had been aggressively courting regional newspaper publishers and offering large sums for their companies."[7] There was strong competition when the Longford Leader Group came on the market in 2002. The sum paid – €9.1m – was fifteen times the company's profits in its previous year of trading. The newspaper with a staff of twenty was selling 13,000 copies each week.

The Leinster Leader group, which published the *Leinster Leader* in Kildare as well as the *Leinster Express* in Laois and the *Offaly Tribune*, paid £2m for the *Dundalk Democrat* in 2000. Two years later, it was reported to have paid €20m for the *Limerick Leader*. The *Tallaght Echo* was acquired for €5m in June 2005 following which the entire publishing group was put on the market

Around the same time the Scottish group Dunfermline Press (Celtic Media) paid €30.5m for the *Meath Chronicle*. The Davis family owners had some months previously failed to conclude a deal with TCH although the Cork-based published had better luck elsewhere. TCH had added the *Kingdom* to its local newspaper portfolio and in 2004 secured the *Roscommon Herald*, its ninth acquisition in eleven years. The deal was valued at between €7m and €8m. When asked to comment on the price paid, the newspaper's owner Brian Nerney remarked, "Enough for a good night out."[8]

When Scottish Media Holdings exited the Irish market in mid-2005 it sold its local newspaper interests to Johnston Press for €233m. Its chief executive said at the time that Johnston Press wanted to be more exposed to "the dynamic Irish economy."[9] And that it certainly did. In September 2005 Johnston Press paid €139m for the Leinster Leader Group and €95m for Local Press Ltd. The deal was said to have represented the highest multiple of profits paid in recent times although one other deal undoubtedly ran it close. In late 2007, Independent News and Media purchased the *Sligo Champion* for €25m – a deal which is now seen as the "last major newspaper deal".[10] The *Sligo Champion* was first published in 1836 – it had thirty four staff when the deal was done in 2007 and had a weekly circulation of 12,574 with previous years profits being at €2m. There was competition from other bidders and it was noted afterwards that, "this sale price is ahead of market expectations and makes it one of the biggest multiples paid for a regional newspaper here."[11]

All this activity in the local newspaper sector was happening in tandem with deals in the radio market. And all this activity made some people seriously wealthy. Not mentioned here are also the start-ups – the new entrants including the Media Group which launched new local papers in the midlands in 2003 – and included, ironically in light of subsequent economic developments, the Bank of Ireland among its investors.

After the party
The role of the British press in the Irish newspaper market is a longtime feature of publishing in Ireland. Many UK media groups – News International, Express Newspapers and Associated Newspapers – publish "Irish editions" of their national newspaper offerings. These titles involve varying degrees of local copy "dropped" into the national newspaper, and replacing UK content with stories produced locally.

Alongside this national involvement the past decade and a half has seen numerous well-known UK media outlets invest heavily in the Irish local newspaper sector. There are still numerous independently owned newspapers published each week in the Irish market. Many of these titles did not have the local scale to attract the interest of bigger publishers in the boom period. Nevertheless, consolidation has placed the ownership of many well-known local titles in the hands of large publishing groups including Alpha Newspaper Group, Dunfermline Press and Johnston Press.

But the investment strategy has turned sour for these new entrants. The story of the decline in Ireland's economic position since 2008 is now well known. The media sector has been badly affected. Local newspapers have not been immune to the declines suffered by national media outlets, or for that matter, local radio stations. Advertising revenues had fallen significantly as have circulation rates. To make matters worse this economic decline coincided with the structural change forced on the industry arising from the expansion of digital activity.

Local newspapers have seen dramatic circulation losses as Table 1 illustrates. Across the local sector newspaper titles have faced difficult market conditions with loses in circulation ranging from a decline of 29% at the *Bray People* to 27% at the *Drogheda Independent* to 42% at the *Munster Express*.

Table 1: Local Newspaper Circulation, 2007 - 2010 (ABC data)

2007	2008	2009	2010	10/09	10/07
475,908	456,586	425,205	399,550	-6%	-16%

The scale of the change in such a short space of time is evident with the *Tallaght Echo*. Sold in 2004 to the Leinster Leader group by its owner David Kennedy for €5m it was subsequently acquired by the Johnston Press as part of its €138m buy-out of the Leinster Leader group. But in 2009 – five years after his €5m sale – Kennedy bought the newspaper back from Johnston Press for less than €1m. But the interesting comment from Kennedy is not about the handsome return rather, "Our current ABC is just under 8,000, but when we sold the paper to Johnston, circulation was nearly 12,000."[12]

The UK publishers have been burnt badly by their entry into the local newspaper market in Ireland, and they now face significant debts – and high interest repayments – on devalued assets arising from their ambitious expansion strategies. For example, Johnston Press, which had such high hopes for its Irish operations but now suffering from a near £400m group debt, sought to off-load the thirteen titles it purchased from Scottish Media Holdings in 2008. Advertising in its Irish titles fell by 23% in 2008.[13] As the company's directors noted:

> "The recession in the Republic of Ireland continued in 2009, and this has significantly impacted revenues. Employment, property and motors were the most significantly affected categories due to high unemployment and low property and motor transactions" (Johnston Press, 2009)

When Johnston Press tried to sell the thirteen local titles in early 2009 the bids received were insufficiently high and the sale was halted.[14] One report estimated that the likely price achieved from the sale – €40m – would be a mere 16% of what Johnston Press had paid for the newspapers only three years previously.[15]

Conclusion

Through aggressive cost control measures publishers such as Independent News and Media have managed to keep their titles profitable. But budget reductions impact on editorial quality – fewer reporters covering local courts and council meetings, fewer FOI requests, greater reliance on "free" copy. Readers do notice, and they ultimately cast judgement by declining to purchase. Moreover, local newspapers face an aging readership; continued competition from free local newspapers and all of this is before considering the 'disruptive change' from the Internet.

In the United Kingdom Ofcom has suggested that the growth in Internet use as the main source of local news has, to some extent, been at the expense of other media. The data suggests that 25% of those accessing local newspaper websites say that they do so instead of reading the print edition (House of Commons, 2010:59). The challenges faced by the debt-laden publishers of local newspapers in Ireland are enormous and these will not abate when the Irish economy eventually emerges from recession. The challenge for Irish society in losing – as seems inevitable – many of these "great instruments of power" – will, however, be more wide ranging and ultimately more serious (Legg, 199: 175).

References

Dooley, Seamus (2011) Only investment in news can save regional newspapers. Paper delivered at Crisis in Ireland's regional newspaper industry conference, University of Limerick, 1 December.

House of Commons Culture, Media and Sport Committee (April 2010). *Future of local and regional media.* Fourth Report of Session 2009-10. Volume I.

Johnston Press Ireland, Director's Report, 2009.

Legg, Maire Louise (1999) *Newspapers and Nationalism The Irish Provincial Press 1850-1892.* Dublin: Four Courts Press.

Notes

[1] Irish Times, 11 June 1999

[2] I am grateful to Professor John Horgan for this information.

[3] Irish Times, 24 June 2005

[4] Irish Times, 24 June 2000

[5] Irish Times, 11 June 1999

[6] Irish Times, 30 June 2000

[7] Irish Times, 12 February 2002

[8] Irish Times, 24 March 2004

[9] Irish Times, 22 June 2005

[10] Irish Times, 13 June 2008

[11] Irish Times, 19 December 2007

[12] Irish Times, 28 January 2010

[13] Irish Times, 12 March 2009

[14] Irish Times, 14 May 2009

[15] Irish Times, 2 April 2009

Note on the author

Dr. Kevin Rafter is a senior lecturer in political communication and journalism at Dublin City University. He worked for many years as a political journalist with the *Irish Times*, the *Sunday Times* and the *Sunday Tribune* as well as with RTÉ, the Irish national broadcaster. He has published widely on media and politics. He is the author of eight books and is the editor of *Irish Journalism before independence: More a disease than a profession* (Manchester University Press, 2011).

From boom to bust: Irish local newspapers post the Celtic Tiger

Tom Felle says that the search for new routes to profitability is continuing – but a solution is yet to be found.

Irish regional newspapers enjoyed never-before-seen profits during the Celtic Tiger boom years up until 2007 as advertising revenues, driven largely by property advertising, fuelled a newspaper profit bonanza. However the economic recession in the latter half of the 2000s caused newspaper revenues to collapse, and with it circulation and readership.

While most local newspapers remain profitable, circulation and readership continue to decline. Like the UK, owners failed to invest in the future during the boom and none have coherent online strategies now. Local journalism itself is under threat as jobs in local newspapers evaporate. The consequences for local communities are profound - less local news will be reported, few courts will be covered, and local government will not be scrutinised. Local newspapers will to struggle for relevance, and eventually for survival.

Boom...

To fully understand what happened in Ireland's economy post 2007, and to understand how it happened so quickly, it must be understood that the Irish economy was a runaway success story across the world for much of the 2000s. A small, English speaking, highly educated and open economy on the edge of Europe turned itself around from a basket case with high unemployment and mass emigration in the late 1980s to GDP growth of on average 6% per year between 1995 and 2007, and unemployment was virtually eliminated (Central Intelligence Agency, 2012). The Good Friday Agreement, which led to lasting peace on the island of Ireland, the introduction of the Euro, low corporate and personal taxes, a light touch regulatory regime and global economic growth all helped, but it was the decisions made by the Irish government to stimulate growth through generous tax concessions on property development that underlined much of the early successes.

41

By the mid-2000s the Irish government, it appeared, had the Midas touch, and newspapers were cashing in. Many of the normal rules of business were simply ignored as profits from advertising revenues rolled in, driven mainly by property, and to a lesser extent cars and jobs. Local newspapers bulged with property supplements, and owners expanded with new titles and supplements, bigger staffs and better offices. Record prices were paid for newspaper titles as groups sought to buy up the market. The prices were high, but banks were keen to lend and mortgages would be easily serviceable so long as advertising continued to grow.

...to bust

The problem was much of the Irish economic success story was a Ponzi scheme, based on a property bubble fuelled by government incentives and cheap credit from banks (O'Toole, 2009).[1] Once the boom ended in 2007, the property market ground to a shuddering halt and with it the rest of the economy. Property prices in the Irish capital Dublin increased by 519% between 1994 and 2007 (Foley, 2010). Since 2007, property prices have more than halved and consumer spending has remained sluggish (O'Brien, 2012). The implications for local (as well as national) newspapers from all of this were profound. Property advertising didn't stop overnight but it slowed dramatically. With it went consumer confidence, and the advertising revenues that had driven the profits of local weeklies simply disappeared.

Circulation tsunami

Irish regional newspaper circulation remained relatively static during the boom years, despite a 16% increase in the population between 1996 and 2006 (Central Statistics Office, 2011). In fact, if a direct comparison is made between circulation and population growth, circulation per capita actually declined in real terms between 1996 and 2006. Much of the population growth can be attributed to the influx of emigrants into the country following EU accession of former eastern bloc countries in 2004. According to the 2006 Irish census, one in ten then living in Ireland were non-nationals (Central Statistics Office, 2006). Local newspapers, it is argued, failed to capitalise on potential new readers by introducing speciality editions to new emigrant populations.

Local newspapers were also failing to attract new and younger readers, most catering instead for an aging market with the tried and trusted staple of local news and sports. While Ireland had changed dramatically in the previous ten years, local newspapers, apart from the mass availability of colour, looked remarkably similar in terms of content. Editors, presumably, were happy with static or small changes up or down in circulation, on the basis that the advertising revenues continued to grow.

The successes of the local newspaper market were intrinsically linked to the success of the Irish economy in the period from 2000 to 2006/07. Newspaper executives did not re-invent the rules of economics, they were living a boom and simply cashed in. Like the Irish government, however, newspaper executives convinced themselves that their newspapers were different. The circulation slumps, the title closures, the advertising plunge that hit the US in the early 2000s and the UK post 2005 would simply never happen in Ireland because Irish people loved their local (and national) newspapers too much. Indeed, for a long time, that appeared to be true.

So when the circulation tsunami did eventually hit Ireland in 2007, it was all the more unexpected. In the four years between 2007 and 2011, audited circulation of Irish weekly regional newspapers dropped by more than a quarter. Among the biggest individual drops in sales were the Johnston Press owned *Leinster Leader* and *Limerick Leader*, down 43% and 28% respectively between January-June 2008 and January-June 2011. The Independent News and Media-owned *Fingal Independent*, a Dublin suburban weekly, sold just 3,319 papers weekly according to its audited figures for January to June 2011, down almost 40% on the same period in 2008. The Galway city-based *Connacht Tribune*, of the few independently owned titles left, dropped 14% between 2008 and 2011, but remained the country's largest selling weekly with 21,000 sales.

Nationally, total audited sales of paid-for Irish weekly newspapers dropped from 431,142 to 330,436, a drop of 23% (Audited Bureau of Circulation, 2007-2011)[2]. Almost immediately a large number of weekly free sheet titles in towns around the country that had set up and traded successfully on a simple economic model of advertising and editorial during the boom years disappeared. Most had no audited figures and none had any brand value or intrinsic community loyalty. The survivors were the long-established paid-for titles, and a handful of long-standing free sheets.

Readership figures for local weeklies make for even more troubled reading because advertising buyers have traditionally kept a much closer eye on readership than on circulation, as it is considered a better measure of impact. In 2003/04, some 75% of Irish adults over fifteen said they read a weekly local, outside of Dublin and Cork cities, according to the Joint National Readership Survey for Ireland. In 2010/11, that figure had dropped to 57.1%, a slide of eighteen percentage points in just seven years, and most of that since 2007 (JNRS, 2003-2011)[3].

The main players
As of 2011, the Irish regional market now has fifty four paid-for and seven free sheets titles that are audited by the ABC (Goodfellow, 2011). Years of Celtic Tiger consolidation saw many titles, held in family ownership for generations, transfer to media groups. Apart from a few independently owned and operated newspapers, the majority of titles in the Irish republic are now owned by five main media groups – Johnston Press, Independent News and Media, Thomas Crosbie Holdings and two smaller operators, Alpha and Celtic Media. *The Irish Times* owns a small stable of Gazette newspapers operating in Dublin suburbs. All are carrying debts, have seen circulation and advertising slumps, and some have already closed titles to try to survive.

Alpha, owned by former Unionist MP John Taylor (now Baron Kilclooney), owns a number of titles in the republic including the *Midland Tribune* and *Tullamore Tribune*. It closed the *Roscommon Champion* and *Longford News* in 2010. The *Champion* had been published for eighty three years in Roscommon, while the *Longford News* was more than fifty years old. Alpha blamed the economic downturn on its decision. Before the closures protests were held outside the offices of both papers by local sporting organisations and community groups, angry at the loss of their local paper (RTE, 2010). The *Athlone Voice*, which was a new Celtic Tiger era paper bought up by Alpha in 2005, also closed. The group had reportedly spent €14.5m buying up titles in the midlands of the Republic in the early 2000s (McCaughren, 2006).

Celtic Media is a small, but significant player in the regional newspaper market in the Irish republic with titles including the *Anglo Celt*, *Offaly* and *Westmeath Independents*, and the *Meath Chronicle*. The company reported significant cuts to its operations, including staff reductions, in its 2009 accounts, the latest available. It recorded a €246,000 profit in 2009, compared with a €1.4m loss the previous year. The group's managing director and former INM journalist Frank Mulrennan has recently begun an editorial outsourcing operation at its Mullingar HQ, and is handling sub-editing and pre-press for a number of smaller titles (Flanagan, 2011).

Thomas Crosbie Holdings, the Cork-based, fifth-generation Crosbie family-owned company, publishes a dozen local weeklies in the Irish republic including the *Nationalist* group in the east midlands, the *Western People* and *Roscommon Herald* in the west of Ireland, the *Waterford News and Star* and *Wexford Echo* group in the south east, as well as its flagship national daily *Irish Examiner*, and weekly politics and economics specialist *Sunday Business Post*.

It expanded greatly during the boom but has seen its profits nosedive since 2007. In 2009 the company wrote down the value of its media brands by €30m, and posted a €6.3m loss in 2010. Journalists and other staff have seen substantial cuts to pay and pensions (Slattery, 2011a). In 2011 the company closed the *Kingdom* newspaper in Co Kerry (Slattery, 2011b) as well as its London-based *Irish Post* emigrant newspaper due to falling sales and advertising revenues. The *Irish Post* was subsequently sold and re-launched following an outcry from Irish emigrants in the UK (Hennessy, 2011a), as well as a Commons campaign lead by Welsh Labour MP Chris Ruane (Hennessy, 2011b).

Sir Anthony O'Reilly's Independent News and Media plc, former owners of the *The Independent* before its 2010 sale to Russian billionaire Alexander Lebedev for £1 (BBC News Online, 2010) has fared slightly better. INM owns fourteen regional titles, the best known of which is the southwest-based *Kerryman* group. Their Irish regional titles remain profitable, despite falling advertising revenues and circulation declines, mainly through cost cutting and being "anal" about their cost base (Webb, 2011).

The parent INM has substantial debts, owing more than €400m (Reddan, 2011). In December 2011 the company announced a further round of pay cuts for senior executives. In interim results for 2011, INM reported that advertising revenues fell by 7.3% across the group, with Ireland faring worst, dropping by 11.1%. Circulation was 2.1% lower at group level and by 3.3% in Ireland. CEO Gavin O'Reilly commented that it was "probably some of the toughest conditions we've ever seen in Ireland" for the newspaper industry (ibid, 2011). In mid-February, 2012, INM announced it was de-registering 12 of its Irish regional titles from the Audit Bureau of Circulation, claiming it was "too expensive" (Greenslade, 2012).

Johnston's folly
It is Johnston Press's Irish story that is most spectacular however. At the very end of the Irish boom in 2007, the Edinburgh-based media company boasted growth in ad revenues of 7.5% in Ireland for their 2006 fiscal year, despite a slump of 13% the same year in the UK. Its Irish success story was built largely on the back of acquisitions of titles, including a reported €140m paid for the *Leinster Leader* group just two years previously, racking up significant debts in doing so. (Noonan, 2007a)

By 2007 Johnston had eleven paid-for titles and ten free sheets published weekly in Ireland. The company's then chief executive Tim Bowdler described its Irish operations as the "star performer", and the company announced plans for new "lifestyle magazines and niche products" in Ireland (ibid). It was a steep rise to success.

When it came, however, the fall was just as steep. Just six months later, in August 2007, Johnston announced a significant drop in Irish advertising revenue. Bowdler was still predicting growth in Ireland, but "not by the same margin" (Noonan, 2007b). Two years later, in 2009, the company announced it was reviewing its entire Irish operation. The *Irish Independent* reported the company planned to sell its Irish titles, however bids for the portfolio of newspapers were not sufficiently high enough. The paper speculated Johnston has spent more than €250m building its Irish empire, while offers to buy the portfolio were less than half the €70m hoped for (Noonan, 2009).

Days later the company, in an interim management statement, confirmed that its efforts to sell its Irish titles were unsuccessful (Johnston Press, 2009). The Irish state broadcaster Radio Teilifís Éireann (RTE) reported Johnston later sold a Co Dublin local weekly, the *Tallaght Echo* back to its former owner for reportedly less than €1m. He had sold the title to the *Leinster Leader* Group, later bought out by Johnston, for €5m in 2005 (RTE News Online, 2010). The same year the company introduced drastic cost-cutting measures including retrenching its sub-editors across many of its Irish titles. In November that year, it closed its *Limerick Leader* printing press with the loss of thirty jobs and centralised its entire Irish printing operation in Northern Ireland (Johnston Press, 2010). The company reported a 29% drop in newspaper advertising revenue in its Irish operations in the first six months of 2010, though that decline had improved somewhat (18.2%) in the same period in 2011. In its latest published interim results, it describes the economic environment in Ireland as "challenging" (Johnston Press, 2011).

Consequences

In the rush to cut costs since 2007, it is local journalism that has suffered most. The consequences of the demise of local newspapers in Ireland are actually quite profound. Local newspapers in Ireland have been, it can be argued, an integral part of local communities for generations. Papers record births, family occasions, local sporting achievements, weddings, birthdays, retirements and obituaries. They have an implicit public service remit, and central role in local democracy, reporting on local politics as well as investigating potential wrongdoing. Felle and Adshead (2009) describe journalists as professional citizens and a watchdog on democracy, while O'Reilly (2009) said they "keep government honest". These attributes are arguably even more important at local level where there is little plurality of media, and less intensive scrutiny of public affairs.

The implications for journalists are also severe. There have already been considerable job losses in Ireland; in the main sub-editors have been outsourced. In the future there will be fewer opportunities for young journalists to get a start in the profession. For those that do remain, pay and conditions are likely to reduce even further. The National Union of Journalists' Irish Secretary Seamus Dooley (2011) revealed that reporters in local newspapers were leaving jobs because they could no longer afford to work as journalists. In one case, he suggested a local newspaper journalist had left to become a security guard, as it was a better paying job.

The very reason many readers buy newspapers – the journalism – is also being diminished. Titles have paired costs to the bone in an effort to survive. Edition changes have been scrapped, papers have shrunk in size and editorial production has been outsourced in a number of Irish regionals. Unlike the UK, where groups like the DMGT have successfully converted loss-making daily locals into potentially profitable weeklies, the Irish locals are already weekly, and going fortnightly would simply make them irrelevant in an era of instant digital media.

Cost cuts have been so deep that in some newsrooms journalists are being inhibited from performing their basic functions. Courts coverage in particular has been hit. In one newsroom a busy court in a large county is not reported on because it is too far from the office. In another, journalists are only sent to cover a circuit court, where cases on indictment may last days, if the newsroom gets a good tip that the indicted person will plead guilty. Freedom of Information Act (FOI) requests are not pursued and few local newspapers have the time to conduct investigative journalism (Dooley, 2011).

"Restrictions on travel expenses had led to journalists being metaphorically chained to their desks. The lack of 'fresh air' journalism leads to an unhealthy reliance on press handouts with no time for follow up stories or developing local contacts. There is little

time for investigative journalism. FOI requests are being monitored on cost grounds. In the area of sports coverage there is an ever-increasing dependence on club PROs, with fewer resources for reports and analysis. The devaluing of press photography and the reliance of free pictures, often of doubtful quality, is another worrying trend…." (ibid).

In reality, this means that justice is being administered away from the public and there is less scrutiny of local government. Fundamentally the role of the journalist and newspaper as the watchdog for citizens is undermined.

Crystal ball

So what now for Irish regional weeklies? The boom time profits are gone forever and until 2014 at least, the Irish economy will remain a challenging market, meaning advertising may continue to decline. The debt hangover remains and, if unresolved, a number of newspapers will fold in the coming years. Fowler (2011) suggests that UK regional newspaper publishers failed to invest in the future when they were cash rich, and now needed to be much more inventive in their approach to ensure survival. It is arguable that Irish publishers are also guilty of this charge. Irish local newspaper content remains largely banal, the page design of many weeklies is poor, and few have any substantial online presence. For those that do, even fewer are making money from their online operations. A minority have tested pay walls, but they have proved largely unsuccessful (Collison, 2011).

In "The Reconstruction of American Journalism" Downie and Schudson (2009) suggest a number of future models for American newspapers, including turning into a free sheet; going hyper-local; philanthropy and going entirely online as alternatives to the declining newspaper environment. While all are technically possible, turning from paid-for into free sheet seems the most likely for at least some Irish weeklies struggling for survival in the short term.

The small scale of most Irish weeklies by comparison with the UK or the US means that the other options are unlikely to be viable. Webb (2011) suggests Independent News and Media is considering a somewhat radical move away from traditional local coverage toward more entertainment and local celebrity news and pictures, what he termed "*Hello!* style coverage of local events".

He also suggests that INM's weeklies will increase their online presence. It is likely that all local newspapers will attempt to increase their online presence, including an increased use of social media. Greenslade (2011) suggests local weeklies have to embrace online as the future, but it is difficult to see any significant return on investment for local newspapers from doing so.

For the foreseeable future Irish local weeklies are committed to their print editions, where circulation declines are inevitable; however predicting how steep they are likely to be is impossible. Advertising agency Mediaforce predicted local newspapers may be more resilient than nationals (Slattery, 2012) though it is likely that newspapers that continue to see sustained circulation drops will find it difficult to attract advertising. Ireland is also likely to follow the experience of the US and the UK where just one newspaper per population area will survive. In Ireland, that will either be the county or large town newspaper.

The director of the Regional Newspapers and Printers Association of Ireland, Johnny O'Hanlon, predicted many more local newspapers will outsource their distribution and may move to tabloid in an effort to cut costs (ibid). Beyond that newspapers are also likely to outsource their back office and production, employing only a key sales and editorial team. Mergers and resource sharing are also likely. The closure of some titles is certain, but ironically that resulting loss of competitors should help those that stay afloat to survive. The online revolution may also, ironically, hurt local weeklies less as readers are more likely to buy printed copies in the first place.

Fundamentally, as Greenslade (2011) suggests, media companies are going to have to eventually separate the journalism from the paper it's printed on. Nobody in Ireland has found a way to do that profitably yet.

Bibliography

Audited Bureau of Circulations 'Irish Regional Newspapers' reports, 2007-2011. ABC: Hertfordshire.

BBC News Online (2010) 'The Independent bought by Lebedev for £1' accessed online at http://news.bbc.co.uk/2/hi/business/8587469.stm on 31 January, 2012.

Central Statistics Office (2007) *Census of Population 2006*. Dublin: Central Statistics Office.

Central Statistics Office (2011) *Census of Population 2011: Preliminary Results*. Dublin: Central Statistics Office.

Collison, Gerry (2011) 'Starting a newspaper: the *Clare People* experience' presented at *Regional Newspapers in Crisis* conference, University of Limerick, 1 December, 2011.

Dooley, Seamus (2011) 'Only investment in news can save regional newspapers' presented at *Regional Newspapers in Crisis* conference, University of Limerick, 1 December, 2011.

Downie, Leonard and Schudson, Michael (2009) 'The Reconstruction of American Journalism'. New York: Columbia University.

Felle, Tom and Adshead, Maura (2009) *'Democracy and the Right to Know - Proceedings from the Department of Politics and Public Administration Conference marking the 10th Anniversary of Freedom of Information in Ireland'* 2009/4. Limerick: University of Limerick Papers in Politics and Public Administration.

Flanagan, Peter (2011) Celtic Media returns to profit' in *Irish Independent*, 19 January, 2011.

Foley, Michael (2009) *Media Landscape Ireland*. Maastricht: European Journalism Centre.

Fowler, Neil (2011) 'Have they got news for you' presented at *Guardian Lecture*, Nuffield College, Oxford, 11 November, 2011.

Goodfellow, Christopher (2011) 'Drowning in online's slipstream' in *Business and Finance*, April 2011.

Greenslade, Roy (2011) 'Crisis? What Crisis? Newspaper publishers still see a future for print,' *Guardian* blog accessed at http://www.guardian.co.uk/media/greenslade/2011/dec/02/local-newspapers-downturn on 16 January, 2012.

Hennessy, Mark (2011a) '*Irish Post* to go back into production after publisher makes successful bid' in *The Irish Times*, 1 October, 2011.

Hennessy, Mark (2011b) 'MPs sign motion on *Irish Post* closure' in *The Irish Times*, 8 September, 2011.

Johnston Press (2009) 'Interim Management Statement 13 May, 2009' accessed online at www.johnstonpress.co.uk/jpplc/mediacentre/ pressreleases/index.jsp?ref=115 on 22 January, 2012.

Johnston Press (2010) 'Interim Management Statement November 10 2010' accessed online at www.johnstonpress.co.uk/jpplc/mediacentre/ pressreleases/index.jsp?ref=143 on 22 January, 2012.

Johnston Press (2011) 'Interim Results for the 26 weeks ended 26 July 2011'. Edinburgh: Johnston Press.

Joint National Readership Survey (2003). Dublin: JNRS.

Joint National Readership Survey (2011). Dublin: JNRS.

McCaughren, Samantha (2006) 'Lord Kilclooney media interests Taylor made' in *Irish Independent*, 4 March, 2006.

Noonan, Laura (2007a) 'Irish papers star for Johnston' in *Irish Independent*, 8 March, 2007.

Noonan, Laura (2007b) 'Johnston ad revenue up on year but slipping' in *Irish Independent*, 30 August, 2007.

Noonan, Laura (2009) 'Johnston reviews all aspects of its Irish newspapers' in *Irish Independent*, 5 June, 2009.

O'Brien, Ciara (2012) 'Property prices continue to slide' in *The Irish Times*, 24 January 24, 2012.

O'Reilly, Emily (2008) 'Freedom of Information: The first decade' in *10th Anniversary Conference of Freedom of Information in Ireland* conference proceedings. Dublin: Office of the Information Commissioner.

O'Toole, Fintan (2009) *Ship of Fools: How stupidity and corruption sank the Celtic Tiger*. London: Faber and Faber.

Reddan, Fiona (2011) 'Profits at INM down 6.3 per cent in first six months' in *The Irish Times*, 27 August, 2011.

RTE News (2009) 'Former Owner buys back Tallaght Echo', accessed online at http://www.rte.ie/news/2009/1211/presswatch-business.html, on 20 January, 2012.

RTE News (2010) 'Protests over newspaper closures in the midlands,' accessed online at www.rte.ie/news/2010/0902/alphanewspaper.html on 24 January, 2012.

Slattery, Laura (2011a) 'Kerry's *Kingdom* newspaper to close with 11 jobs lost' in *The Irish Times*, 13 January, 2011.

Slattery, Laura (2011b) '€6.3m loss for Crosbie Media Group' in *The Irish Times*, 12 November 2011.

Slattery (2012) 'Local papers hoping to turn a new page in 2012' in *The Irish Times*, 5 January, 2012.

Webb, Joe (2011) 'Independent Newspapers approach to the challenges in regional newspapers' presented at *Regional Newspapers in* Crisis conference, University of Limerick, 1 December, 2011.

World Factbook (2012) *Ireland.* Central Intelligence Agency, accessed online at https://www.cia.gov/library/publications/the-world-factbook/geos/ei.html on 29 January, 2012.

Notes

[1] While much has been written about this, see O'Toole (2009) for a comprehensive analysis of the Irish economy and its foibles in the 2000s.

[2] For full details see individual Audited Bureau of Circulations six monthly reports for Irish weekly newspapers, 2007-2011.

[3] See Joint National Readership Survey (2003) and (2011). Dublin: JNRS

(Note: only newspapers that are members of the Regional Newspapers and Printers Association of Ireland are included in this survey).

Note on the author

Tom Felle is a former Independent News and Media journalist and has worked as the *Irish Independent's* midlands correspondent. He started his career with the Galway city-based *Connacht Tribune* in the West of Ireland and briefly worked for Associated Newspapers. He has worked as a journalist in Australia and in the Middle East and has contributed to a wide range of international publications on foreign affairs and political issues. In 2006 and 2007 he was Beirut Bureau Chief of the Lebanon News Agency. He teaches newspaper reporting and is Head of Journalism at the University of Limerick, Ireland. His email is tom.felle@ul.ie

The men who killed the regional newspaper industry

Few journalists have had the opportunity to bet their house on buying their own newspaper. Chris Oakley took the chance – and here he tells of where it all started – and where it may all end.

A luncheon. Seated around the long table in the Garrick Club are the great and, probably by their own estimation, the good of the regional newspaper industry – past Presidents of the Newspaper Society, current and former chief executives of major groups, members of families running newspapers founded by their ancestors, whose titles survive and, in some cases, still prosper today.

Among them is one remarkable, indomitable man who over the last 50 years has built a thriving newspaper group, one small title at a time.

A fellow guest leans closer to whisper. "Around this table," he says, "are the men who killed the regional newspaper industry."

It's a good joke. All the more so because, like all the best jokes, it contains more than a grain of truth. It's also unfair because among those guilty as charged are those whose stewardship of titles, whose understanding of what regional newspapers are really all about, whose vision and determination should be signposts to the future.

I do not know in which category my fellow guest would place me. Some would say I and my team started the acquisition price spiral, which has left the biggest regional newspaper groups saddled with unsustainable debts.

In mitigation, I would claim we left the titles we briefly owned in much better shape than we found them; that we left them with a roadmap for the future.

In the beginning

Half a century ago, I walked through the glass-panelled front door into the linoleum-covered reception area of the *Sevenoaks Chronicle*. In front of me were two young women who took it in turns to receive advertisements brought to the counter or to take incoming phone calls. That was how most advertisements reached the printed page – written out and handed over by readers for the classified or births, deaths and marriages columns or by the business people who, for the most part, ran one shop, one motor dealership, one estate agency.

To my right, behind a wooden partition which reached almost, but not quite, to the ceiling were the editorial team – a chief reporter, three senior reporters, a sports editor, a photographer and a junior reporter, soon to become one of two. In a small back office, filled with pipe and cigarette smoke, were the editor and his deputy.

This was the team for a weekly, selling twelve thousand copies in three geographical editions. It was one of three weekly newspaper offices in this town of fifteen thousand people. The independently owned *Sevenoaks News* closed in 1981, and the county paper, the *Kent Messenger*, no longer has an office and staff in Sevenoaks but happily survives in the same family ownership.

As the *Chronicle's* new junior, I earned three guineas a week less ten shillings to pay for my typewriter, but I could earn an extra £1 by loading the company van on a Thursday night and delivering the bundles of newspapers to newsagents. Even then, managements knew how to value journalists – £1 for two or three hours' work as a van driver, £3 3s (£3.15 in today's money) for a sometimes seven-day week as a journalist.

I knocked on the doors of families whose mothers or fathers, grandparents or children had died, collected a picture and wrote an obituary. I stood at the lych-gate during funerals to note down the names of mourners. I delivered wedding forms to couples whose banns had been read at churches in the town and its surrounding villages.

It was a different world then. Sevenoaks Magistrate's Court sat one morning a week; now it sits five days a week in three courtrooms; at the police station, the desk sergeant simply passed over the incident book for reporters to note down reported crimes or, more often, "incidents" that never reached a courtroom. There were no police press offices and no Filkin Report.

Parish, town and rural district councils met in the evenings. The councillors had proper daytime jobs and politics rarely, if ever, entered the council chamber. Reporters were expected to clear their notebooks before going home and still be in on time in the morning. So council meetings ending at 10 pm – to give councillors time to get to the pub for last orders – meant a long day and no opportunity to flirt with a police officer over a pint.

Weekends were spent covering a football match or, in the summer, dodging between a cricket match and a local fete or flower show, getting the names of all the class winners and runners-up. School sports days and plays were photographed, reviewed, the names of actors and competitors listed – all without the need for a Criminal Record check.

The world was different – but what was local then is local now, as Sir Ray Tindle's 220-plus newspapers demonstrate every week. Then, as now, local meant something that involved or affected you, your family, your friends, your neighbours, your team, your club, your street, your town or village. You expected to see faces you knew in the pages of your paper, to read names you recognised, to be alerted to decisions and events that might impact your day-to-day life or your budget.

Names and faces or, to add a qualification, correctly-spelled names and faces were the foundations on which the *Sevenoaks Chronicle* and all successful weeklies were and still are constructed and that requires feet on the ground, journalists visible and accessible in the communities they serve.

Fifty years ago, much the same was true for the regional dailies serving Britain's larger towns and cities. They now face more difficult challenges but, outside the conurbations, life is local – as Johnston Press used to say, before it began shutting offices and herding a reducing number of journalists into hubs, the newspaper equivalent of battery farming. It's cheap, but it's not quality.

Recent Newspaper Society research found 80% of people spend more than half their life and more than 90% of their money within five to ten miles of where they grew up. Even though we can and do instantly read the tweeting inanities of celebrities across the globe or watch the latest YouTube freak show, most people still have local roots, creating a market that can be profitably served.

The opportunity has not gone unnoticed. Below the radar, the local void left by the retreat of major publishers is being filled by new publications, some weekly, some monthly, some in newspaper format – like the excellent *Saddleworth Independent*, run by a former member of my team, the ever-energetic Ken Bennett – some in pocket-size magazine format, like the *Redland and Westbury Park Directory*, in suburban Bristol. They are packed with the sort of advertising the *Sevenoaks Chronicle* might once have carried and, as paginations grow, the breadth of their content expands.

The beginning of the end

In many ways, these small publications are how local newspapers began – a title launched in a town or city, sometimes with an eye to making a profit, sometimes to provide a platform for a particular viewpoint, political or religious. Often one title would lead to another being launched by the same businessman in a neighbouring area and so, over the years, families built up portfolios of titles in communities surrounding their homes or estates.

In the latter half of the last century, many families sold their titles to larger groups. Some regional newspapers became parts of businesses whose principal interests lay elsewhere, like one of the largest regional groups, Westminster Press, which was owned by the banking and book publishing company S. Pearson and Son, until it was sold to Newsquest in 1996.

But some family groups still remain, like the Cumbria-based CN Group, in the careful stewardship of the Burgess family since 1815, or the Wolverhampton *Express and Star* group, bought by the Graham family in 1902 from its Liberal Republican founder Andrew Carnegie. Generally speaking, they are in better shape than titles owned by major groups in spite of arguably having fewer resources to cope with difficult economic times and competition for readers and advertisers.

It was only as the century drew towards a close that regional newspapers became hot takeover targets and, briefly, one of the darlings of the Stock Market. And, at this point, I and the fellow defendants in my team step into the dock.

Goodbye America, hello venture capitalism

It was in April 1991 that I realised I would probably soon be unemployed. This was not a happy prospect. Ex-editors with a year's experience as a managing director do not find it easy to land new jobs that will support the lifestyle to which they have just become accustomed. So how did I find myself in this uncomfortable position?

In 1989 I was headhunted by the American owners of the *Birmingham Post and Mail*, the *Coventry Evening Telegraph* and a group of Midland weeklies to become editor-in-chief of the *Post*, *Mail* and *Sunday Mercury*.

At the time I had been editor for almost seven years of the *Liverpool Echo*, producing an irreverent, campaigning tabloid as closely tuned to the quick wit and challenging nature of Scousers as my talented team of journalists could make it. We had exposed corruption, brought about a change in the law to allow the seizure of drug dealers' assets, pioneered a telephone helpline for abused children, helped the city win Freeport status, investigated the football disasters at Heysel and Hillsborough.

We worked with Brian Leveson QC, as he then was, to defend the *Echo* in a contempt of court action for preventing the early release by a mental health tribunal of a killer on what many believed were spurious grounds. We won and I hope Mr Leveson remembers now that newspapers can be a positive force and do more than just irritate publicity-seeking celebrities who have something to hide.

It was the most enjoyable job I have ever had, but the time had come to move on and I was interested in training to become a managing director in what at the time looked like a growing group. Weeks later, I was acting managing director of the *Birmingham Post and Mail* and confirmed in the role after about six months. So much for training!

A year later, Ralph Ingersoll's international media company faced difficulties. American titles were sold and it became increasingly clear that the same was likely to happen to the Midlands titles. Six of us came together to attempt a management buy-out of the titles. None had ever raised money in the City; none had ever bought a company; we did not even have the cash to pay our advisers – they worked on a success fee basis; most of us had to take out personal loans which would have bankrupted us in the event of failure to fund the purchase of our equity. Seven months later we owned what became Midland Independent Newspapers.

Events during a contested acquisition are never crystal clear but we believe that we outbid Emap, the *Daily Telegraph* and a major German publisher. We know that a rival, American-led buy-out team was given a period of exclusivity to complete the purchase of the titles. Indeed, our own newspapers reported that the American team had bought them and each member of our team was given his leaving date.

We succeeded because we remained loyal and committed to each other and because of the unwavering support of our principal private equity backer Candover, in the person of Colin Buffin. The price paid was £125m, a world record at the time for a media management buy-out, and twenty three times the total group's annual profit.

The *Financial Times* commented that we had wildly overpaid and forecast that the inexperienced management team would be gone within six months with the company unable to meet the commitments resulting from the financial structure. That prediction was made the more feasible when Birmingham City Council withdrew its advertising, worth more than £1m a year, from the Birmingham titles because it objected to critical coverage by the *Evening Mail*, announced it was setting up its own newspaper and awarded the print contract to a rival publisher.

The deal, however, set the benchmark for regional newspaper prices. Vendors aspired to get at least the same multiple of profit; acquirers found banks, bondholders and shareholders prepared to fund deals at that level and beyond. The seeds of the destruction of a large part of the regional newspaper industry were sown... but for a decade or more they lay dormant.

It's the content, stupid
The Iliffe family launched the *Midland Daily Telegraph* in Coventry in 1891 and acquired the Birmingham titles in the 1940s. The landmark 1965 building in Colmore Circus, Birmingham, says much about how families regarded their titles and their expectations for the future. On a practical level, the basement press hall was designed with space to install at least one, if not two, extra press lines to cope with the expected increase in demand for the titles and any new ones which were launched. The 14th floor entertaining suite with its own kitchens and two small flats could accommodate up to 100 dinner guests. On the management floor was a ballroom, complete with sprung floor and, when it was in regular use, glitter balls.

By the 1980s, however, the ball was over, the expectations dashed. Sales were falling and profits disappointing. The morning *Birmingham Post* – founded in 1857 and the first regional newspaper to turn a profit of more than £1m in the 1960s – was on the point of collapse. Britain's only free daily newspaper had been launched in competition. The Iliffe family's Yattendon Trust, while retaining smaller titles, sold the Midlands' newspapers to Ralph Ingersoll for £60m.

Ingersoll recognised the need for change, including a £20m investment in colour presses in Birmingham and Coventry, and supported re-staffing the *Birmingham Post* and its conversion back from tabloid to broadsheet. Profits improved and, had his fortunes not changed in America, he might have persevered.

Our buy-out pitch to potential backers was simple: a promise to triple the profit and double the profit margin within four years. The funding structure put together by Candover was conservative, judged against later models, with almost 50% equity and the rest bank debt and mezzanine funding. It still left little room for failure.

Our plan was hardly original:

- To reduce costs but without cutting editorial or sales forces
- To use the latest technology to improve our titles and increase efficiency
- To take loss-making titles into profit
- To stabilise or increase the sales of paid titles

Two and a half years later, as the company approached flotation on the London Stock Exchange, we had more than made good on our promise – ahead of time. Profits stood at more than £16m with a margin of more than 20%, making MIN one of the most profitable newspaper groups in Britain.

The improvement was brought about while the economy, under John Major's government, was stagnating and claims by the then Chancellor of the Exchequer, Norman Lamont, to see "the green shoots of recovery" were widely ridiculed.

How was it done?

The business model for paid daily regional newspapers has always seemed fairly simple. Advertising accounts for between 60% and 80% of revenue. Cover price revenue does not meet the cost of production and distribution. Nonetheless circulation is critical: the more readers, the greater the likely response for advertisers, although a weakness has always been the impossibility of tracking that response accurately.

The key to paid circulation or the readership of free titles is content, original, relevant and interesting to the target audience…which means investing in adventurous editors and quality journalism, something the buy-out team unsurprisingly had no difficulty in supporting since four of the six had an editorial background.

It also means carrying the advertising that pulls in readers – situations vacant, property and motors. It is no coincidence that the highest sale day for most regional dailies was the day they carried job advertising or that the *Birmingham Post's* highest sale day was Saturday, when the upmarket property supplement appeared. Without the underpinning of these key advertising categories, maintaining sales becomes significantly more difficult, as today's publishers have found.

All our efforts were tuned to getting our titles into the hands of more readers and securing their loyalty. More than £750,000 was invested in canvassing and sampling to get the *Birmingham Post* to a wider audience. The target thirty thousand plus circulation was never consistently achieved but readership, often at the workplace, rose to 5.2 per copy.

The first newspaper loyalty card in Britain was launched in affluent suburbs of Birmingham to build the penetration of the *Evening Mail* in those areas important to advertisers. The card gave readers who ordered the paper six nights a week discounts at local retailers. Sales of the *Mail* stabilised at around two hundred thousand.

The *Coventry Evening Telegraph* launched innovative home delivery schemes, driving household penetration above 70%, the highest of any regional daily. Loss-making weeklies, haemorrhaging money so severely that the banks set quarterly targets for improvement with a right to insist on closure if two consecutive targets were missed, were returned to profit within a year by reducing production and back office costs and, more significantly, re-focusing and re-vitalising the sales teams.

More than £250,000 was invested in new colour processing, replacing a complete unionised department with journalists using Apple Macs to create colour separations, the first time this had been done in the UK. The workforce was cut by 30% to 1,300 – but the number of journalists and sales people actually increased.

All this created the headroom to acquire titles, mainly free and many loss-making at the point of purchase, from Peterborough to Burton to Derby. New titles, such as a regional TV listings magazine, were launched.

With pressroom salary costs reduced by 22% and press availability increased by 30% by more flexible working, the acquired titles were printed on presses which would otherwise have been idle. Contract work was brought in to fill remaining downtime – including Birmingham City Council's title as part of a deal which saw council advertising return to the *Evening Mail*, a change of policy brought about by the lack of response to advertising in the council's own newspaper.

By 1994, MIN's titles were going into three million homes each week and had two million more readers than any national newspaper in the Midlands. That success was down to people, people who really understood the newspaper industry – not just the buy-out team of finance director John Whitehouse, commercial director Julian Day – a *Post* and *Mail* Newsboy of the Year in 1967 – operations director Joe Holmes, editorial director Terry Page, and Ernest Petrie, managing director successively of Coventry and Birmingham, but great editors like Ian Dowell, of the *Evening Mail*, innovative marketing manager Mark Hollinshead, now a key figure in Trinity Mirror's senior management team, IT pioneers like the late Alan Bott, no-nonsense commercial leaders like Roger Chappell and relentless promotions managers like Ken Bennett and Dominga de la Cruz and, of course, the sage advice of our chairman, Sir Norman Fowler.

Everyone in the company had a stake in its success. Shares were given to all staff with more than minimal length of service.

Local newspapers have to be run from the ground up, not the top down. Our style was to agree targets for the year and give managers and editors the tools and the freedom to achieve them. As Julian Day told *The Times*: "The strength of local newspapers is their localness."

Twenty-four months after buying Midland Independent Newspapers, well ahead of schedule, we were ready to float the company on the Stock Exchange. At a listing valuation of £200m, the shares were over-subscribed. The deal that was doomed to fail remains among the top six for Candover with a return of 40% per annum for investors.

Shares can go down in value

Great things were expected of Midland Independent Newspapers plc. Floated at a profit to earnings ratio of twenty times in March 1994, it was at a discount to other regional publishers trading at twenty four times earnings.

Financial comment in *The Times* suggested that, even if the company did very little, the group would benefit from a recovery in the advertising market; that there were further acquisition opportunities in the East Midlands and that the management team had a good track record of improving the performance of acquired titles. But dealing with a large number of institutional investors was markedly different to sharing a vision with a private equity investor working towards an agreed goal some years ahead.

I did not believe that newspaper profit margins could be advanced, consistently quarter by quarter. A 20%-plus margin looked to be sustainable in the foreseeable future but anything much above that would fluctuate with conditions in the advertising market. A permanent commitment to an ever-higher margin could only be achieved by short-term decision making, which would be damaging to the newspapers in the longer run. I had no interest in taking those decisions.

In my view, newspapers needed to diversify into related but counter-cyclical activities to help protect them from movements in the advertising market. We bought a magazine, exhibitions and conference group, catering for sectors as diverse as public housing and the surface coating industry and as close to recession proof as it was possible to get. It was – and, as far as I know, still remains – a sound profitable business, but its margins were half those of regional newspapers and the City did not like the deal.

We looked at various acquisition opportunities but prices were spiralling upwards and we would not pay an unjustifiable price to please the City. The MIN share price drifted down. We came close to buying the *Nottingham Evening Post* and its associated titles, owned since 1857 by the Forman family, but were thwarted when Conservative Ministers over-ruled the then Monopolies and Mergers Commission and cleared Northcliffe to buy the titles, giving the *Daily Mail*-owned group a monopoly of daily regionals across the East Midlands.

In 1996 we negotiated to buy Emap's sixty five under-performing regional newspaper titles, a deal where we could clearly see how to bring about value-enhancing performance for our shareholders. The acquisition would have required a substantial rights issue. On the morning that I was to shake hands on an agreement with Robin (later Sir Robin) Miller, Emap's then chief executive, I was called to a breakfast meeting with MIN's principal institutional shareholder. I was told they would not support the deal by taking up their rights. Without that support, we could not go ahead. The titles were sold to Johnston Press for £200m. At that point, we knew MIN was transformed from predator to prey.

We continued to look at ways to diversify, becoming the first regional group to experiment with local television – a move into the crazy world of Kelvin MacKenzie's Live TV. Topless darts, the weather forecast in Norwegian or delivered by a dwarf who used a trampoline to be able to point to the north of Scotland, a stripping business reporter who removed an item of clothing each time she reported a falling share price – only a stammering newsreader was ruled out.

Our local TV output was more conventional but failed to command a big enough audience to win advertiser support...but it did open the door to David Montgomery, then CEO of Mirror Group. After widespread City enthusiasm as he cleared the wreckage left by Robert Maxwell, the Mirror's previous proprietor, and substantially increased the Mirror titles' profitability, Montgomery was now under pressure to find new ways of advancing profits and margins. We provided an answer. In July 1997, Mirror Group Newspapers paid £305m for MIN – and I became a Mirror director.

A glimpse in the Mirror

My office in the Canary Wharf tower was known as the ejection chamber. No one who occupied it lasted more than six months. Kelvin MacKenzie gave me the benefit of his advice. "You need to get in early in the morning to grease the stairs for the other directors," he said. With Piers Morgan as one of the humbler executives, no tower would have been tall enough to accommodate the competing egos.

My responsibility was for the MIN titles, magazines and exhibitions and the Mirror's Scottish and Belfast titles, which together contributed about 50% of the group's profits. My buy-out colleague Ernest Petrie became MD in Scotland and, over the following months, profits improved.

At the time, the Mirror was energetically undermining its market-leading Scottish stablemate, the *Daily Record*, by lifting its exclusives, advertising them on TV and slashing the Mirror's cover price to 10p. The *Record* was allowed neither to advertise on TV nor to cut its cover price. The objective was to bolster the *Mirror's* total UK sale and so protect its share of advertising spend and to slow the advance of *The Sun* in Scotland. Predictably, it failed to halt *The Sun* and destroyed the *Record's* market dominance.

My largely ineffective trips around the Coventry, Birmingham, Glasgow, Belfast and London circuit were interspersed by strategy meetings, the highlight of one being a video of a naked Tory MP cavorting with his young girl lover, recorded by a camera hidden in a wardrobe, and of another being some succinct criticism from Kelvin MacKenzie.

The editor of *The People*, Bridget Rowe, held up a copy of the magazine *Woman* in one hand and the dummy of a new Sunday supplement in the other and asked directors to comment. "Well," said MacKenzie, "in your right hand you have a copy of Woman, a successful, well produced magazine for women; in the other hand, you have a crock of shit." End of meeting.

Before the ejection chamber could be fired, United News and Media, owners of the *Daily* and *Sunday Express* titles, announced the sale of its regional group with its flagship *Yorkshire Post* title. Having so recently acquired MIN, Mirror Group was not in a position to bid - but Candover, recalling its financial return on MIN in 1994, was.

Second time lucky

Shortly after Candover's £360m bid for the newspapers which became Regional Independent Media was accepted, and I was announced as chief executive, I bumped into the family owner of one of the industry's larger groups. I grant him anonymity as I recall his disobliging remark: "You got lucky once," he said, "but you won't again."

And we didn't...because we never "got lucky" the first time. We had a plan to deliver a promise and we delivered it. Now we intended to use substantially the same plan to deliver a new promise.

The *Yorkshire Post* was founded in 1754 as the *Leeds Intelligencer*, one of Britain's first daily newspapers. It was taken over by Yorkshire Conservative Newspaper Company in 1865, with the clue to the reason for the takeover in the company's name. In 1969, the company was bought by United Provincial Newspapers, which owned newspapers across the North and subsequently became United News and Media when it acquired the national Express titles.

Whether Candover outbid Trinity for the titles or whether UNM preferred the certainty of a deal which avoided the need for a Monopolies and Mergers Commission clearance is uncertain. What is certain is that on the night the deal was signed, UNM threw a party to celebrate getting rid of a troublesome asset, the growth potential of which had, in UNM's opinion, been exhausted.

For me, walking into the concrete monstrosity that is the *Yorkshire Post* building as chief executive and, in small part, owner was indescribable. Twenty years earlier I had been a down table sub-editor there on the *Yorkshire Evening Post* and later deputy editor of the *YP* for four years.

First, we had to build a management team. I like a blend of experience and naivety, intelligent young managers prepared to challenge the accepted way of doing things. Sir Norman, since ennobled as the Lord Fowler, agreed to be our chairman again; Ernest Petrie joined as my deputy, Julian Day, who largely wrote the business plan, became a non-executive director, and Colin Buffin again represented Candover.

Then there were the new faces. Sue Laverick, who had started her career on the *Yorkshire Post* and was financial controller of UPN became group finance director; Steve Auckland, now MD of Northcliffe, became assistant group managing director; Marlen Roberts, who had worked with me in Liverpool as a successful tele-ad manager and became a rising star in Northcliffe, was commercial development director; Alison Stock, the *Yorkshire Post* IT manager became IT director with the task of dragging the group's IT up to date, centralising it and substantially reducing its costs; Lisa Hanson joined as HR director to bring experience of cost reduction and contract negotiation in heavily unionised environments.

The funding structure was more aggressive than that for the MIN deal, leaving less headroom for failure to achieve the acquisition business plan. International bondholders who invested alongside Candover were reassured when the credit rating agencies – much in the news this year – improved their rating of RIM to BB after the first 12 months, which saw profits rise by 15% on turnover up by 6%.

The end of year report had a familiar echo from the first year of MIN:

- Nearly £4m reduction in annual costs achieved without any industrial action
- Investment in the flexibility and colour capability of the presses
- Investment in re-launching two of the group's daily titles and launching new weeklies
- Acquisition of weekly titles on the Scottish borders and regional business magazines
- A successful bid for the group's first radio licence
- The largest training and development programme in the group's history
- Shares in the company for a large number of staff

Investment in quality and content, acquisition of under-performing titles at a sensible price, diversification into related areas of publishing with different revenue streams and different economic cycles to the core business, lower operating costs in all areas except editorial and sales, a major effort to equip staff to deliver outstanding performance and to enable them to benefit from their commitment to achieving the group's vision – these were the keys to MIN's success and to that of RIM.

There was, however, one new element. Home penetration of the Internet was low outside Greater London in 1998 but we recognised both the opportunity and the threat to our newspapers. Marlen Roberts, who had been MD of AdHunter, the regional newspaper industry's far-sighted initiative to upload motors, property and recruitment advertising to the Internet, was appointed MD of Regional Interactive Media. By 1999, sixty sales and development staff were working on eighteen websites aiming to be the definitive source for local information, services and shopping and another forty staff were in the process of being recruited.

We believed our ownership of the local information franchise, our instant brand recognition, our relationship with readers, buyers and sellers made us ideally placed to capitalise on Internet opportunities. We could also use our newspapers to provide constant and free promotion for the sites.

In the first year of operation we uploaded one million vehicle advertisements, three hundred and fifty thousand job advertisements and two hundred and fifty thousand properties for sale and achieved 12m page impressions. Our revenues grew from nothing to £500,000.

The strategy was supported by Candover but unpopular with other investors who believed, correctly but shortsightedly, that money invested in the Internet could instead have fallen to the bottom line. By 2001, Internet revenues stood at just under £2.5m and the division was on the point of breaking even.

RIM's investor views were echoed by shareholders in other regional newspaper companies, with the result that the AdHunter project became mired in confusion and starved of investment, a situation replicated in the response to the Internet of publishers' own titles.

With the market unwilling to acknowledge the threat of the Internet, the valuation of regional newspapers continued to rise driven by the imperative of publishers such as Johnston Press, Trinity and Newsquest to acquire and so be able to demonstrate profits rising continually at a pace beyond anything which could be achieved organically.

In early 1999, RIM put together a proposal to buy Mirror Group, then the lowest-rated newspaper stock, with a plan to increase profits of the merged companies from £157m in 1999 to £220m by 2004. The approach did not succeed. Instead, Mirror Group merged with Trinity in what was, in effect, a takeover by the regional group.

Other titles came to the market – Portsmouth and Sunderland Newspapers and Southnews among them – but in the view of the RIM team their valuations were incompatible with building rather than gutting the business.

By 2001, RIM's operating profit was more than £44m compared with £25m in 1997, the year before acquisition. And on September 11 of that year, at a breakfast meeting I shook hands with Tim Bowdler, the CEO of Johnston Press, on an agreement to sell RIM. I walked from the meeting to our London office – arriving just in time to see the second airliner fly into New York's twin towers. As the towers came crashing down, so did the deal. The fear and uncertainty, which swept the financial markets, made the purchase impossible for Johnston Press to finance. But the market demand for Johnston Press to grow, the need for its acquisitions to be ever larger if they were to have a significant effect upon the company's results and the scarcity of other targets, brought Tim Bowdler back to the negotiating table early in 2002.

In April of that year, RIM – except for its business magazines and associated events – was sold to Johnston Press for £560m, roughly the same multiple of profit as Candover had paid in 1998. But, although the City did not appear to recognise it, the world had changed in those four years. *Autotrader* was a growing threat to private classified motors' advertising and increasingly targeting dealers; Internet competitors were beginning to make inroads into regional newspapers' core market of situations vacant and property; Fish4, the successor to AdHunter and the regional newspapers' best hope of warding off the new operators, was paralysed by a lack of investment and direction.

Johnston Press dismantled Regional Interactive Media, making most of its staff redundant. Marlen Roberts now owns and runs the UK's largest regional business publisher with digital revenues which grew 60% in 2011; her RIM team own and run a digital agency which numbers Coca Cola among its clients and handled more than £200m ecommerce transactions last year.

The newspaper spending spree did not stop with RIM. In 2005, Johnston Press spent £350m on acquisitions and another £160m on *The Scotsman* the following year. The *Glasgow Herald*, the *Daily Telegraph* and the Northcliffe group all came on the market between 2003 and 2006 with DMGT turning down more the £1bn for Northcliffe.

The willingness of banks to provide loans on ever more arcane assumptions – cashflow forecasts for five or more years ahead – helped to ensure the valuation of newspaper groups did not reflect the new reality. They do now. The current market capitalisation of Johnston Press is £40m and that of Trinity is £125m.

There can be life after death

Mourners for the regional newspaper industry of old are in the cemetery and we may not have to wait long for the hearses. First to arrive will be the big city dailies which face multiple misfortunes. They are almost exclusively owned by publicly-quoted companies which have huge debt burdens to service while attempting to maintain or improve year-on-year profits and margins at a time of falling revenues.

As a result, costs continue to be cut in ways which have rendered regional dailies less readable and less relevant. Editorial workloads have been increased to service online media while staff has been reduced to a level where the generation of original, well-researched material or the undertaking of local investigations is almost impossible.

Remote printing has led to "evening" titles having deadlines the previous afternoon. The argument that this does not matter because the advent of the Internet means such titles can no longer break news is specious. Other media, such as local radio and TV, have been able to break news ahead of newspapers for decades, but readers still expect to find the day's most important stories covered in their own regional daily.

Sales and household penetration have already fallen below a level where they can produce an acceptable response for advertisers. To use Birmingham as an example, sales of the evening paper are now around forty thousand a day in a city of one million.

Local or regional newspapers need to be able to reflect the identity of the community they serve but in most major cities that community identity has fractured into different and often conflicting ones, represented by ethnicity, race, religion, culture and economic divisions.

No daily newspaper, particularly one with a limited ability to editionise because of editorial cuts and artificial printing schedules, can now, for example, meet the needs of the majority of people in Birmingham.

Most regional dailies have in the past been profitable on, at best, three days a week – Wednesday, Thursday and Friday – supported by situations vacant, motors and property advertising. All three categories have now largely moved online and, if they use the regional paper at all, do so simply as a branding exercise.

Converting evenings to weeklies, as Northcliffe is doing, may save smaller titles in places such as Bath, Torquay, Scunthorpe and Exeter but is unlikely to offer more than a temporary reprieve for big city titles like the *Birmingham Post* and the *Liverpool Daily Post.*

Only the family-owned dailies in smaller, more remote cities with a more coherent community identity and with no debt burden are likely to survive.

Weeklies with their lower cost base and lesser dependence on national, property, motors and jobs advertising stand a better chance. Those chances are greatly improved the further their circulation area is from London and, to a lesser extent, other major cities because community identity remains stronger in more rural communities.

Survival chances are best for family-owned weeklies. Those owned by publicly-quoted companies face similar cost-reduction challenges to their sister dailies with major reductions in their editorial staffing levels, unrealistic production deadlines for remote printing, closure of local offices and, in many cases, editorial decisions taken many miles from the communities they serve.

It is no coincidence that Audit Bureau of Circulation figures published in February 2012 show that 84 of the 693 paid and free weeklies increased sales or distribution in the last half of 2011 and the worst performing titles, losing almost 20% of their sales, were all bar one owned by Trinity.

The last decade of the twentieth century and the early years of the present one was a golden age for newspaper owners. Advertising spend was growing rapidly, the TV and radio inventory was limited, the Internet was in its infancy and newspapers were the obvious outlet for the rising expenditure. In the main, the record profits of those years were not invested for the future but returned to shareholders.

That golden age will never return. Perhaps no one can honestly claim to have recognised fully the competitive pressures that the Internet has brought. However, if the industry had supported Fish4, regional newspapers could now have the largest and best used property, motors and situations vacant sites…and online estate agency RightMove would not be worth more than even the biggest regional newspaper group.

Instead, managements reacted to the Internet as their predecessors had to the launch of free newspapers decades earlier. Then they either ignored them or launched their own free titles, restricting them so severely to avoid cannibalising the advertising of their paid titles that they offered no competition to the independent free papers. Eventually these entrepreneurs had to be bought out at huge cost by the established titles.

Exactly the same scenario has played out with the Internet. At first it was largely ignored; then management launched online sites but severely restricted them to avoid cannibalising their print titles' advertising. Even now, many groups shy away from using the power of brands built up over a century or more and invent new names for their websites. Most give away their only trade-able commodity, local news. The free newspaper solution is not open to today's newspaper owners. They cannot afford to buy out the online operators.

But all is not black. Those newspapers which are not heavily indebted still produce enough cash to provide their family owners with an at least comfortable income, as they have done for generations.

New entrepreneurs – and, of course, Sir Ray Tindle – have recognised this and responded by launching highly-localised weekly, sometimes monthly, titles. It is fiendishly hard work to get them off the ground and individual profits are small but, just like the first family owners, each title can be the building block in an expanding group.

There are examples in every region, reflecting local life in the way the *Sevenoaks Chronicle* did half a century ago. They will never be a private equity investment vehicle, never a City favourite, but they remain a good lifestyle investment – which is how many regional newspapers began.

The verdict
In a couple of decades, managements who have overpaid for acquisitions, over-promised to City investors and failed to recognise the threat and opportunity of the Internet have come close to destroying an industry.

You be the judge of the extent of the MIN team's culpability in creating the financial climate that brought this about.

The paid-for local press grew up to alert and to protect individuals, to build and bind communities, to defend and campaign for those in need of support. Where can they turn now when planners slice up their neighbourhoods, Tesco bulldozes their tennis courts and the local school or library is closed?

A pillar of localness is crumbling. Perhaps the new entrepreneurs will restore it but, for the time being at least, the real losers from the financial folly of the past decade are communities up and down the country which are now worse informed than a century ago, a depressing outcome in what is supposed to be the age of information overload.

Note on the author
Chris Oakley CBE is a journalist and former regional newspaper editor. He is a past president of the Newspaper Society and the Guild of British Newspaper Editors (now the Society of Editors). He chairs a multimedia regional business publishing company, a digital agency specialising in ecommerce, the commercial activities of The Royal Armouries and is the finance trustee of the charity Television for the Environment which makes programmes for international transmission. He runs his own media consultancy based in Brussels.

Rethinking what local means to the audience

Traditional publishers know they need to deliver news and advertising in the way that an individual reader wants to consume it, says Kent Messenger Group editorial director Ian Carter. The challenge is how.

On the wall of the chairman's office at KM Group headquarters pride of place is given to the first edition of the *Maidstone Telegraph*, the paper that would become the *Kent Messenger*.

Launched on New Year's Day in 1859, the *Telegraph* set out its stall in a single column editorial nestled alongside the railway timetables and adverts for cheesemongers and snuff suppliers.

"The Cheap Press has now become an established fact," it stated. "Maidstone, with its population of 28,000, offers a fair field for the establishment of a cheap newspaper.

"The *Maidstone Telegraph* will be a close and observant recorder of public events, a fearless opponent of public abuses and a straightforward advocate of public claims."

In the following 153 years Maidstone and its surrounding district has changed greatly – the local media landscape even more so.

In 1859, the *Telegraph* editorial team would have taken confidence from the knowledge their readers were never more than the turn of a page away from a familiar face.

For a community that lived, worked and socialised with their neighbours, life truly was local and their weekly newspaper reflected all that mattered to them.

The KM Group of 2012 remains family-owned and fiercely committed to Kent.

The company has grown to encompass newspapers, radio stations and websites serving almost every major conurbation in the county, stretching from Dover and Thanet in the east across to prosperous Tonbridge and Malling in the west.

But though our guiding principle remains unchanged – to make Kent a better place to live and work – we have had to rethink what local means to our audience.

Our newspapers have grown at the same rate as the towns and cities they serve, but as people's horizons expand the challenge for the KM Group has been to ensure our products remain as vital to people's lives as the *Maidstone Telegraph* was all those years ago.

By definition, we cover a tightly defined geographical area – Kent and the unitary authority of Medway, the latter comprising of the towns of Chatham, Rochester, Gillingham, Strood and Rainham.

So how do we meet the needs of the modern day *Kent Messenger* reader, who may think nothing of the commute to London to work or socialise, and who is more likely to be found at the Emirates or Stamford Bridge than following the fortunes of Maidstone United?

And how do we balance that challenge against the needs of those areas where community spirit still runs deep, such as the Isle of Sheppey – an area where life is local to the extent that legend tells of one octogenarian who has never even visited the 'mainland'?

The answer is to accept that the reader, not the publisher, defines their own boundaries and their own areas of interest.

We can no longer take a 'one size fits all' approach to our media, and have had to loosen the traditional shackles to allow our audience to receive news and information in a manner of their choosing.

Sir Ray Tindle, the 84-year-old publisher of more than 200 weekly newspapers, believes that "if you had a newspaper for every street it would sell," adding: "The average person isn't interested in the wider area but they are very interested in their immediate locality."[1]

For many of our readers and many of our newspapers that is still the case.

There remains a huge demand for our printed products. More than 100,000 KM newspapers are sold every week, and late in 2011 we bucked the industry trend for closure and consolidation by launching a new paid-for newspaper in the growing town of Sittingbourne.

In the right market and in the right conditions, this can still be the route to success.

There is still a substantial audience who treat our traditional weekly newspapers as the first port of call for their news, with the 'happy and sad' adverts on our BMD pages as important as the choice of front page splash.

But equally there is a growing audience whom we will not reach through these traditional methods.

In order to grow and flourish, we know we need to deliver our news and advertising in the way that an individual reader wants to consume it, rather than relying on our editors to provide a weekly summary of the news we believe they will be interested in.

In truth, this is not new territory for the company. The KM Group has never been backwards in exploring new avenues to reach audiences.

We decided at the end of the 90s that local evening papers - particularly those close to London - were a challenged business model.

At the time we published the daily *Kent Today*, which had formerly been known as the *Evening Post*, covering the whole of the county.

We began the process of exiting the daily newspaper market by converting the Friday edition of *Kent Today* for the weekly *Medway Messenger*.

Two years later we dropped the other daily editions of *Kent Today*, introducing a Monday *Messenger* to start the week. What had once been a struggling daily title was now a strong bi-weekly product.

The wider newspaper industry is now following a similar path, hoping it can transform a time-poor, dwindling daily readership into a solid weekly audience.

Newspapers from Exeter to Scunthorpe have taken this approach over the past year, with further big guns expected to follow suit in 2012.

However, the KM Group's withdrawal from the daily market was no simple retreat – at the same time we were experimenting with reaching our audiences in new ways as we began to transform the company from a straightforward newspaper publisher into a multimedia operation.

This transformation began at the end of the 90s when we were relatively early adopters in the digital age.

After experimenting with a variety of options at the tail end of that decade, we launched www.kentonline.co.uk in the year 2000, with the site acting as an umbrella for its various weekly newspapers.

The launch of *Kent Online* saw died-in-the-wool newspaper reporters and advertising teams awaken to the possibilities of the digital world. Today, *Kent Online* has an audience of 350,000 unique monthly visitors and remains a beacon of excellence in the industry.

This transformation continued when KM Group expanded into local radio, with the acquisition of a local station in Thanet.

The following four years saw stations in Canterbury, Folkestone, Dover, Maidstone and Medway and Ashford join the fold and now all operate under the kmfm banner.

Now we are on the next stage of that journey, with a snapshot of the KM Group in 2012 showing a company offering its news services in a variety of ways designed to meet individual readers and listeners' needs.

Our radio stations – their output unashamedly populist and commercial – deliver news in 60-second bites every hour to listeners who may never have paid for one of our newspapers.

Kent Online, meanwhile, offers readers the opportunity to find the news that is relevant to their lives, from pan-Kent headlines down to local village gossip.

Our editorial – and increasingly our commercial teams too – are plugged fully into the world of social media, with Twitter feeds and Facebook sites delivering our news to tens of thousands more people.

Users of our *What's On* website, which launched in 2011, define their own areas of interest, setting their own parameters for search results. Similarly, contextual advertising means our customers can define which online visitors are shown their adverts.

This functionality will now expand across our other digital services, whether people are accessing them through desktop computer and laptops or, increasingly likely, their phones or tablets.

As people gain the ability to select their geo-tagged news from postcode level upwards, it really will be the age of self-editing.

None of that diminishes the importance of print, which will continue to be at the heart of the KM Group for years to come.

Here too though we must continue to develop our editorial approach. We know that in today's 128-page *Kent Messenger* we can no longer assume readers will see a recognisable face on every other page – maybe not even every edition.

Nor will our weekly newspapers be the natural environment for breaking news stories.

Instead, our editors are charged with finding those subjects and topics that really do cut across everyone's lives – the areas of interest that, whether people feel it or not, make them "local".

We have long worked on the basis that the best way to capture new readers is when they put their roots down and start families.

Accordingly, education, health, transport and crime are at the forefront of our editors' minds when setting their news agenda.

When plans were mooted to move maternity services from Maidstone to Tunbridge Wells, the *Kent Messenger* acted as the focal point for the anger felt at the proposals.

Over many years, the *Messenger* fiercely fought the plans, fearing it would lead to the inevitable downgrading of all services in Maidstone.

The same battle rages today in Canterbury, where similar proposals would mean no more babies being born in the historic city's hospital.

It is these such campaigns that will ensure those print titles serving the main population centres in Kent remain relevant.

But that will be only one strand to our multimedia offering. No journalist can think of themselves as a reporter solely for one of our print titles. Readers expect more, and our teams have to be as comfortable grabbing a 30-second audio quote, filing video footage and Tweeting a 140-word court update as they are writing a 400-word page lead.

However people in Kent choose to define what is of interest to them, and what local means to them, the KM Group's role is to ensure it is their first port of call.

Note
[1] Ray Tindle interview, journalism.co.uk January 2012

Note on the author
Ian Carter is editorial director of the KM Group, a family-owned publisher with newspapers, websites and radio stations across Kent. He is a former senior broadcast at BBC News Online, editor-in-chief at Northcliffe South East and assitant editor at the Argus, Brighton.

Innovation on the streets of Manchester

It is time to stop being dazzled by technology and start considering the practical value of multimedia publication to serve audiences with a wide range of demands, says Ian Wood.

Innovation and transformation are not virtues in themselves – they only have value insofar as they provide a constructive response to change. Visions of the future have often focused on the index of possibilities created by new technology. This has led to an array of impractical, pointless and commercially naïve proposals.

What has become clear is that we on the *Manchester Evening News* should not be driven by the novelty of technological advance but, rather, regard it as one factor in a far more significant process – the change in the nature and expectations of our audience. The way people define their locality, their communities and themselves is the real issue with which the media industry needs to be concerned if it is to respond appropriately and profitably.

The networks people use are increasingly diverse. Of course, they remain interested by what happens close to where they live and work – but new, geographically disparate communities are facilitated through the web and which create a new dimension to the notion of "local". It is necessary for media organisations to serve this new reality if they are to move from the traditional business of informing and entertaining readers to providing a new offering which engages with an audience comprising not only readers but also viewers, users and commentators.

This realisation allows a business like MEN Media to understand we are no longer simply just trying to tell the best stories, it is now also imperative that we tell those stories in the best possible way. Success depends on delivering a wider range of quality content to a far more complex audience when, where and how it wants it.

What this has meant in practice at MEN Media has been a root and branch reform of editorial organisation and extensive innovation in both online and print products. These reforms have necessarily been accomplished against an industry-wide background of falling revenues, digital migration of advertisers and readers, diminishing print circulations and, of course, declining resources – part of the changing audience landscape involves a shift in when, where and how people are willing to pay.

Therefore, the response by MEN Media has been an attempt to adapt content and delivery methods to appeal to this more diverse audience while, at the same time, creating a new model of efficient working practice reflecting our changing capabilities.

This chapter provides a brief overview of the innovation and transformation which has taken place at MEN Media in recent years, both in terms of organisation and philosophy, to respond to the changes we face.

Background to the changes

MEN Media incorporates the *Manchester Evening News* and twenty weekly newspaper titles distributed in and around the Greater Manchester region. Until March 2010 MEN Media was owned by the Guardian Media Group (GMG) and also included the local television station Channel M as well as a number of commercial local radio stations. MEN Media was sold to Trinity Mirror plc in 2010 but Channel M and the radio stations remained in GMG ownership, severing editorial links.

How editorial is organized

There have been significant changes in the way MEN Media deploys both its content gathering staff and its production teams in recent years. In general terms this has involved a series of redesigns of the newsroom structure from a network of traditional newspaper offices to a multimedia operation staffed by a single editorial team serving all products.

In the last five years the MEN has moved between four different newsrooms which have produced content for daily and weekly newspapers, web, radio and TV. Although these moves were disruptive they provided a series of opportunities to refine the design of the newsroom and implement new working practices.

The key feature of the new newsrooms, which has underpinned multimedia publication, has been the development of the "hub".

Initial attempts to create a single base for all managers of all media platforms encountered some obstacles due to the overambitious size. Later versions have been more successful and are a vital factor in our ability to provide effective multimedia publication to serve a diverse audience.

The hub places the priority on function (e.g. news, sport, features, business) rather than on format (e.g. print, web, radio or TV). Only by organising the newsroom in this way can MEN Media exploit the strengths of each platform – whether for speed of publication of breaking news or for competitive advantage of exclusive content – and thereby serve and engage all elements of the audience.

Practicality demands that functions be separated to create manageably sized hubs where everyone can hear what is going on (to be within eavesdropping range), but each hub must incorporate all formats.

How content is gathered

In 2009 all MEN Media's weekly newspaper headquaters were closed and staff moved into the MEN Media offices in central Manchester. This move created controversy within the communities the titles served and posed a significant challenge to maintaining the quality of engagement and content.

Initially each team effectively replicated their existing operation within the Manchester office. Each title continued to be edited and run independently from all other titles. However, in 2010 MEN Media moved all operations from its central Manchester offices to its new base in Chadderton, Oldham. As part of this move the organisation of the newsroom was radically revised to integrate the weekly teams into a broader MEN Media resource.

A new organisational model was devised to maintain local content while serving the multimedia interests of the business. Reporters were no longer allocated to specific titles but to media neutral district teams serving specific areas (e.g. Salford, Tameside, Oldham, etc). The district teams were responsible for providing all the content from the patch for all MEN Media products – whether the MEN, the weekly title or the website.

A further media neutral team of reporters focusing on specialist subjects was also established to serve those interests which transcend geographic boundaries (e.g. education, health, transport, technology).

By doing this we created a coherent multimedia approach to gathering content which is capable of engaging with communities of all types through all media platforms. We avoid counterproductive internal competition or duplication between titles, there is a clear expectation for each reporter to gather content for all publishing platforms – web or print (daily and weekly) – and communities of all types can still identify with a dedicated reporter.

This media neutral approach to content gathering required a fundamental change in the structure of newsroom management and in the role of the hub.

The traditional role of editor of the weekly titles was redefined. Each district team of reporters is now led by a district head whose focus is entirely on content generation and engagement with communities. District heads sit on an expanded hub and are managed by a central head of content who coordinates their activities and establishes priorities to meet the demands of the various platforms (MEN, weekly title and web).

How production takes place

While content gathering was organised on a media neutral, geographic basis there was a clear need to adopt a different approach to production activities to achieve greater efficiency.

The responsibility for page production, which previously had taken up much of the time of weekly editors, was assumed by the new role of district page editors. These members of staff are organised as a pool and allocated to meet the needs of the production cycle for each product. Each title has a senior page editor who stays with a specific series of titles to maintain consistency.

In the past year most of the weekly titles have undergone a redesign to create a uniform layout in order to achieve greater efficiencies with production staff moving between titles. While the redesign raised some debate among readers its impact was monitored and had little identifiable negative impact on circulation. In some cases the design (particularly choice of colours) was modified after liaison with readers which was seen as a positive engagement.

Online innovation
Online innovation has been a key area of development. We have recognised the need to exploit the unique strengths of online publishing and the new opportunities it provides to reach both traditional and new audiences. The development of the MEN Media digital strategy was designed to be an integral part of the content gathering and publishing processes.

The debate over online publication in newspaper offices seems to have been dominated by quantitative concerns – when, where and how much to publish – which in turn has led many into the futile web-first vs print-first argument.. At MEN Media we recognised the need to adopt a more qualitative approach and distinguish between types of content to maintain the value of all platforms. To this end a distinction is made between live and exclusive content. Live content is published online at the first opportunity creating a constant flow of fresh material. Exclusive stories are managed in a different fashion with parallel publication in print and online at a time deemed to create the maximum overall benefit.

Specific online initiatives have dramatically improved our ability to interact with our audience and react to what is creating the most interest. We, like all newsrooms, have sought to exploit this opportunity to allow us to create more compelling and relevant content.

User comments are an important source of interaction and are regarded as a valuable form of content alongside journalist-generated articles. Although there is a clear correlation between the volume of interaction and overall site traffic, the issue of monitoring and managing the nature of comments to maintain legal, ethical and brand values is a thorny one which remains a point of debate. At present MEN Media maintains a pre-moderation strategy.

A further major advance in the ability of newspapers to tell stories better has been the rise of live blogging. MEN Media has successfully exploited this in a range of situations including for coverage of the 2011 riots, sports events, traffic disruption, extreme weather conditions, a range of protest marches held in the area and local and national election counts.

One significant use of live blogging which has attracted an audience has been the coverage of local council meetings. A reporter provides live commentary on the proceedings, often attracting contributions from participating politicians and members of the public. This has reinvigorated the coverage of local politics and provided communities with a new forum with which to engage with the democratic process.

Live blogging can be regarded as one aspect of a wider trend toward using social media as a tool to connect audiences with content. Twitter feeds are now run by a wide range of reporters along with the main content desks with comment and breaking news.

Social networking sites like Facebook have also created another point of contact with an ever expanding audience with no interest in our print products.

Incorporating these activities into the normal working day while applying uniform standards for the quality of content and scrutiny has provided new challenges.

Print innovation

A characteristic of MEN Media's recent approach has been to identify new possibilities for print publication to gain greater advantage from existing markets and to exploit niche opportunities.

Certainly, the introduction of a part-paid part-free distribution model for the *Manchester Evening News* in 2006 has been well documented and has proved its value in supporting distribution as well as advertising revenue.

More recently there have been a number of further initiatives. The launch of two new weekly titles in Trafford last year reflected a belief that there was an untapped demand for quality newspapers to serve specific communities. The *Sale and Altrincham Advertiser* and the *Stretford and Urmston Advertiser* have successfully competed for readership and advertisers with the rival *Messenger* titles in the same areas.

In November 2010 another new title was launched in response to demand from the business community. The *Greater Manchester Business Week* magazine targeted a gap in the market left when Crain's shut its business newspaper in Greater Manchester. Creation of the *Business Week* magazine was part of an overall expansion of MEN Media's business coverage in the MEN, the weekly titles and, in particular, online.

The editorial business team grew significantly and the management structure was reformed to create a single unit providing content for all outlets. A new online platform was launched to create a common web resource for all print products which was capable of successfully challenging the main source of web based competition in the region.

Broadcast innovation

One further innovative step worthy of mention was the incorporation of television production into the MEN Media newsroom. Although ultimately unsuccessful, the ultra-local appeal of Channel M generated audiences in excess of 300,000 each week in the Greater Manchester area and offered an alternative to the regionwide alternatives offered by the BBC and ITV Granada.

Since it was founded in 2000 Channel M operated a separate editorial team in several separate buildings. There was some cooperation but on an ad hoc basis. However, in 2008 Channel M's entire news operation was moved into the MEN Media newsroom alongside print and web journalists. This was regarded as an extremely innovative move at the time and involved live broadcasts being made from the newsroom and a senior member of the television news team being based on the news hub. A representative of the radio stations also followed, although the reporting team remained based in a separate building.

The move toward incorporating broadcast content also prompted a reform of the conference structure to move away from the old newspaper format of looking ahead to the next day's paper but instead created a "live" element to consider continuous publication online as well as serving the different deadlines of television and radio. The arrangement ended with the sale of MEN Media to Trinity Mirror plc.

It can be argued that Channel M was ahead of its time – the new framework for local television currently being proposed by the DCMS as well as the rise of "smart" television sets may well provide a widespread expectation for local television content and accessibility through an appropriate delivery platform that could make the Channel M model viable in the future.

What does it all mean?
The recent history of MEN Media demonstrates that quality multimedia content can be generated by a newsroom which is also adapting to the pressures of the challenging economic environment. It also demonstrates how a proactive approach to seeking new sources of revenue is an alternative to cost reduction.

The MEN Media newsroom now provides a highly efficient model for providing content to serve a diverse audience through a range of media platforms. It maintains personal engagement of reporters with a geographic patch, allowing them to develop contacts and knowledge, while avoiding allegiance to specific media platforms or titles. It also creates a truly multimedia environment where the needs of all media platforms and audiences are recognised – with breaking news stories being speedily published online and exclusive stories being managed to appear in the most appropriate print titles in a coordinated fashion to gain the maximum editorial and commercial benefit.

Ultimately, the experience at MEN Media demonstrates how we are successfully equipping ourselves to engage with the full spectrum of audience. Perhaps it is high time the traditional "Read all about it" cry of the newspaper seller be updated with "Watch all about it, listen all about it and talk all about it".

Note on the author

Ian Wood was deputy editor of the Manchester Evening News until January 2012. He joined the paper's newsdesk in 1998, working his way up to be appointed news editor in 2001. In this role he took over responsibility for refining a working model of convergence and developing a multimedia publishing strategy for the group. In 2011 he led the launch of the Greater Manchester Business Week magazine. Ian now works as a freelance journalist.

Towards a newspaper for every street

Andrew Adamson outlines the launch of the *Pembroke and Pembroke Dock Observer*, and explains why an increasingly local focus is paying dividends.

The 1st July 2011 saw a new local newspaper, the *Pembroke and Pembroke Dock Observer*, launched by the Tenby Observer group, part of Tindle Newspapers. The *Pembroke and Pembroke Dock Observer*, together with the *Tenby Observer* and *Narberth and Whitland Observer* form the Tenby Observer group, covering South Pembrokeshire.

Throughout their history the towns of Tenby, Pembroke and Pembroke Dock have shared interests, and throughout the century-and-a-half of the *Tenby Observer*'s history it has covered news relevant to both areas. Over this period the masthead and title have reflected this. 1860 – *Tenby and Pembroke Dock Observer*, 1867 – *The Tenby Observer and Pembrokeshire Chronicle*, 1949 – *The Tenby Observer and District Reporter*, and in the 1970's the Observer group included editions, one of which was the *Pembroke and Pembroke Dock Weekly News*.

Toward the end of the 1970s the paper was called the *Tenby and West Wales Weekly Observer*, and was, most unfortunately, in trouble. In January 1978 the *Daily Telegraph* carried news of the paper's difficulties and it was following this article that Sir Ray Tindle took ownership of the paper two months later, reverted it back to its original name, the *Tenby Observer*, and the paper has gone from strength to strength ever since.

Sir Ray's philosophy is a simple one for local newspapers, local people, local names, local events, local places. He wanted nothing to happen in Tenby that wasn't in the *Observer*. This is the basic format for all of our titles, and one that we religiously follow.

I've often exaggerated that his ideal would be a paper for every street in the town, with every person living in that street in the paper, every week. While I think I'd struggle to claim it was my idea, I will mention that he did say something very similar to Hilary Gavin, for journalism.co.uk, "The average person isn't interested in the wider area, but they are very interested in their immediate locality. If you had a paper for every street, it would sell. You couldn't do that, but you could do it for every town."[1]

Why we set it up?

Over recent years we strived to include as much content, including as much community-generated content as possible, and while our main area is Tenby, Pembroke and Pembroke Dock are still areas relevant to our readership. As the *Observer* is sold in Pembroke and Pembroke Dock, we found that increasingly the community there would voluntarily submit their news to us, as they found that it was more than likely to be published. Furthermore, local businesses had no cost effective platform for them to advertise. This left them searching for other options to promote their businesses. Market research carried out locally highlighted this fact that their options were indeed limited and few and far between and a long way from cost effective.

We also found that as the volume of submitted news increased, so to did the affection and popularity of the *Tenby Observer* in Pembroke and Pembroke Dock. This gave us the confidence and the opportunity to seriously consider the case for a Pembroke and Pembroke Dock 'only' newspaper, the aim of which was to carry all the local community-based news which was clearly not being published by any of the larger county titles. Add this to the potential support from local traders wishing to reach their local community and we were confident we could deliver and match the demand from all quarters for a truly local paper for Pembroke and Pembroke Dock.

How it has worked

With the *Tenby Observer* already popular in Pembroke, our main aim has been to increase the relevance for Pembroke and Pembroke Dock. As well as the title, it was important for us to include more news from the towns and ensure that the new paper was relevant to the community.

We contacted clubs and societies, sports teams, charities and gave out sheets with contact information to all town councillors to ask that if they had any story or news report from the community or aforementioned groups that they wished to see in print that they contact us. Two groups in particular have supplied regular features/photos which have proved to be very popular, the Pembroke and Monkton Local History Society with photos from days gone by, and a local Pastor, Rob James with his thought of the week.

All papers in the *Tenby Observer* series have common sections, but we strived to make the early pages of the paper as specific to Pembroke and Pembroke Dock as possible. We wanted the communities to perceive this as their paper, and use it as the first port of call for reader generated content.

As well as the editorial content, we felt it was vital to get the support for the new title from the small local businesses. After all, advertising revenue will help increase the resources to grow the paper, and give us the ability to carry more content. We tried hard to make sure that all local businesses knew about the new paper, and had a new truly local media in which they could advertise to local people. Many business owners are also active members of their communities, so it doubled as an excellent opportunity to ask them to send us any news they could.

Why it has worked

In the Pembroke and Pembroke Dock area, the new title has approximately doubled our circulation and penetration within those areas, and is still increasing. Prior to the *Pembroke and Pembroke Dock* Observer launch, our area coverage of Pembroke was approximately 20%; with the increased sales that the new title have given us, that has increased to an estimated 40%.

This increased coverage has also improved awareness about the paper and the service it offers; it has helped make sure that the news content hasn't dropped over time. The reporters have made sure they've stayed in contact, and the communities themselves have continued to send us their news. As we have made every effort to include everything we can, the clubs and societies have indulged us; the content coming from the communities shows that they value this new local title as their own. We have ensured we continue to keep it local, relevant and personal to the whole communities of Pembroke and Pembroke Dock.

Lessons to others

The *Pembroke and Pembroke Dock Observer* has succeeded partially due to the fact that we were able to establish it without incurring large costs. It's an area where we have found that we were able to provide a new, or greatly improved service for local readers, which in turn has given small local businesses an extremely cost effective way of promoting directly to their customers, and us a constant revenue stream to support and grow this new title.

Pressure on newspapers to steady falling circulations has not helped the pressure on editorial teams to produce the big story that helps boost sales, but at the local level it is as important to keep the news relevant to the local readers. I'm afraid I must admit that I am not a journalist; I found it interesting to hear Professor Jay Rosen discuss the difference between cosmopolitan and provincial journalism, and the requirement for provincial journalism in a local newspaper. It is core to the role that local newspapers play in their communities.

One of the things without which the Pembroke and Pembroke Dock Observer would not have succeeded is the use of reader generated content. We do rely on the community to submit their news, but for our part we try our best to make sure it always sees print. Without a doubt, this contributes to the perceived "community ownership", it gives locals a vested interest in the paper, and increases the affection for it. The best salespeople in the world are the next door neighbours. Who better to sing the new title's praises?

It is interesting to note that many successful online blogs also find reader-generated material a useful source for editorial content; it appears to be a similarity between us.

The Future

There is no doubt that the future for local newspapers includes some tough times, and I think it also fair to say that the exact model for local news is not resolved. While it may be entirely possible that print circulations will continue to decline, I believe that there is cause to be optimistic. There is still a certain prestige in the local printed media, and for me the favourable reaction and increased circulation by the *Pembroke and Pemrboke Dock Observer* shows the value that local people still place in their papers. The model we try to follow, set out by Sir Ray Tindle, of faces, names and places is one that still has a place in today's, and tomorrow's, media landscape.

Note

[1] Journalism.co.uk tindle interview

Note on the author

Andrew Adamson is general manager of the Tenby Observer group, which include the *Tenby Observer, Narberth and Whitland Observer* and *Pembroke and Pembroke Dock Observer*.

Media on remote islands
– local in the extreme

On the South Atlantic British island of St Helena, a new law allows a Media Commission to close down any newspaper that breaches its rules. A long association with remote islands has taught Simon Pipe that life for journalists in such places is different - and sometimes, bizarre.

The studio of Radio Weka was through a side door off the ladies' lavatory in Waitangi, the tiny 'capital' of the Chatham Islands. It wasn't glamorous. At some point, someone had stuck egg cartons to a section of the studio wall to soften the sound, but that was the nearest it came to soundproofing.

It's often said of small communities that you only have to cough and everyone knows about it; if someone pulled the chain in the ladies' loo when the microphone was open, the entire population really did share the experience.

The gale-blown Chathams lie in the South Pacific Ocean, 500 miles off New Zealand, of which they are nominally a part. They're nearly three times the size of the Isle of Wight, and in the early 1990s were home to about 700 people - white Europeans, Maori, and the few surviving native Moriori. On shearing days, you could add a few sheep to Radio Weka's audience profile.

My career changed the day I walked into that ladies' lavatory, in the Centennial War Memorial Hall (actually, there was another door from the outside, but I didn't always use it). My appreciation of local media changed too. A few months earlier I'd been doing casual shifts in London, as a feature writer on *Today*, now one of Mr Murdoch's growing stable of defunct national newspapers. I had no intention of becoming a broadcaster, and certainly no plans to go back to community journalism. On the other hand, it had taken only a few weeks in London for me to discover, after years of striving to become a tabloid hack, that it wasn't really me. Then my wife announced we were going travelling, and that was that.

As it turned out, my afternoons in front of the microphone at Radio Weka were to lead to 18 years at the BBC, mostly working in local radio but with a strange stint at the World Service, producing and presenting a programme for the Falkland Islands. And now I find myself experimenting with an online news service[1] for another extremely isolated community, 5,000 miles away on St Helena, in the South Atlantic – although my real readership may turn out to be just down the road.

What do we mean by 'local'? When it comes to remote islands, the word doesn't have the same connotations as it might in mainland Britain. In fact, island people often have to travel far from their homelands in search of work, so 'local' doesn't necessarily even mean listeners or readers are contained in one place. In the case of St Helena, many of them are in Swindon, which is known on the island as Swindolena.

And people in small, very isolated communities have different expectations of their media; it doesn't bother them that there are no audio clips in the news bulletins, and they don't care about slick jingle packages.

I couldn't get this across when I went for my first interviews with the BBC back home to England. It was my radio experience, rather than my 14 years in journalism, that got me the interviews in the first place, which says something about the BBC local radio of the time. Had I gone out interviewing people, they wanted to know? A nice idea, but Radio Weka was a little outside the comprehension of the suited BBC execs: the studio had been built by the New Zealand Telecom man in his spare time, and he hadn't seen the need for recording and editing gear. My daily show started whenever I wandered up to the studio, and finished when I felt like going home again. I thought it best not to trouble the suits with too much detail.

The informality of it all was captured by the Kiwi broadcaster Gary McCormick, whose impromptu weather report for us appeared on a TV documentary. He made a point of coming in through the ladies' toilet. His visit can be seen on the first of two clips on the website of NZ On Screen[2], a spin-off from a charity that funds local television production.

'The studio key's hanging on the door. Just let yourself in'

Radio Weka's day always started the same way, with the voice of Robin Williams calling "Goood Mawnin' Veee-et-naaam" across the islands. Nobody seemed to think this was odd. Steve Locke, the Telecom man, would then do an hour's show, which somehow included a news bulletin from Radio New Zealand; after that, he would load the multi-disc CD player with six albums and programme it to play them three times through. Most days, that was the output. There were no other stations within range.

One morning, I heard *It's My Party And I'll Cry If I Want To* about five times and could take no more. I phoned Steve at work. "The CD player's packed up," he said. "We've sent it to New Zealand for repair. It'll be gone six weeks." He'd borrowed a replacement, but it would only take one disc, so we were in for six weeks of party compilations. Steve could tell I wasn't happy. "Why don't you change the CD?" he suggested. "The key to the studio is hanging up inside the back door of the bank. Just let yourself in."

It was just as he said. After a few visits, the people at the bank suggested I should say a few words into the mic, so I did. The next time, they suggested I should switch it on.

There wasn't a lot to talk about. If something bad happened, talking about it on the radio would have been in poor taste. If it was good, everyone knew anyway. I did do "world news", when I could get some, but there weren't any newspapers in the Chathams, and this was in the days before the internet. There were, however, thrice-weekly cargo flights to Wellington airport, loaded with fish. The pilots had to stay "air side" at the airport, where there was no news stand, but one of them agreed to scoop up any papers he could find in the waste bins, and fly them back. That was pretty much my only source of news, outside of the twice-daily bulletins from New Zealand. The BBC people thought recycling newspaper stories without checking them was legally shaky, but we were 500 miles out in an ocean - who was going to know?

We weren't entirely unaware of what was going on in New Zealand. Surprising as it may seem, the Chathams did actually have a nightly television service for its 700 residents. This began with the six o'clock TV news, which ran at a quarter to seven, thanks to a kink that had been made in the International Date Line so that the Chathams were merely 45 minutes ahead of New Zealand time, rather than a day behind. There was also a mainland programme called *Sixty Minutes*; with the adverts taken out, it only lasted 40. The rest of the night's output was made up of video tapes of TV shows - mostly British - sent out from Wellington. The station was operated by volunteer members of the Chatham Islands Radio and Television Society. Their job also involved typing up adverts, which appeared on screen in text form. Thus my wife was able to advertise on TV for the loan of a spinning wheel, and someone called Bob asked people to look out for a wrench that fell off his truck on the Owenga road. Interesting spellings were seen as part of the night's entertainment: one job advert asked for people to do "male sorting".

Sadly, the minutes of a Chatham Island Council meeting of 2009 reported that Radio Weka had effectively ceased operation[3], and few islanders were still watching programmes from the TV station: the islands had come within the reach of the all-conquering Sky TV. In November 2011, the minutes[4] recorded that only 30 households continued to rely on the local service, making it possibly the smallest television service in the world. At the start of 2012, its future was uncertain: the transmission gear needed maintenance costing $NZ50,000, but closure was not inevitable – it was thought to have twice that amount in the bank.

We did have one big story while I was on the Chathams. I nearly missed it, because I happened not to be among the drinkers at the pub who watched in mild surprise as a large Korean trawler steamed full-speed across the bay and straight up the beach. It was dark: the captain thought he was sailing between two islands. The resourceful islanders rescued the crew, and then the many tonnes of frozen fish in the hold. I was hoisted aboard: the conditions were horrible, and I was able to describe them on air when I got back to the studio. I also appealed for people to bring clothes and blankets for the shivering crew. It was my first experience of what live radio could do, and it was exciting. It was too bad I didn't eat fish.

Islands are like that when it comes to news: there's not much in the way of crime and council stories, but when things do happen, they are often quite extraordinary by mainland standards. For the journalist-cum-broadcaster, working in such an intimate community is highly gratifying, in a way that mainland journalism never could be. When I walked home from the Radio Weka studio, people would shout out their thanks for the show. They knew who I was, because everyone knew everyone.

On the down side, in a place like the Chathams it was easy to cause offence without knowing how, and a couple of times, I did. But you don't need focus groups and audience research to get to know your listeners. Once, I spent an afternoon on Pitt Island with the champion shearer. My programmes were all right, he said, but he wasn't so happy when I played heavy-metal music: "It makes the sheep aggressive."

Further from anywhere than anywhere else in the world
Three years later, my wife and I were sitting in a pub in Milton Keynes, where I was the district reporter for BBC Three Counties Radio. In every sense, it was about as far as it was possible to get from the rough-and-ready Chathams. One of my wife's fellow doctors, knowing of our interest in islands, mentioned that a job was going for a locum general practitioner on St Helena, a British Dependent Territory in the South Atlantic. We'd made up our minds before we'd even finished our drinks. Ant got the job, and then we had to fill out a form with lots of personal details - including information about my occupation. "A journalist? Oh dear. That might be a problem," said the lady at the recruitment agency in Northern Ireland. She agreed that "producer" would be acceptable. Events were to prove her misgivings well-founded.

St Helena is "further from anywhere than anywhere else in the world," as Julie Blackburn neatly put it in The Emperor's Last Island, her book about Napoleon's exile there. The island rises abruptly out of the sea, far to the west of Angola, just ten miles long and six miles across. There is no other land within a thousand miles, save the even-smaller island of Ascension.

In January 2012, work started on building St Helena's first airport, at a cost to the British taxpayer of at least £200 million; for us, though, reaching the island in 1996 involved a six-day sea voyage from Cape Town. The island came into view before dawn but even so, a small huddle of returning islanders were up on the bridge to see it take shape in the darkness. One had not been home for 40 years. Eyes were moist.

With a population of 5,000 people - mostly descended from slaves - St Helena was very different in character from the Chathams. In Jamestown's elegant main street and the island's crumbling fortifications, evidence of British colonial heritage was all around.

After a few days, I found my way up to the studios of Radio St Helena. It was not like Radio Weka. The station was 30 years old, and generously funded by the St Helena Government - which meant, indirectly, by the UK. It had staff. It even had a broadcast van, equipped with mobile studio and transmitter. There was no breakfast programme: television had only just been introduced, and had yet to provide real competition for evening output.

St Helena used to be a listening station for the British secret services, diplomatically known as the Diplomatic Wireless Relay Station. The 'staff up at Piccolo Hill' would monitor radio broadcasts in Africa. When the relay station closed down, it provided Radio St Helena with its first transmitters - still in a side room, but no longer used. The radio station building was far out of town, a couple of thousand feet above sea level. This was because the producers sometimes had to climb the transmitter mast when it went wrong (so they told me).

Tony Leo, the veteran station manager[5], was friendly but curiously reluctant to let me do any news reporting, even as a volunteer. Later on, I learned that there were sensitivities. I would, however, be allowed to make some soft feature items. Three ships of the German Navy were about to anchor in the roads, and I was invited to do a piece on it. I pulled all the stops and produced a report that ran for a good 22 minutes, not a sound effect missed out. I think the islanders were rather taken aback.

And then something unexpected happened. Tony phoned me at home and asked if I'd cover a protest march, over plans to withdraw free transport for government employees (which meant nearly three quarters of the working population). It was due to start in a matter of minutes. I had one of Radio St Helena's battered reel-to-reel recorders on loan, so I grabbed it and ran the half-mile into Jamestown - without the microphone. The protesters were just poised to set off for The Castle, where His Excellency the Governor worked at a desk below a large Union Flag, but the leaders held up the entire march so I could run back to get the missing magic stick. I was astonished by this, but the marchers were even more amazed that a reporter had been allowed to cover their demonstration. Past protests had simply not been mentioned in the media, I was told.

Afterwards, I was allowed into The Castle to interview an official - someone I came to like, actually - and was told that if my resulting report was not entirely fair and balanced, I would not be allowed to broadcast any more. It was as direct as that.

A technical confusion meant that when my report was broadcast, it contained long silences, where my audio had been dubbed on to the wrong bit of the tape. The islanders - known as Saints - were untroubled by this. A few nights later, at the Blue Hill invitation dance, one senior government employee said how well the report had gone down. But what about the long silences? "Oh we all knew what that meant," he said. "Those were the bits that were cut out by government."

This wasn't some despotic dictatorship. We were on British soil, under a British administration, in the late 20th Century. And to be honest, I wasn't convinced that censorship was genuinely still imposed, except by island journalists themselves. They certainly believed there were stories they could not report, but there was another factor: they were employed directly by the government they were reporting on, and people who lost their government jobs often had to leave the island to find work.

Nearly two decades later, however, columnist Vince Thompson was to recall in the *St Helena Independent* that a restraining hand on island media had been justified as "legitimate control of a government resource."

The blurred line between a free press and government funding

The island does now have free journalism - up to a point. In fact, by the early years of the present century it was remarkably well-endowed with local-cum-national media (on St Helena, they're the same thing). The population was sliding to below 4,000, but the remaining islanders could enjoy two weekly newspapers, and two radio stations. The *St Helena Herald* and the old radio station were funded directly by the government, but the rival *St Helena Independent* and Saint FM were set up as a commercial operation. They too came to receive significant income from the government, but in the form of advertising and payment for promotional services – for which The Castle pays a reduced rate. Their editor, a Swedish exile named Mike Olsson, is un-cowed by this financial connection; in fact, he is proud to have been a thorn in the government's side. I suspect he is equally proud of having been arrested on one occasion, for receiving leaked paperwork relating to a business in which the government was a major shareholder. He is a self-taught journalist with more than a hint of frontier spirit about him, though not all islanders appreciate his abrasive editorial style. His organisation's website is candid about its curious editorial situation:

"The relationship between Government and the press has always presented an interesting mix of colonial rules and supposed 'freedom of the press'. The present St Helena News Media Services is, to a degree, recognised as an organisation independent of Government but ironically remains for the most part, funded by the organisation it strives to separate itself from. The line between a free press and a government-run media is a blurred one on St Helena."[6]

In Britain, MPs and media commentators have recognised that legal regulation of the Press raises difficult issues. Actually closing down a newspaper would be pretty well unthinkable.

Not on St Helena. The Media Standards Ordinance 2011[7] allows the St Helena Government to "terminate production" of any newspaper that is deemed by a Media Commission to have breached editorial codes on harmful, offensive or defamatory content. The Commission will be able to summon witnesses under oath; and if they don't co-operate, then "the power of the Supreme Court [of St Helena] to punish contempt of its authority is extended to include a power to punish contempt of the Commission."

And these are the sanctions allowed under the ordinance:

in the case of a complaint against a broadcaster, a recommendation to the Governor that its broadcasting licence be revoked or restricted;

in the case of any ongoing publication, an order that such publication be discontinued.

The Media Ordinance does require the Commission to "have regard to the Constitutional rights to freedoms of opinion and of expression." As of January 2012, though, the new Governor of St Helena had yet to announce when the new law would come into force.

In reality, the power to close down a newspaper is not needed. The government can simply withdraw its advertising, which almost certainly would have the same effect.

Towards the end of 2011, a new, community-owned media organisation came into being: the St Helena Broadcasting Corporation. It aims to launch a local television news service by 2014. It also plans three radio channels - one speech-led, one for music and entertainment, and the third for the BBC World Service.

Stakeholders in this not-for-profit body include representatives of St Helena's modest private sector, the Chamber of Commerce, island charities and the youth service, among others. The funding is coming from the government[8], but under a "service-level agreement". This includes paying for radio output to be relayed to Ascension Island and the Falklands, where many Saints go to work - commonly leaving home, and sometimes their children, for a year at a time. Programmes will also be streamed on the internet for the benefit of Saints now living overseas – about a thousand of them in Swindon.

There is also to be a new newspaper, though Stuart Moors, the chairman of the corporation, could not give firm details at the start of 2012: "We are intending to have a newspaper, but not necessarily once a week. We will have an online version - not just a pdf of the paper, much more of an online magazine. How that is charged for is still under discussion. If it's free it's a bit difficult to make revenue, but it's not doing its job if people don't read it."

The SHBC came about because the existing media had come to be seen as a problem that could no longer be ignored. Government press releases and reports from island organisations tended to be reproduced word-for-word, and both papers often lifted the same stories, verbatim, from foreign newspapers and broadcasts. Reports of executive council meetings were written not by journalists, but by the Governor - and again, reproduced word-for-word, in the newspapers and on both radio stations. The result was that much of the two papers' content was identical - and the government was funding both of them. Many islanders bought copies of each of them.

The *Herald* and Radio St Helena were left marking time, waiting to be killed off as soon as their replacements hit the streets and the airwaves. "They have never really proved their independence from government, and very few people wanted to work for them any more," said Stuart Moors. "On the opposite side, the *Independent* has not got a great reputation with the government. There are some supporters who feel they are at least questioning the government – Mike [Olsson] has achieved something in that - but it's gone too far."

Mike Olsson and his St Helenian wife share a flat over the production office, in an elegant Georgian building in Main Street, Jamestown. From its windows, he can look across the street to the offices of his adversaries in The Castle. Living over the shop is handy for a working life that involves getting up early to present the weekday breakfast programme, then switching roles to become newspaper editor; and on Saturday nights, doing the late show.

Mike puts most of the newspaper together, and there are two staffers working primarily for the radio station. But for the most part, Saint FM is kept on air by more than 40 volunteers – some of them still at school. Much of the content in the St Helena Independent is likewise written by unpaid contributors (including, occasionally, me). One columnist, a retired businessman, writes until he's run out of things to say, then fills out the space with mostly-smutty jokes. They're very popular.

There has been much talk of "citizen journalism" in the UK, but on St Helena, that's pretty much the way it's always been. Saint FM was the brainchild of Johnny Drummond, who had been the art teacher up at Prince Andrew School when I knew him, but then became editor of the *Herald*. Sadly, he died shortly before his radio station went live in 2005. He left money for it in his will.

When I briefly returned to the island in 2009, the *Herald* chair was occupied by a talented, highly-literate young lady named Kerisha Stevens. She was 19 years old, and editor of a national newspaper.

The chief executive of the new broadcasting corporation is also a newcomer to journalism, though he has run his own photographic studio on the island, and made videos. He has a tough job, judging by the advert:

"The first thing the successful candidate will do is to create a winning team of Producer/Journalists who can deliver media excellence. The SHBC will also demand technical competence, commercial acumen and a high level of drive and energy. Specific experience of on-line media delivery and managing a media company would be a distinct advantage."

Curiously, given the independent status of the SHBC, applications were handled by the government.

On an island with a population of 4,000 - plus a diaspora of perhaps 10,000 more Saints overseas - they were unlikely to find a native islander experienced in every aspect of the job – and business experience is the most difficult quality to secure in St Helena. But the Saints have always been adaptable. The news reader I worked with at Radio St Helena also helped run the fire service. The news editor had done a variety of jobs, and went on to take up the fight against alien plant species. Tony Leo, the station manager, was also a wedding photographer, and chairman of the St Helena farmers' group.

The last time I saw Tony at Radio St Helena, he was standing by the open door with a carrier bag wedged over his head, and was rolling up his trouser legs.

It was raining heavily, and he was about to step into the long, wet grass outside. He'd brought his goat to work, and now he was taking it home again.

Notes

[1] Pipe, S. (2012) *The Island That Was Eaten by Goats: Life on the Remote British Island of St Helena – Viewed from a Distance* [online]. Available from http://www.thegatesofchaos.wordpress.com [last accessed on 31 January 2012]

[2] NZ On Screen (n.d.) *Heartland, Chatham Islands, 1993 television documentary* [online]. Available from: http://www.nzonscreen.com/title/heartland-chatham-islands-1993 [last accessed on 31 January 2012]

[3] Chatham Islands Council (2009) *Minutes of the Ordinary Monthly Meeting of the Chatham Islands Council, held in the Council Chambers, Tuku Road, Waitangi, on Thursday, 19 March 2009: Item 5.2 Community Trust of Canterbury Funding.* Available from: http://www.cic.govt.nz/pdfs/councilMeetings/CICMinutesMarch2009.pdf [last accessed on 30 January 2012]

[4] Chatham Islands Council (2011) *Minutes of the Ordinary Monthly Meeting of the Chatham Islands Council, held in the Council Chambers, Tuku Road, Waitangi, on Thursday, 10 November 2011: Item 9.1, Chatham Islands Radio and Television Society.* Available from: http://www.cic.govt.nz/pdfs/councilMeetings/cic-council-minutes-101111.pdf [last accessed on 30 January 2012]

[5] Drummond, D. (2002) *Tony Leo "Signs Off" after 29 years in Radio Broadcasting*, St Helena Herald, October 2002. Available from: http://www.sthelena.se/tony/tony.htm [last accessed on 31 January 2012]

[6] St Helena News Media Services (2005) *Saint FM, The Heartbeat of St Helena: How it all started* [online]. Available from: http://www.saint.fm/part1.htm [last accessed on 29 January 2012]

[7] St Helena Government (2011) *Media Standards Ordinance: An ordinance to regulate media services, to establish a media commission to monitor and enforce media standards, and for purposes connected therewith or incidental thereto.* Available from: http://www.sainthelena.gov.sh/data/files/resources/719/Media-Standards-Ordinance.pdf [last accessed on 27 January 2012]

[8] St Helena Government (2011), *Executive Council report, 2 November 2011.* St Helena Government website. Available from: http://www.sainthelena.gov.sh/news.php/439/exco-report-2nd-november-2011 [last accessed on 27 January 2012]

Note on the contributor

Simon Pipe began his career in local and regional newspapers in the West Country. After a period of travel, he joined BBC local radio in 1994, ending his career in 2011 as a senior broadcast journalist at BBC Oxford. He also worked for BBC News Online and produced the BBC World Service programme, Calling The Falklands. A return visit to St Helena in 2009 resulted in a dispatch for the BBC's From Our Own Correspondent programme. In 2011 he became an MA student at Coventry University.

Section B. New ways of serving the audiences

Ian Reeves

Every now and then throughout the 1980s and 1990s, a group of highly-influential regional newspaper editors would put aside a day to gather in a conference room at one of their HQs. They called themselves the 120 Club.

And for a few hours they would park their editorial, commercial or geographical rivalries and allow themselves a free and frank exchange of views on a variety of topics concerning the industry.

In the early 2000s, they allowed me to join one of their sessions as an observer, hosted on that occasion by the Newcastle *Evening Chronicle*. It was one of their final meetings, and a fascinating insight into the preoccupations of the men – and one woman – at the helm of the half-dozen or so top-selling newspapers in the country.

The editors talked about editorial campaigns, staffing issues, advertising revenue, government policy, digital strategies and much else besides. Occasionally, I was asked to leave the room when a piece of information deemed too commercially sensitive for the pages of *Press Gazette* was about to be revealed. They were passionate, experienced and commercially savvy.

What strikes me now about that meeting, a decade or so later, is that there was no palpable sense of the maelstrom into which we were all heading. Yes, there were concerns about sliding circulations – at that stage a year-on-year drop of a couple of per cent wasn't unusual. And all of them were painfully aware of the margins that their publishing bosses demanded of their businesses. But the first Internet bubble was in the process of bursting, and there was a feeling that the principles that had served their newspapers so well, in some cases for well over a century already, would continue to underpin them.

Things look somewhat different in hindsight. Only one of the people in that room is still editing a regional newspaper. Most are no longer in the industry at all, having left for more lucrative careers in communications or having been swiftly sidelined when they became too outspoken about their corporate masters.

I don't know whether their successors meet in the same way. If they do, they certainly don't call themselves the 120 Club any more. Back then, to be invited you had to be editing a newspaper selling more than 120,000 copies a day. Today, most feel lucky if they shift more than 50,000.

Press Gazette, the industry's weekly newspaper for which I was covering the meeting, went out of business in 2006 and later returned as a monthly title with one sixth of its former staff roster.

Should we have seen it coming? Were we complacently fiddling while the bonfires were already alight around us?

I don't believe so. The technologically-driven social and commercial upheaval that followed was so drastic, so fundamental that nobody could truly have predicted where it would lead.

At the time of the meeting I've described, Google was just two years old. YouTube wouldn't exist for another five years. Mark Zuckerberg was only sixteen, and wouldn't launch Facebook until he was twenty two. Craigslist was nothing more than an email listing of things for sale in San Francisco.

Yet all of these things have transformed the media landscape in astonishingly short order, and in ways that even their founders could not have predicted.

None of them has journalism as part of their DNA.

So this section attempts to looks through the smoke and the debris for the models that journalism might use to forge a new future from the wreckage of the old. It starts with the successor of the editor who hosted that 120 Club meeting. Paul Robertson, who in turn left the editor's chair of the Newcastle *Evening Chronicle* last year, kicks us off with an impassioned defence of journalism as the glue that binds communities together. His predecessors would have wholly endorsed his message.

Likewise the contribution from John Meehan, another passionate editor of many years' standing, who urges publishers to treasure and nurture their core newspaper products while intelligently developing digital complements, using social media tools to enhance the public's trust in their journalism.

Justin Scholsberg then takes a close look at the corporate ownership structure of the regional press, pointing out how the consolidation of the industry has often been at the expense of the local communities their newspapers were set up to serve.

Tor Clark takes us back to the origins of the UK newspaper industry in the seventeenth and eighteenth centuries, and suggests that perhaps a return to some of that early focus on tightly defined local communities might pay dividends.

All of which brings us to one of the key words in most analyses of journalism's future: hyperlocal. David Baines examines from an academic perspective the key hyperlocal experiments so far, including those by *The Guardian*, the *New York Times* and Northcliffe Newspapers, among others.

And then we move on to those heroic pioneers who are attempting to forge a hyperlocal future with business models of various shapes and sizes. Richard Coulter has put print at the core of the *filtonvoice*, a quarterfold monthly magazine for the twelve thousand people of his town. It's early days, but he believes the signs are promising. Meanwhile the founders of *Lichfield Live*, *Pits n Pots* and *Saddleworth News* all adopted a digital strategy for their hyperlocal offerings. Ross Hawkes, Richard Jones and Mike Rawlins respectively offer fascinating insights into the triumphs and disasters of hyperlocal start-ups.

Sarah Johnson takes a look at another hyperlocal blog, one started almost by accident by Jonathan Turton in 2010. *West Hamsptead Life* now boasts four thousand unique visitors, albeit as a "labour of love" for its creator.

Another taking the non-profit approach is Tom O'Brien, creator of MyMuswell. Frustrated by the lack of useful local information available during the London riots in the summer of 2011, he set about building a community platform which residents of Muswell Hill would adopt as their own.

All of these brave souls are utilising the power of digital technology – web tools and social media platforms – to make geographical connections for a local community.

And if none has cracked the economics of it yet, there are at least some positive signs. One figure in particular struck me in Richard Jones's piece about *Saddleworth News*. He was reaching twenty thousand people with news about a population of twenty four thousand people. That's quite some market penetration.

But it's not only geographical connections that can bind a community. Jay Rosen, one of the most forward thinking members of the journalism blogosphere has an idea that he calls the 100 Per Cent Solution. It starts (and ends) with the proposition: 'What if we could cover all of it?' The 'it' in question could be college football matches. Or gigs by local bands. Or church sermons. Or election hustings.

But as Rosen says, it's the resulting innovation that then brings its own rewards: "In trying to reach the goal you immediately run into problems. To solve those problems you often have to improvise or innovate. And that's the payoff, even if you don't meet your goal."

It's a long way from the 120 Club to the hyperlocal experiment. But in their own way the innovators in this chapter have the same ideals at heart as those editors did. To make journalism matter to a community. And to find a sustainable way of allowing it to thrive.

The glue holding communities together

Paul Robertson was at the sharp end editing one of the UK's leading regional dailies. Here he tells how his company attempted to adapt to changing times.

During the Leveson Inquiry, the public would be forgiven for thinking that all journalists are cheating, uncaring reprobates out to destroy anyone and everyone. Nothing could be further from the truth. The vast majority are hard working, passionate about their jobs – determined to expose wrongdoing and uncover injustice but, equally importantly, to promote and support the local people and communities they serve. They are appalled by the phone-hacking scandal and the damage it unfairly does to their own reputations.

The expensively assembled inquiry will, by its very nature, concentrate on the celebrities, the high profile ordinary people badly wronged by the national media such as the McCanns and Dowlers. What it has largely ignored – an accusation which can be levelled at Parliament too – is the real crisis that is happening among those operating at regional and local level, where the journalists play by the rules.

MPs and others have been up in arms about the proposed cuts to local BBC services – understandably so – yet what about the birthplace of those stations' journalism?

You can hear the pages turning on air as the local newspapers form the basis for any regional radio station's news, sport and entertainment coverage as well as its phone-ins.

It is the regional newspaper journalists who sift through council agendas, talk to contacts, bother to attend magistrates courts, community events, schools and workplaces. They and their families live and work in the towns and villages they serve, where contacts are made and the consequences of what they write are keenly felt.

When people turn to local brands
The pages of the local paper in print and online continue to be the home of original journalism – a force for good but all that is threatened by the

acceleration of circulation decline, the damage being done to the perception of journalists and the lack of a clear strategy from companies which give the perception that their shareholders are more important than their readers and advertisers,

Trusted brands, with a fantastic heritage, pillars of the community loathed by some but loved by many. Even in the face of twenty four-hour news coverage, when a major event happens on their doorstep it is the local brands people turn to. This was clearly demonstrated during my time at the *Evening Chronicle* in Newcastle when gunman Raoul Moat went on the run for a week and became the focus of an international media frenzy.

From the moment the first shot was fired in a quiet Tyneside suburb, injuring his ex-girlfriend and killing her new boyfriend, the team covered every cough and spit of the drama with fresh angles to stories for the newspaper and a rolling service through the website and social media – and in particular Twitter.

It was thanks to local contacts, the fact we lived in and knew the area and people trusted us that we were able to lead the way without resorting to the cheque-book journalism which inevitably saw the nationals buy up Moat's surviving victims.

Long after the incident, it was the local paper which supported the launch of injured policeman PC David Rathband's charity, covered the police inquiry, the subsequent court cases, the inquest and asked difficult questions of the police, social services and all those involved in the incident in which Moat ultimately shot himself having eventually been cornered and tasered by police.

The dedication of the team on the ground resulted in brilliant coverage, rewarded with big increases in sales and online hits. To me, it proved in turbulent times the local media is still relevant and has the talent to capitalise on the biggest of stories.

The move to overnight printing did mean the Chronicle missed out on PC Rathband's tragic death in March 2012 in-print, which, judging by the paper's Twitter account prompted complaints and raised awareness among many readers who thought their evening paper was printed on the day that actually it isn't - a further reason for some not to buy but log on instead.

This should not tarnish such a brilliant performance on the Moat story; it should inspire confidence that local newspapers can not only survive but also thrive.

However, forces are at work, which could make this extremely difficult, and unless there is focus, support and a deliverable strategy, more local newspapers will go to the wall before it gets to that point.

Case for the defence
In July 2011, a month before leaving the *Evening Chronicle* in the days leading up to the closure of the *News of the World*, I found myself on local television and radio constantly defending what local and regional journalism stood for. I became so angry at the negative portrayal. Like every decent-minded person in

the country, our professional journalists were appalled at the abuse of press freedom undertaken by the *News of the World.*

It was a damaged brand – morally bankrupt – which brought shame on our industry and the threat of further legislation and regulation that will make it more difficult to do the job. Yet its closure was a major shock – a newspaper, which until this outrageous scandal had a well-earned reputation for investigative journalism mixed with celebrity gossip, sport, and campaigning, gone.

A free, independent, scrutinising press has long played a key role in the democracy of this country at both a local and national level. In the acres of newspaper coverage, in Parliament with MPs baying for News International's blood and most notably among the, at times, holier-than-thou television coverage, this has been overlooked during the phone hacking debates.

PCC is taken seriously

It is hugely disappointing that few have drawn a distinction between the way most journalists operate and the culture exposed at the *News of the World.* I know of no regional or local newspapers that act in this way. Do they get things wrong? Yes. The difference is they put them right through direct contact with complainants, correcting errors in print and carrying readers' views on our coverage in letters and Feedback columns.

Contrary to the impression given that little attention is paid to the industry watchdog – the Press Complaints Commission – nothing could be further from the truth. A letter from the PCC is taken extremely seriously; complaints dealt with as quickly as possible in the hope a satisfactory resolution can be reached. No journalist wears any such letter as a badge of honour, as no editor relishes having to publish in a prominent position any adjudication against their newspaper.

Of course, there are times articles are written about individuals and organisations they don't like – that is part of the media's job. But local newspapers also champion the region they serve, the people within it, highlighting the great deeds of local people, being a critical friend to those who work to make their particular area a better place to live, work and do business.

Local newspapers are the only media which regularly cover courts, councils, criminal investigations, which report on schools, help raise the profile of charities with extensive coverage, and which campaign on issues which matter to readers. As Geraldine Allinson, the President of the Newspaper Society, said in a speech in 2011: "The fact is the role of local newspapers cannot be replicated by any other medium.

"No-one else can scrutinise those in authority and underpin the local democratic process the way we do. No-one else can support and reflect the aims and aspirations of the local community and campaign on its behalf. And no-one else can give a voice to local people who want and need to be heard."

Need for focus and a strategy

Yet for how long are we going to be able to argue the case? Sadly every day there is news of job losses among journalists and regularly closures of titles attracting little attention outside the trade and the affected communities. Almost every newspaper centre with one or more daily has seen the evening title printed at the same time as its sister morning, while there is an increasing trend of once proud dailies becoming weeklies.

A strong weekly, backed up by an interactive website could be a success, provided the owners support the editorial and commercial teams with cash and time to give it a chance. In Newcastle there was a "clear blue water" strategy aimed at ensuring differentiation between *The Journal* and the *Evening Chronicle* – a challenge in any multi-title newsroom.

Armed with marketing information, each title had its own dedicated team working to a publishing strategy which complemented each other with a fierce but friendly rivalry, resulting in distinctive newspapers with character. Financial pressures and structural change put this well-defined strategy, using brands with more than 100 years' heritage, in the spotlight and a series of decisions were made which was to change the face of journalism in Newcastle and potentially threaten the real local feel of each title.

Staffs merged so those who had grown up with loyalty to one title were forced to quickly get to grips and understand the characteristics of the other. Reporters were required to write different styles for different titles, designers and subs following suit and for a time there was a painful period to manage change.

The mantra was exclusives yes, secrets no, with more intelligent forward planning, sensible placement of stories where they would have the most impact and collaboration at all levels became the norm.

It was not just editorial. Being aware of the difficulties facing our commercial colleagues operating in the same local market place was more important than ever. There was a clear need to be more supportive, without compromising independence and integrity.

The madness of free content

A Dunkirk spirit ensued, so despite the cuts, changes and pressures, newspapers continued to be produced – but in the same cut-throat environment that saw sales spiralling downwards and boardrooms wrestling with how best to tackle it.

The utter madness of uploading all content online for free continued as the attempts to monetise websites proved only moderately successful. However, more discerning advertisers were looking for alternatives to monopolistic newspapers charging higher prices for smaller audiences and, in the process, the cash cow that was classifieds – in particular situations vacant – was slaughtered – having a dramatic impact on the bottom line.

In an industry of innovation – local newspapers quickly adopted social media, such as Twitter and Facebook not only as tools for newsgathering but also to interact with the audience. User generated content brought a new dimension to publishing and there was a real opportunity to once again begin reclaiming some of the ground lost due to the explosion of alternative sources of news and information, using brands which were recognised, trusted and still strong enough to be a significant player in the crowded marketplace.

Yet, the economic situation, the need to make profits to service increasingly high debt levels and the fact print still remained the place where most revenue was generated despite the migration of classified, has seen what could be a fatal delay for many in adapting to changing consumer demands. You only have to travel on your local transport system to see the change. Not so long ago the train carriages and bus seats were filled by people reading their local newspaper.

Today those same people are using their Kindles, mobiles and iPads – spaces where very few local newspapers have gone because they don't see it making a return – short-sighted thinking which has become the norm.

There is no doubt too that the clear blue water has become increasingly muddied as content is duplicated across titles from the same stable. The marketers may say there is little crossover readership but, from my own experience, many family, friends and acquaintances did get both *The Journal* and *Chronicle* but no longer do so. When I ask why the main reasons given are "it is because they are the same" and "I can get it for free on the web" but that is not what either the owners or the marketers want to hear.

Local life under pressure

Newsagents continue to close apace, while new outlets which people frequent less often – garages, supermarkets expand. It is a difficult conundrum for distribution.

But again, to cut costs, most newspapers are now distributed wholesale rather than dedicated local teams, in fewer numbers and less areas to reduce waste.

Taking two hundred copies out of van routes doesn't appear too drastic but it all adds up, as does the lack of a coherent, cost-effective home delivery service. Just like the Post Office, the pubs, the independent high street stores – all part of local life under intense pressure, many closing, so the local newspaper – many of who fight to save those facilities face a fight themselves. But they still have more eyes and ears on the ground than most media outlets in terms of journalists, readers and other staff.

The multi-skilled single newsroom at its best allows a flexible approach, where resources can be targeted effectively. It has improved diary management and forward planning. No longer are there two reporters and photographers turning up to every event from the same centre or to the same court case to hear the same evidence.

Having said that, there are times when it is still desirable, perhaps even necessary, such as covering a football match with personality writers whose opinions are valued by a particular title's readers.

If this is to be maintained then everything must be done to protect and in some cases beef up the content operation again even if, and I say it with a heavy heart, all production is outsourced. Pages can be produced to template from anywhere in the UK or indeed in the world but local, unique, relevant content has to be gathered from the town, cities and villages served by the newspaper.

How do we sustain local newspapers?

In *InPublishing* , November 2011, (and also in this book – see page 103), former *Hull Daily Mail* editor John Meehan talks about sustaining journalism in the regions. It is thought provoking, well argued and, while there are points for disagreement, it largely reflects my own views on the future way forward.

He points to the unique place the newspaper has in the community as compendiums of local life while the printed word gives credibility to the digital format and it is this point which is probably the most pertinent.

Meehan writes: "Regional media businesses have spent years agonising over 'the Internet'. What do we put on it? Who does it? How do we make money on it? All are valid questions, but the constant questioning and lurches of direction are paralysing the industry. It is fiddling while Rome burns."

Local newspapers have a proud record of championing important causes, promoting local businesses, holding decision-makers to account, unmasking those who commit crimes in the neighbourhood as well as the unsung charity workers – with regular up to date information which can be trusted and relied upon.

In a world of global communications, there needs to be more recognition that no two places are the same – what matters to people in the suburbs of Newcastle is not necessarily the same as in London, Manchester, Birmingham, Cardiff or Glasgow.

As I have already stated, there have been many efforts to streamline and rationalise the work being done in newsrooms around the country – some of which makes sense.

Whether it is delivered in print, via a website, mobile device, a new form of television or a technology not yet even available, content generation and managing material coming through active engagement with the audience should be protected at all costs.

Towns, cities and villages will be poorer, less democratic places without their local newspaper in whatever form it takes. Almost everyone agrees but too many are reluctant to enter the debate and make a difference. Platitudes don't pay the bills or wages.

MPs can help by changing the legislative framework and ownership rules – they should take a closer look at who covers the issues they are talking about in their constituencies away from the Westminster bubble and perhaps gain a better understanding of what it would mean to them to lose the local news source.

The phone-hacking scandal and the attention being paid to it means the crisis in local newspapers is likely to be largely ignored for the foreseeable future, by which time it could be too late.

Sky has joined the fray with its video-led website pilot in Tyne and Wear. If successful, it is certain to be rolled out to other areas. In many ways, thanks to the resources at its disposal, Sky Tyne and Wear is doing news on the web in a way newspapers have failed to do.

Local television might play its part, but only if the brands with heritage, trust and a relationship with their audience engage and shape its future along with a viable financial model which may require initial subsidy to ensure plurality.

Failure to act will mean local newspapers, so often the glue which holds communities together will become unstuck and society will be a much poorer place as a result. As media consultant Jim Chisholm said in Press Gazette in December 2011, much of what has happened to our newspapers has been self-inflicted, but the products remain profitable.

He argues: "Yes there are tough times ahead, but this doesn't mean they can't be exciting and positive if we start making some brave, positive decisions about the future of news." And I agree.

Note on the author

Paul Robertson was editorial director of Trinity Mirror North East and editor of the Newcastle *Evening Chronicle* (2002-2011). Previously he was editor of the Teesside *Evening Gazette* (2000-2002) and held numerous positions on the *The Journal*, Newcastle including chief reporter, head of content, sports editor and deputy editor.

Innovative ways to sustain community journalism

It's tough, John Meehan says, but if the industry gets on the front foot, ways through the malaise can be found.

It was more than a little ironic – within days of the announcement that I was leaving the regional news industry, I was asked to write a detailed article about its future.

So why take heed of someone who has headed for the exit? Well, mainly because I remain hugely passionate about local and regional journalism and believe that it can and must continue to be one of the cornerstones of our society.

Until now, all but four of the 28 years of my career as a journalist and editor have been spent in regional media. The other four were with a news agency focused strongly on the regional market. I've decided on a career change – everyone should do that every now and then to stay fresh – but my heart remains in regional journalism. I may return to it one day and I am desperately anxious that it doesn't just survive, but thrives.

By the way, notice that I haven't referred to local and regional newspapers. I much prefer the term regional media. That's because the future of the industry cannot be focused predominantly on print. The platform is not important – the content is.

The industry's corporate structure is certain to change, when conditions allow. That may well include the welcome emergence of new independent publishers but, irrespective of ownership, what is really important – no, absolutely vital – is sustaining vibrant, independent, commercially viable journalism focused on local communities. Without it, those communities and the free, accountable society we treasure will be diminished immeasurably. So what should be done to sustain this journalism? I suggest the following:

We're all in it together

To the outsider, the industry can look like a war zone – management and workers constantly fighting, throwing accusations and insults amid a culture of suspicion and hostility. It's counter-productive and corrosive.

The truth is, we're all in it together (yes, I still refer to "we" as if I'm inside the industry!) and we will only address the challenges facing us with a unity of purpose. It starts with leadership from the very top and that has been somewhat deficient in some parts of the industry. The troops in the trenches need to see real leadership, confidence, openness and engagement. I know they will respond, if given reasons to believe in their leaders.

There are positive signs. Northcliffe Media MD Steve Auckland is "walking the walk" and has put a new emphasis on communication and talent development. Johnston Press has made the brave appointment of former BBC and Microsoft digital executive Ashley Highfield as its new MD. He is certain to usher in profound change to that company's culture.

But it also requires a new approach on the newsroom floor. Journalists must stop fighting losing battles and allowing the National Union of Journalists to send them over the top into the machine-gun fire.

Most journalists realise the industry is under intense pressure and requires fundamental change. They must be part of that change, however uncomfortable that is.

Focus on what really matters

The industry has understood that it can no longer afford all that it used to have. Much peripheral activity has been dispensed with or outsourced. Where the paper is printed doesn't matter; nor where the ads are set; nor where editorial production takes place. Reduced manpower and funds must be focused on what really matters and what must stay local – content, sales and marketing. If there is a cheaper, more efficient way of doing anything else, adopt it. Otherwise you are wasting scare resources, time and attention.

Treasure and develop the newspaper

We should remind ourselves of the power and influence of our core products. Local and regional newspapers have generations of positive heritage; tremendous brand recognition and loyalty; significant readerships; and considerable influence within the communities they serve.

The newspaper is the physical manifestation of the brand. It is the banner under which to rally. It gives credibility to the digital platforms. It is a true pillar of any local community. So we simply must continue to focus on developing the core title. Make it exceptional in quality and relevance and ensure the cover price reflects the value it offers – 50p plus for dailies; £1 plus for bumper weeklies.

I support totally converting smaller dailies to weeklies. It is commercial logic to offer readers and advertisers a substantial weekly compendium of local life, rather than a flimsy daily offering. I suspect we will see many more titles go weekly over the coming months.

Newspapers in major towns and cities have greater longevity as dailies – long enough, I believe, to make the transition to digital copy sales via tablets. But, in the meantime, quality and relevance must be paramount. And beware focusing on C2DE readers – what is sometimes seen as the core readership of city dailies. Drop the tabloid treatments, learn restraint as well as impact, and move upmarket – that's where the money and a sustainable future lies.

Integrate intelligently

Regional media businesses have spent years agonising over "the Internet". What do we put on it? Who does it? How do we make money on it? All are valid questions, but the constant questioning and lurches of direction are paralysing the industry. It is fiddling while Rome burns.

I suggest we should simply accept that digital media is now all-pervasive and must be embraced totally, in newsrooms and in advertising sales departments. Six years ago my editorial team in Hull embraced video journalism – not as an end in itself, but as a means of changing the culture and working practices from print-obsessed to a multi-media mindset. It is disappointing that the industry has failed to make the great leap forward to genuinely integrated multi-media publishing. Yes, I know the prolonged economic crisis has been a major factor, but the truth is that we have failed to transform in tune with the world around us.

So let's integrate print and digital, but it must be done intelligently. Throwing all of our print content on to the web – or even the best of it – is total madness. It's simply cannibalising unnecessarily our already under-pressure print sales and readership.

But the other extreme – focusing almost exclusively on the paper because it's what pays the rent now – is a road to nowhere. At best that will achieve greater longevity for the printed product, but it will not maintain or grow audience, or sustain journalism.

We simply have to develop differentiated, complementary and cross-promotional print and digital platforms – many consumer touchpoints, united by brand. We must identify what content is most relevant and works best on which platform. We should make decisions based on consumer behaviour and preference, but also influenced by what drives the greatest commercial return, now and going forward.

For example, why upload to the web the newspaper's exclusive in-depth splash? Surely it's better to refer to it online; promote the paper's unique content; and drive conversation and follow-up angles on the website and via social media. Hardly rocket science, but does anybody do it routinely? Indeed, are they allowed to?

And, while on the subject of digital, I am astonished by the scarcity of regional media activity on tablets. Lately I have become convinced that newspapers will migrate in significant proportion to mobile devices. The iPad is a game-changer for media and the Apple device and the multitude of copycats will continue to improve in experience and functionality, while reducing in price. I believe the printed newspaper will survive, but I suspect ten to fifteen years from now more people will read tablet equivalents.

Crucially, it is accepted that people will pay for content on tablets and e-readers like Amazon's Kindle. Sustaining journalism will require the public to pay for it and for the industry to stop pandering to the digital freeloaders. Shouldn't we begin to occupy this territory?

Become a trusted voice and influencer across social media

At one time, community issues were debated almost exclusively through the news columns and letters pages of local papers. Not any longer – now the debate rages every day, every hour, every minute across social media networks. Facebook is the platform of choice for millions to conduct their social interactions. Twitter is an amazingly powerful news machine and story source. LinkedIn connects movers and shakers in localities as well as industry sectors.

Editors and journalists must use these platforms, but with clarity of focus. Don't just join the idle chit-chat. There's no value in a meaningless "I'm down the pub" tweet. Engage personably with users to promote the brand and its continuing relevance; extend your circle of trusted contacts and sources; share knowledge; and influence the community. Above all, remind your social media followers and friends of the unique appeal and content of the newspaper!

There's also a major, directly commercial opportunity. Local publishers can act as trusted, knowledgeable guides to help local businesses engage with social media and benefit from it.

Create an all-company commercial culture

This is simply essential. Journalists can no longer turn their noses up at anything advertising-related. Like it or not (and they should embrace it, if only for reason of self-preservation) journalists have to play their full part in the commercial development of the business.

That means understanding that our editorial content has real value to commercial clients. They will pay for it, but expect quality, time and attention. At the *Hull Daily Mail* we brought in more than £200,000 for the business over two years through our Bounce Back campaign, with commercial partners funding and influencing our coverage. No one sold their soul to the devil; the business earned new revenues; the partners appreciated the involvement; and we built lasting relationships.

We must also make commercial content choices – what is most commercially beneficial; most relevant to our audience; unique to us? More of the same will get us nowhere. And being commercial also means appreciating the value of relationships with the business community. Win friends and influence people in local business networks and you will find the effort repaid.

Finally on this point, it's clear that we can no longer pay our way just by selling advertising space. Our customers have too many alternative options and expect so much more. We have to step into their shoes, understand their businesses and markets, and develop and deliver print and digital marketing campaigns that work for them and for us. It's a major change that will require a transformation in skills, culture and, probably, personnel within commercial teams.

Flex your un-used, or under-used, muscles

When advertising just came to us the business model was simple – reach readers by reporting the news and sell that readership to advertisers. But that isn't sufficient now or going forward. Regional publishers need to flex different commercial muscles and build up others that have grown weak through under-use. I believe there are significant opportunities to develop and extend our brands without drifting from the core competencies of journalism, sales and marketing.

An obvious example is events. Johnston Press identified this opportunity some time ago and now makes significant revenues from high-margin events, ranging from business awards, to country pursuits and pet shows. All of them also reinforce the brand. It's good to see other publishers taking heed.

Another major opportunity is public relations and marketing. An enormous industry has developed in PR while the mainstream news industry has declined. I recall two years ago at the Society of Editors conference Neil Benson, Editorial Director of Trinity Mirror Regionals, suggested regional publishers should launch PR agencies. It prompted a predictable "selling out" outcry on trade websites, but he was right. Recently in Hull we launched an arm's-length PR company focused on the emerging renewable energy industry. It's making good progress and the Hull editorial team welcome it as a positive move to diversify the business.

Collaborate to mutual benefit

The turf wars of the past belong in the past. To have a sustainable future regional publishers must understand that the way forward is collaboration across the industry. Our enemies are not other regional publishers. Individually we are weak; together we are stronger and better able to counter the challenges of the likes of Google or Craigslist. The message seems to have hit home, certainly in terms of press utilisation and the adoption by other groups of pure play platforms such as DMGT's Jobsite.

There are opportunities at a more local level too. It's interesting to note that two of my former colleagues, Steve Anderson-Dixon and Phil Inman, are now running the neighbouring publishing businesses of Trinity Mirror and Midlands News Association in the West Midlands. I genuinely don't know, but I would not be surprised if they found ways to co-operate to mutual benefit. I would be amazed if they got worked up about scrapping against each other for sales of the *Birmingham Mail* or Wolverhampton *Express & Star* in the Brummie suburbs.

Make a big noise

In the attention economy blandness is death. Regional media can't just report. It has to make a big noise, through campaigns, events and partnerships. Be your local community's cheerleader in chief – evangelise life is local and promote consistently the immense value you bring to your locality.

For example, just before I moved on, the *Hull Daily Mail* launched the "Battle for Brough" to save nine hundred jobs under threat at the BAE Systems plant at Brough. It's an uphill battle, but the campaign has energised the local community and enhanced the newspaper's reputation.

Shout up for the industry

We are, far too often, our own worst enemies. We focus on negatives – e.g. falling circulations – rather than positives – robust readerships. We fight among ourselves rather than uniting to address the industry's challenges. And "pundits" within the industry – albeit mostly from the national sector – predict our doom.

We've got to get on the front foot; accentuate the positives (they do exist); and shout out for our industry. And that includes fighting much harder for a fair deal from Government and the regulators. Much has been said in favour of the regional news industry, but little has been done to actually support it. We don't want subsidy, just the opportunity to develop, including through changes of ownership and consolidation.

The recent decision to effectively scupper the sale by Northcliffe Media of newspapers in Kent to the Kent Messenger Group was a disgrace. Did the industry kick up enough of a fuss about it? Did the NUJ protest? I believe we have to be much more proactive and purposeful in fighting for a fair deal for an industry that employs thousands of skilled workers and is more vital to the Big Society and community wellbeing than any other.

A substantial agenda for sustainability

So that's a substantial agenda to achieve sustainability for regional journalism. Some of the issues are being grasped; on others the penny has yet to drop. Sometimes I observe things in this wonderful industry that have me shaking my head, but more often I see reasons for optimism. I believe regional journalism will survive and thrive. And belief is what the industry needs above all to find a sustainable future.

Note on the author

John Meehan was formerly Editor of the Hull Daily Mail and Regional Editorial Director of Northcliffe Media's North East region. He is now a media and communications consultant. This chapter first appeared in *Inpublishing* magazine in November 2011.

Co-opting the discourse of crisis: Re-assessing market failure in the local news sector

Now is the time to re-imagine the models of journalism and to forge a very different future, argues Justin Schlosberg.

Forty years ago, as a wave of death and consolidation swept the provincial press, a study of the roles of the provincial press in the UK found that they carried out four central functions that were being lost as closures and mergers diminished local press: 1) fostering a sense of community identity and cohesion and facilitating individual integration; 2) conveying political, institutional and cultural information and analysis and creating a historical record of community affairs; 3) providing a platform for debate and complaint; and 4) publicising goods and services available, situations vacant, and announcements and notices (Jackson 1971).

Since that time mortality and consolidation have continued to plague the local press. The Newspaper Society has reported that 101 local newspapers closed between January 2008 and June 2009 (Fenton 2010). But the problem is at least as much qualitative with local news consumers complaining of a decline in editorial content both in terms of standards and in proportion relative to advertising content. This presents challenges not only to the newspaper industry, but – as Ofcom recently noted – to broadcast media as well because of their reliance on print coverage for local news: "We have recognized the critical role that local newspaper journalism plays in delivering public purposes. Local newspaper journalism not only underpins the delivery of local news on other media, but also makes a key contribution to the national news agenda" (Ofcom 2009).

The challenges facing local news provision have not gone unnoticed and the UK Government has put local television, at least, at the heart of its cultural plans. Having rejected the previous Labour government's proposals for Independently Funded News Consortia (IFNCs), it has now committed itself to a policy centred on commercial growth in local television services. Initially these services will support only 10 to 12 local television stations, although the government has expressed belief that the number will increase later. However, part of the proposals included a commitment to significantly relax local cross media ownership rules enabling one media sector to cross subsidise another less profitable one. Whilst this may appear to be a sensible response to market conditions, it will also likely result in increasing consolidation of ownership and business rationalisation that may, once more, diminish the ability of news to respond to the professed news needs of local communities.

But the effects of consolidation on local news provision have been side-lined by over-attention to the disruptive force of technology – and the Internet in particular. To be clear, the causes of the crisis are myriad and further research is needed in order to provide a substantive picture of their relative effects. But this chapter argues that there has been too often a presumptive emphasis on technological disruption (and secondarily, cyclical pressures) which has considerably distorted the picture. Moreover, it has allowed de-regulation and great swathes of resource cuts in operational journalism to go relatively unchallenged in policy debates over the future of local news.

The discourse of crisis

The very notion of crisis in respect of public interest journalism has long permeated the discourses of academics, activists, lobbyists and policy makers alike. Its manifestation in terms of a broken business model has been well documented, particularly in respect of the local news sector (Currah 2010; Fenton 2010). The effects in turn on news content and operational journalism have been shown to be of endemic proportions (Davies 2008). In economic parlance, the problem amounts to market failure and in particular, the structural decline in the revenues of traditional local news business models.

The idea of the Internet as a disruptive force has been a prominent theme in both business and academic literature over the last decade (Castells 2001; Lessig 2003; Funk 2004; Lessig 2004; Downes 2009). Much of this literature draws on both the discourse of "threat" and "opportunity" in relation to the Internet's impact on markets and industry. Optimistic accounts posit the threat as targeting incumbent and monopoly power, with a resultant shift in favour of new entrants and niche markets (Anderson and Anderson 2009), ultimate consumer sovereignty (Tapscott and Williams 2008) and a new economics of abundance (Jarvis 2009). More critical accounts conceive of the threat in relation to creeping mechanisms of control by "old business" in the new economic landscape through copyright expansion (Lessig 2003), commodificiation (Mosco 2004), new forms of concentration (Mansell and Jarvery 2004), pay-walls and content discrimination (Wu, Dyson et al. 2007), and personalisation (Sunstein 2001).

What all these accounts share in common is a conception of the Internet as wreaking havoc upon millennial capitalism, ushering in a new age of thriving competitive markets and/or new forms of monopoly control. In 2009, an extensive project by the Reuters Institute for the Study of Journalism concluded that "increasing commercial pressure, mainly driven by the inherent characteristics of the digital revolution, is undermining the business models that pay for the news" (Currah 2010: 5). The growth of online news consumption, particularly amongst younger age groups, has likely played a part in accentuating a long-term decline in newspaper circulation.

At the same time, migration of advertisers to online search engines has left print outlets facing a double assault on revenues. The Advertising Association has forecast that the press advertising market is likely to shrink yet further by between £700m and £1.6bn by 2019 with the regional press taking most of the impact (Franklin 2009). But the decline has also been greatly exacerbated by the financial crisis which has combined with changing consumption patterns to create the "perfect storm" for the newspaper industry.[1] For some commentators, notably Emily Bell (former digital media editor at the *Guardian*) the online threat to the commercial news industry was posited as both catastrophic and terminal:

> *'In the UK, five nationals could go out of business and we could be left with no UK owned broadcaster outside of the BBC. We are facing complete market failure in local papers and regional radio. This is systematic collapse not just cyclical downturn.'*[2]

The above quote is indicative of a sustained discursive focus on technological and cyclical disruption amongst news producers, as the principle if not exclusive cause of enveloping market failure.

Commercialisation and market failure
But we do not need to look into the annals of history to see that market failure in local news is not just about technology and recession. Recent research focusing on the perspective of news consumers presents a rather different picture to that painted by industry analysts (Media Trust 2010). Far from abandoning traditional local news formats for the Internet, consumers continue to place a premium value on high quality print journalism and declining demand is attributable at least in part (and somewhat paradoxically) to elements of commercialisation and consolidation within the sector. This has left local news consumers with the perception that local papers – where they still exist – are no longer "local" in terms of the physical presence of journalists, and in terms of addressing the kind of issues that really matter to the community in question. Such perceptions reflect long-term patterns of industry consolidation which have left many communities either without a local newspaper at all; with titles that are run remotely from regional consolidated offices; or with free sheets dominated by advertising and recycled content.

The failure to deliver high quality local news – indeed market failure itself – appears to be linked fundamentally to the marketisation of news, resulting in less staff doing more work and undermining both operational journalism and the provision of news in the public interest:

> *"They [leaders of the big regional press companies] performed just as they were obliged by the ruthless logic of an economic system that demands ever-increasing profits. To do that they kept a close eye on the "costs", ensuring that the staffing of mechanical jobs involved in newspaper production were pared to the bone."*[3]

In other words, reinvestment in their product and recognition and development of the product's value was superseded by market ambition and the desire to deliver extensive profits to shareholders. This is a trend that has continued, given only added impetus by the flight of advertisers to online search. Franklin cites an ABN Amro Bank report in July 2008 that states, "One saving grace for Trinity in recent years has been management's ability to surprise on the cost base, with a strong discipline to go out and cut out the 'fat' and (some would say) even the muscle. We expect this trend to continue, as indicated by management yesterday, that there will be a £15–£20m restructuring charge taken in 2008 to pay for further cost cuts" (2009: 3), meaning of course, more redundancies.

Much of the articulated crisis in local news, by focusing on technology (and the Internet in particular) as the main cause of the problem, has allowed an over simplification of the debate and diverted attention away from some of the more structural indicators of decline. Part of the problem is that commercial news providers have tended to pin the digital threat on free content providers with formats similar to their own. The competitive threat posed by these providers – namely public service broadcasters – has been portrayed as one of the chief obstacles preventing news providers from monetising online content. According to the chairman of News Corporation (Europe and Asia), "dumping free, state-sponsored news on the market makes it incredibly difficult for journalism to flourish on the Internet"[4] But in reality, the main competitive online threat to commercial news providers stems not from free content providers, but search engines that have been luring advertisers away from news markets altogether with dynamic pay-per-click models.[5]

In an attempt to hold on to what's left of advertising revenues in the print domain, newspaper groups have compromised the value of their titles from a consumer perspective. This in turn has no doubt made local newspapers even less attractive to advertisers who above all seek large, regular and attentive readerships. Thus, commercialisation of the type outlined above, may have backfired and cast a double-edged incision into revenues – reducing both consumer subscriptions and advertising. What seems certain is that local audiences have not been deserting local newspapers because they can attain the same value for free on other platforms. They have been deserting them because the local paper has *lost* its value in respect of the criteria discussed above. This raises the spectre that much of the crisis in relation to failing business models in local news may have been self-induced, at least to the extent that effective provision is simply not conducive to the dynamics of large scale corporate ownership structures.

Consolidation and decline

The closure of the *Long Eaton Advertiser* (that served a community in Derbyshire) provides a case in point. Owned by Trinity Mirror, which returned profits of £145.2m in 2008, the title was closed down in 2009 with its owners citing "difficult trading conditions"[6]. According to Jeremy Dear, former head of the National Union of Journalists:

> *"The Long Eaton Advertiser was not a victim of the recession, even though it had seen a huge fall in advertising revenue – it was a victim of a failed corporate business model for news. This is the model that has been encouraged by politicians through deregulation and by turning a blind eye to the effects of mergers, indebtedness and excessive profiteering on citizens' rights to information."[7]*

The implication is that decreasing demand for the paper had at least something to do with Trinity Mirror transferring its offices to Tamworth (in Staffordshire, some thirty six miles away) and progressively commercialising its output prior to closure.

Long-term macro-economic perspectives suggest that market concentrations proceed in waves but ultimately on a single and permanent trajectory. A global study of mergers and acquisitions over several decades states emphatically that "The pace of corporate combinations may ebb (as it did in 2001) or flow (as it did in the 1990s) but consolidation is unstoppable. Its progress is continuous and inevitable" (Deans, Kroeger et al. 2003). The local news industry has proved to be no exception and waves of consolidation long pre-date the Internet (Curran and Seaton 2009). There is also evidence to suggest that consolidation and resource cuts are often more about profit maximisation than surviving cyclical pressure, let alone digital disruption.

In 2006, *The Times* reported that the Trinity Mirror Group, one of the largest owners of local news titles in the UK, had axed three hundred jobs in spite of a "buoyant"" market.[8] Similar cuts were made to the group's newly acquired *Manchester Evening News* (*MEN*) outlet in 2010. The paper had reported significant profits and was well on the way to paying off the group's investment. According to one representative of the National Union of Journalists at the *MEN*:

> *"Over the past few years, journalists at the Manchester Evening News and weekly newspapers have seen that when business is good, management cuts our jobs, when business is bad, management cuts our jobs and then when business is improving, management cuts our jobs. Different management, same philosophy."[9]*

The financial crisis certainly did not prevent supposedly cash-strapped corporations from continuing to make large-scale acquisitions. In 2010 Trinity Mirror acquired GMG Regional Media, publisher of thirty two titles, from the

Guardian Media Group for £44.8m[10]. The acquisition led to a 17% rise of profits within a year to £123m and a record pay packet for the group's chief executive of £1.7m[11]. Despite this, the cautionary rhetoric persisted:

> *"Although 2010 proved to be as challenging as we expected, we made good progress in rolling out our new operating model, integrating GMG Regional Media and increasing profitability and margin whilst managing extremely volatile revenue trends throughout the year. Many of the challenges we faced in 2010 remain in 2011."*[12]

The discourse of crisis in relation to the digital economic threat has not been mere ineffectual rhetoric. It has been routinely invoked to justify widespread industry concentration, wholesale cuts in resources and investment, as well as deregulation and liberalisation of media ownership rules that have led to further consolidation. The public debate that waged over the BBC online news proposals in 2008-9 illustrates the influence of such arguments on policy decisions. Following an outcry from the regional commercial press lobby, the BBC Trust rejected the proposals which were put forward in response to "license fee payers wanting better local services".[13] Arguments against the proposals rested on a conviction that they would raise a barrier to commercial competition in a nascent market, leaving local online news audiences with a "very strong BBC and nothing else"[14]. But despite the red light given to the BBC, there has been little sign since of commercial players expanding in the markets they feared would be off limits.

Yet local Johnston Press, one of the big five newspaper groups that own eight hundred of the twelve hundred titles in the UK, with eighteen daily newspapers, two hundred and forty five weekly newspapers and a raft of specialist print publications, has recently declared that its future lies "in digital", threatening to continue the cull on journalists which the National Union of Journalists estimated at more than 230 in 2010 alone, and continuing with its policy of collapsing local titles and pushing them to out of town premises.

At the *South Yorkshire Times* (a Johnston press publication) the journalists staged an eight-week strike from July to September 2011 after a plan to make eighteen journalists redundant, cut the editorial staff by half and merge editors across papers owned by the group with key operations being run from Doncaster. Once a key protagonist in the promotion of local news it has now closed several newspapers and runs many others on minimal staffing, from remote locations. The journalists have labelled this a "call centre approach'" to news that operates on the basis of remote access resulting in a vastly inferior product and subsequent nose-dive in sales and circulation. The company has a £388m debt burden brought about by empire building and asset stripping through healthier economic times. During this period they ruthlessly acquired titles then just as ruthlessly consolidated and cut their resources to make the most of scale economies. Once the advertising revenue all but disappeared they are left with local newspapers that are not local and have precious little news.

Towards a more sustainable future

Co-optation of the crisis discourse has also likely had tangible and substantial effects in expanding copyright regimes and further de-regulating media markets. It lies at the root of a real crisis resulting from newsroom cuts that have severely disempowered journalists and undermined their autonomy (Fenton 2010). Its distortion lies in its emphasis on the Internet's disruptive qualities as the origin of crisis, rather than cyclical pressure or even the corporate strategies of publisher conglomerates themselves. It distracts attention from the real drivers of concentration which have more to do with the dynamics of monopoly capitalism than any technological disruption. This is particularly the case with the symbolic goods industries – central to the knowledge economy – that depend on ever-increasing scale to obviate risks associated with the production of "novelty" (Garnham 2000).

As the economic forces affecting media and information providers lead to greater consolidation, reducing the sustainability of local and regional information providers, and concentrating information provision in the hands of national providers, we are also witnessing a push for the oversight and provision of many public services to move from central government to the regional and local levels, with more localised self-governance appearing in provision of education, transport, and health care. This creates in turn the need for more local information and debate. Thus, at a time when needs for greater local news and information is rising, less is being provided.

But the market failure of a conglomerated local news industry needn't sound the death knell for the local newspaper. Indeed, it may well create new opportunities for alternative models of funding and providing the kinds of local news services that are truly valued by local readers. The *Camden New Journal*, for instance, is cooperatively owned and its managing editor cites independence as the key to its survival. "Today, we are managing, but it is because we can survive on a small net profit. A big company would not tolerate our performance. They would close us down."[15]

If corporate models are failing journalism because of a priority on the bottom line, on high profit margins and shareholder returns that has ultimately had a detrimental impact on the quality of news journalism, then the starting point for alternative models to address these concerns would seem to be fairly clear. We must begin with the connection of news to democracy – an acceptance that news provides the vital resources for processes of information gathering, deliberation and analysis. The ability of news to support democratic practice also hinges on a conception of independent journalism in the public interest (which the recent hacking scandal in the UK has thrown into sharp relief). In other words, what is in the public interest in relation to the provision of news for democracy to thrive?

Independent journalism then also rests on journalistic integrity – how can we provide the environment that is required to enable journalists to do the job most of them want to do – to scrutinize, to monitor, to hold to account, to interrogate power, to facilitate and to maintain deliberation? To firmly establish the relationship between journalism and democracy requires a move away from a model based on excessive profits for a few shareholders and towards more collaborative-partnership models that prioritize these three elements – the relationship of news to democracy; independent news journalism in the public interest; and the freedom to pursue professional journalism of integrity. It is not then simply an issue of making the new online environment more profitable. It is not simply about charging for online content. But it does have something to do with new technology considered in the context of ethical journalism, economic viability, plurality (of content and ownership) and power.

A journalism and newspaper industry fit for the digital age needs to consider models that have been hitherto largely ignored. Particular emphasis should be placed on establishing new ownership models rooted in the local community, harnessing local innovation and enthusiasm. Co-operatives, public ownership and trusts are some of the possibilities that require further research and attention. New structures of governance could be designed to protect and preserve the quality and diversity of news content. This type of governance would need to safeguard the independence of the news organisations, but could also increase the involvement of civil society within local communities. There is a crucial role for foundation grants and local or national government subsidies for genuinely local, genuinely independent news which prioritises the public interest.

Current debates over the relative power of the Murdoch empire and News Corporation's interests have thrust to the fore concerns over the relationship between control of the media and power to influence social and political institutions that are key to a healthy democratic life. Without a much tougher attitude towards media concentration and the pursuit of meaningful diversity, current public interest considerations are unlikely to be strong enough to confront aggressive liberalisation and marketisation. Research on local news is little referred to in this regard but could not be more relevant. Protecting the public interest requires both a more determined stance on media concentration and a more imaginative approach to securing media diversity, one that is based not simply on economic benefits but on the advantages of stimulating vigorous debate and critical perspectives and securing widespread political representation.

Sole reliance on fully commercial enterprises for the delivery of news and current affairs journalism that purports to be for the public good and in the public interest has proven to be problematic. Old models of journalism are outmoded and equally problematic. But so too is dumping the cause of the crisis on the doorstep of new technology. Independent, not-for-profit (or not primarily for profit) newsrooms are critical to the survival of local news and the promotion of local democratic wellbeing. Only when we are able to re-imagine a post-corporate, not-for-profit, independent news media freed from the shackles of commercialism that prioritises the relationship with democracy and exists primarily to aim for this ethical horizon will the true value of local news in the digital age be realised.

References

Anderson, C. and C. L. t. Anderson (2009). *The longer long tail: how endless choice is creating unlimited demand.* London, Random House Business.

Castells, M. (2001). *The Internet galaxy: reflections on Internet, business, and society.* Oxford, Oxford University Press.

Currah, A. (2010). *What's Happening to our News?* An investigation into the likely impact of the digital revolution on the economics of news publishing in the UK. Oxford, Reuters Institute for the Study of Journalism.

Curran, J. and J. Seaton (2009). *Power without responsibility: the press and broadcasting in Britain.* London, Routledge.

Deans, G. K., F. Kroeger, et al. (2003). *Winning the merger endgame: a playbook for profiting from industry consolidation.* New York; London, McGraw-Hill.

Downes, L. (2009). *The laws of disruption: harnessing the new forces that govern life and business in the digital age.* New York, BasicBooks.

Fenton, N. (2010). *New media, old news: journalism and democracy in the digital age.* London, SAGE.

Franklin, B. (2009). *The future of newspapers.* London, Routledge.

Funk, J. L. (2004). *Mobile disruption: the technologies and applications driving the mobile Internet.* Hoboken, N.J.; [Chichester], Wiley-Interscience.

Garnham, N. (2000). *Emancipation, the media, and modernity: arguments about the media and social theory.* Oxford, Oxford University Press.

Jackson, I. (1971). *The provincial press and the community.* Manchester, Manchester University Press.

Jarvis, J. (2009). *What would Google do?* London, Collins.

Lessig, L. (2003). *The future of ideas : the fate of the commons in a connected world.* New York, N.Y., Vintage Books; London : Hi Marketing.

Lessig, L. (2004). *Free culture : how big media uses technology and the law to lock down culture and control creativity.* New York, N.Y., Penguin Press.

Mansell, R. and M. Jarvery (2004). New Media and the Forces of Capitalism. *Toward a Political Economy of Culture – Capitalism and Communication in the Twenty-First Century.* A. Calbrese and C. Sparks. Oxford, Rowman and Littlefield.

Media Trust (2010). *Meeting the News Needs of Local Communities.* Available at www.mediatrust.org/uploads/128255497549240/original.pdf (accessed 23 January 2012).

Mosco, V. (2004). Capitalism's Chernobyl? From Ground Zero to Cyberspace and Back Again. *Toward a Political Economy of Culture – Capitalism and Communication in the Twenty-First Century.* A. Calbrese and C. Sparks. Oxford, Rowman and Littlefield.

Ofcom (2009). Local and Regional Media in the UK. London, Ofcom.

Sunstein, C. R. (2001). Republic.com. Princeton, N.J. ; Oxford, Princeton University Press.

Tapscott, D. and A. D. Williams (2008). *Wikinomics : how mass collaboration changes everything*. London, Atlantic.

Wu, T., E. Dyson, et al. (2007). "On the Future of Internet Governance." American Society of International Law **101**.

Notes

[1] R. Greenslade, "We journalists are not to blame for the decline of newspapers", *guardian.co.uk*, 3 October 2008. Available at: http://www.guardian.co.uk/media/greenslade/2008/oct/03/1 (accessed 20 September 2010).

[2] E. Bell, quoted in *Polis* blog. Available at http://www.charliebeckett.org/?p=864 (accessed 16 April 2011)

[3] R. Greenslade, "Answer to economic crisis in newspapers is not more consolidation", *thisislondon.co.uk*, 19 April 2009. Available at: http://www.thisislondon.co.uk/standard-business/article-23669660-answer-to-economic-crisis-in-newspapers-is-not-more-consolidation.do (accessed 20 September 2010).

[4] J. Murdoch (2009), *MacTaggart Lecture*, speech to Edinburgh International Television Festival. Available at http://image.guardian.co.uk/sys-files/Media/documents/2009/08/28/JamesMurdochMacTaggartLecture.pdf (accessed 7 August 2011).

[5] T. Heaton, "Local media in a postmodern world: Failure at the top", *digitaljournalist.org*, October 2008. Available at http://digitaljournalist.org/issue0810/local-media-in-a-postmodern-world-failure-at-the-top.html (accessed 3 February 2012)

[6] NUJ (National Union of Journalists), submission to the Culture Media and Sport Select Committee Inquiry on "The future of local and regional media". Available at http://www.publications.parliament.uk/pa/cm/cmcumeds.htm#reports (accessed 23 January 2012)

[7] J. Dear, "What would Rupert Murdoch say about that?" *redpepper.org*, February 2010. Available at http://www.redpepper.org.uk/what-would-rupert-murdoch-say/ (accessed 3 February 2012).

[8] R. Morrison, "Stop press: The sad Decline of local newspapers", *The Times*, 28th February 2006.

[9] D. Ponsford, "As the profits pile in from MEN Media, why indeed is Trinity Mirror cutting yet more jobs", *pressgazette.co.uk*, 2nd August 2010. Available at http://blogs.pressgazette.co.uk/editor/2010/08/02/as-the-profits-pile-in-from-men-media-why-indeed-is-trinity-mirror-cutting-yet-more-jobs/ (accessed 3 February 2012)

[10] O. Luft, "Trinity Mirror to close Nine Midlands Papers", *guardian.co.uk*, 1 July 2009. Available at: http://www.guardian.co.uk/media/2009/jul/01/trinity-mirror-to-close-midlands-papers (accessed 14 November 2010); Newspaper Society, "History of British Newspapers", *newspapersoc.org.uk*, 2010. Available at: http://www.newspapersoc.org.uk/Default.aspx?page=304 (accessed 22 September 2010).

[11] M. Sweney, "Trinity Mirror's Sly Bailey received £1.66m package in 2010", *guardian.co.uk*, 5th April 2011. Available at http://www.guardian.co.uk/media/2011/apr/05/trinity-mirror-sly-bailey-pay-package (accessed 26 April 2011).

[12] Sly Bailey, chief executive of Trinity Mirror, quoted in The Newspaper Society, "Trinity Mirror profits up 17% on the back of GMG acquisition", 3 March 2011. Available at http://www.newspapersoc.org.uk/03/mar/11/trinity-mirror-profits-up-17-on-back-of-gmg-acquisition (accessed 29 April 2011).

[13] Dianne Coyle, quoted in BBC Trust press release (June 2008)

Carolyn McCall, Chief Executive of the Guardian Media Group quoted in testimony presented to Parliament Commons Select Committee for Culture, Media and Support (July 2008)

[14] See http://newmodeljournalism.com/2010/03/eric-gordon-the-camden-new-journal/ (accessed 3 February 2012)

Note on the author

Justin Schlosberg is a media activist, researcher and visiting tutor based at Goldsmiths, University of London. He is the author of *Power in the Dock: Media Spectacles of Accountability*, forthcoming in 2012 from Pluto Books

The demand will remain but what about the supply?

The big groups' ambitions to maximise profits may have squeezed too much life out of their newspapers, says Tor Clark, yet he believes that consumers still have a wish for their core product of local news.

The obituaries of the UK regional press continue to be written[1]. Each set of ABC[2] figures shows significant circulation declines for our largest regional publications. Formerly thriving daily newspapers have been converted to weeklies, weeklies and frees closed. Newspapers' advertising revenues have declined, editorial staffs have shrunk and offices closed.

Academics and leading journalists have chronicled the decline of the regional press[3] while the Newspaper Society[4] and the large companies which own most of the UK regional press continue to assure advertisers and the City it is still a buoyant and significant medium.

So what actually is the position? What are the reasons for the decline and what hope is there for vibrant local journalism in the UK in the future?

The golden age of the regional press

All UK journalism was originally local. In the late seventeenth and early eighteenth centuries small printers in small towns started producing newsletters containing all manner of information, most of the news, ironically, not local at all.[5] Over the centuries this was organised into what we now recognise as newspapers. The purpose of many was often to promote their owners' political or religious views, or to sell the products of local entrepreneurs. These papers were often owned by local worthy and monied families and remained so well into the twentieth century[6]. Not all survived, but by the second half of that period those which had were well established.

Without competition, communities were served by regional morning, evening and weekly papers. Broadsheet morning papers such as the *Yorkshire Post*, *Northern Echo* or *Birmingham Post* had prestigious reputations. Weekly paid-for papers serving defined areas were simply the Bible for local people, their news parochial, their staff well known and part of the community. The paper itself "one of the family".

This was the golden era of the evening paper. Much of its circulation was locked in by home delivery. In towns and cities street vendors would sell the paper to workers on their way home from their factories and offices. The papers would be read on the bus, tram or train home then passed around the family. The biggest papers sold in their hundreds of thousands[7].

This comfortable normality lasted for much of the twentieth century, despite changes in ownership. Larger companies had started to form, with the Harmsworth and Berry family enterprises in particular creating empires in the inter-war years. But even until the 1970s there were many titles still in family ownership. But from this point, the various companies began to form into the Big Four[8] we know today, with family organisations taken over by larger firms, such as Johnston Press[9], Trinity Mirror and Newsquest.

Going out with a bang

Before the recession of the early 1990s, all was relatively well in the regional press. Its ownership was becoming more concentrated, but was still diverse. Circulation was high. It was well-staffed and lacked competition, with only local radio and regional TV scratching the surface of its unique selling point, the plentiful supply of local news to local people. Local commerce made good use of its platform to supply a growing consumer demand.

But with hindsight the early 1990s recession was the beginning of the end of the good times. Circulation fell and advertising revenue declined. Newspapers cut staff and traditional practices to save money. But when the UK came out of recession cuts made in the early 1990s were not reversed. Corporate managements recognised their papers had survived on smaller staffs and budgets in tough times and reasoned they could continue as times got better. And times got much better.

In the past, typically under local family management, newspapers were there to serve the community. In some years they made a good profit, in lean years they might not. It didn't matter. Over time the enterprise sustained itself. By the early 1990s the Emap mission statement recorded it wished to be a media company with profit margins of 20%. Emap owned high-margin low-staff businesses such as magazines, radio stations and exhibitions. Its small papers, with their high headcounts, made 5-15%, so 20% was an ambitious target[10].

But maximising gains from staff cuts, improving technology to further reduce manpower and then riding the wave of the late twentieth early twenty-first century boom, for a short period of perhaps ten years the UK regional press made money like never before. The "mission" of 20% margins was being easily surpassed by the late 1990s, particularly by the fourth biggest regional publisher of that time Johnston Press, which doubled in size in 1996 with the purchase of Emap's newspapers.

Johnston companies trimmed costs to the bone, maximised "business synergies" and pushed local advertising rates as high as they would go, netting declared margins of 35% or more. Management of the other big players, Trinity Mirror, Newsquest and Northcliffe, saw these margins and demanded them of their own executives. For many running regional papers it became the curse of "Johnston's margins".

Here were regional conglomerates operating super-slim and efficient businesses, squeezing as much cash out of their local markets in a boom with little to no competition. Between 1995 and 2005 three of the four biggest businesses had almost completely changed hands, creating even more cost savings in the newly merged conglomerates.

The five big advertising categories – homes, cars, jobs, classified and display – all prospered. But at the height of the boom, with its corresponding skills shortage, the category which grew most was situations vacant jobs advertising. What had once been a few pages at the back of the paper often became a huge regional supplement. The night of the jobs pull-out in evening papers was the biggest seller of the week, often with thousands of additional sales to people who wanted to change jobs to cash in on the good economic times.

In sits vac advertising many market-leading papers had a monopoly and could charge top prices for employment advertising. The UK regional press enjoyed a huge spurt, fuelled largely by the enormous margins generated by this advertising. A colour page, which might cost a local estate agent a few hundred pounds, could be sold in smaller chunks to firms needing to fill jobs for several thousands of pounds. It was a gold mine and several regional press companies became the darlings of the stock market as their shares rose and rose on the back of ever-increasing profits.

Changing times

But it wouldn't last. Two developments would end the golden days for ever. One was changing social trends, the other the arrival of the Internet.

Newspaper companies knew society was changing. Their research showed as more people went to work they had less leisure time, fewer minutes to read a paper six nights a week. As the media became more sophisticated, so people had other sources of news. As people migrated away from their home areas looking for better jobs so their connections to the area in which they lived broke down, and with it their desire for strictly local news.

The businesses recognised these issues in the 1990s and came up with editorial strategies to keep readers interested, largely by increasing local news, which local reader surveys always said was readers' top priority. But by this time the balance sheet was king and the big companies needed ever-increasing profits to fund their acquisitions and meet City expectations. From the boardroom's perspective, though falling circulation was worrying, the papers continued to make big profits, often from employment advertising.

Soon web-based advertising took huge, profitable chunks of regional advertising away, never to return. Jobs ads were the biggest casualty. Specialist websites replaced generalist newspaper pages. In the NHS, which had paid thousands of pounds to the local and trade press every week to advertise its many vacancies, once its managers realised they could advertise those jobs on their own websites for nothing, its business left for good.

Car sales went to specialist publications and websites, estate agents set up their own websites which offered tours of the properties rather than just a picture, and the old faithful miscellaneous sales disappeared to specialist websites like e-Bay.

Many newspaper executives did not realise the scale of the impact the Internet would have on their advertising nor did they seek a compelling local alternative until it was too late. The arrival of the Internet also created a generation used to reading news on a screen rather than on paper.

This was one, admittedly major, problem, but another largely ignored but equally significant issue was the big owners' failure to realistically reduce their profit ambitions despite the obvious fact the economy had seismically changed.

Even though huge swathes of fantastically profitable advertising had deserted newspapers, publishers still wanted unrealistically large profit margins. The decade between 1995 and 2005 was regional newspaper advertising's golden era, but it was a bubble. After the advertising left, the economics of the regional press went back to normal, indeed below normal if the desertion of readers to the Internet is taken into account. But many boards needed big profits to pay back the loans they had taken in the boom years to buy more papers, make cuts and synergies and drive up profits. It was a vicious but unsustainable spiral.

Faced with their desire to maintain large margins many newspapers closed offices, reduced the numbers of journalists – often by non-replacement but also by redundancy – centralised whole operations, such as sub-editing, moved printing to huge regional plants, closing local print works, and finally reduced the frequency or even closed their papers. Newspapers were still the best news source in town, but with fewer journalists to fill more pages, they were often forced to fall back on dull, easy news.

Many papers stopped routinely covering courts and councils, reporters stopped leaving their offices, stopped finding out what people were talking about in the pubs and clubs of their communities and as a result many papers ceased to be compelling. The reporters still working in the regions were often paid so little they only used the local press as a two-year stepping stone to more lucrative careers in better paid areas of journalism, or often the dark arts – and much better pay – of public relations.

Faced with a readership declining because of their looser ties with the area in which they lived and a younger generation never likely to convert to local newspaper readers, it was precisely the wrong time to cut staff to such a point that many ceased to have time to cover their local areas in sufficient depth.

Some journalists can be blamed for an unwillingness to leave their desks and go out to meet real people in the normal course of their work, but most remained dedicated and conscientious, just trying to fill their papers with less and less help. Email traffic and clever PR people (often former journalists themselves) filled this gap with easy copy, the phenomenon which became known as "churnalism"[11].

Readers and advertisers deserted the regional press for social and technological reasons at just the time owners were asking their pages to be filled by fewer journalists often with an impact on the quality of the content. This decline may have happened anyway, but most frustrated journalists involved believe they could have done more to arrest the decline of their medium had they had sufficient resources to generate the compelling, pro-active content necessary to engage and retain readers.

Interestingly the big evening papers have lost many more readers, faster than their local weekly paid-for cousins. For example, the *Leicester Mercury* sold around one hundred and ten thousand papers every night in 1990, but twenty one years later that total had halved. The *Northamptonshire Evening Telegraph* still sold forty thousand papers a night at the same time, and it too halved over the same period. But sitting midway between them and covering some of the same areas, the weekly *Harborough and Lutterworth Mail* sold around ten thousand papers a week in 1996, and still around that number fifteen years later, enjoying a good increase in the intervening period. The picture of well-established weekly papers managing to hold-up circulation even in today's difficult climate offers hope for the future.

Back to the future?

So what does the future hold for the regional press after what has been a particularly depressing seven or eight years of cuts and decline?

The Internet hasn't been all bad for local news. Whilst physical sales of newspapers have declined dramatically, so use of their websites has risen incredibly. Local newspapers are still usually the first port of call for local news online. They have not lost their dominance of local news largely because they mostly still have the best news-gathering networks and the trusted brand on which to publish it. Their brands may prove their saviour.

The regional press still has a large audience of news-consumers, but whereas in the past they paid for their papers, now they access them free online. That lack of a cover price, plus the on-going problem of desertion of advertising spend means newspapers are still struggling to come up with a good model to monetise their content online. In an effort to try a subscription rather than advertising model, pay walls have been attempted, most notably recently by Johnston Press, but these were limited experiments which did not provide any long-term answers. Pay walls would be a solution if they worked, but even marketed well their value is questionable[12].

One USP local newspapers do have is their archived local content, economic, business and advertising data as well as local news stories, and it may be this archive material has a greater long-term subscription model value than has previously been realised[13]. But in the short-term all regional publishers are still looking for a decent model to make their day-to-day online presence pay.

Another scenario if large publications did decline or fold would be that smaller hyperlocal websites might spring up offering local news from a low cost-base. This would, ironically, return local news-gathering to its origins. This is beginning to happen in some areas, as other parts of this book outline, sometimes successfully, sometimes less so, and it remains to be seen how realistic a model this will prove to be.

Of course the game is far from over for the local press. Talented and committed journalists are still labouring away on their beloved papers and if big publishers reduced their desire for huge profit margins and returned to the days of smaller, but sustainable profits, many papers, especially the smallest, are eminently viable. Other sectors have weaned themselves off unsustainable profit margins and adapted well to this new era – and it might not be too late for the regional press to do the same.

If the big owners cannot do that because of their own financial positions and heavy gearing, if they sold these papers back to their communities, without the expectation for continuing unrealistic margins, there could be a long-term future for local media, as multi-platform providers of news and advertising.

What is certain is that local people still have an appetite for local news, the more compelling the better. Whether that can be supplied to them in future, who will supply it and who will pay for it remain the big questions.

Bibliography

Aldridge, Meryl, (2007) *Understanding the Local Media*, Maidenhead: Open University Press/McGraw Hill

Davies, Nick, (2008), *Flat Earth News*, London: Chatto & Windus

Engel, Matthew, (2009) 'Local papers: an obituary' *British Journalism Review*, 20(2), pp. 55-58

Fowler, Neil, (2011) 'Time for a radical change in who owns the regions' in *Press Gazette*, December 2011

Franklin, Bob, (ed) (2006) *Local Journalism and Local Media*, London: Routledge

Franklin, Bob, & Murphy, David (eds) (1998) *Making the Local News: Local Journalism in Context*, London: Routledge

Freer, Julie (2007) 'UK Regional and Local Newspapers,' in Anderson, P and Ward, G. (Eds) *The Future of Journalism in the Advanced Democracies.* Hampshire: Ashgate

McNair, Brian (2010) *News and Journalism in the UK* (5th edition). London: Routledge

Newton, David, and Smith, Martin (1999) *The Stamford Mercury: Three Centuries of Newspaper Publishing*, Stamford: Shaun Tyas

Riley, Edward (2006) *Life is Local, The History of Johnston Press*, Edinburgh: Johnston Press

Temple, Mick (2008) *The British Press*, Maidenhead: Open University Press/McGraw Hill

Williams, Kevin (1998) *Get Me a Murder a Day*, London: Hodder Arnold

Notes

[1] See Engel (2009) for instance

[2] The Audit Bureau of Circulations – see its website http://www.abc.org.uk/

[3] See Franklin, B., (2006), Temple, M., (2008) and Fowler, N., (2011) for example.

[4] www.newspapersoc.org.uk

[5] See for example Newton, D., and Smith, M., (1999) *The Stamford Mercury*

[6] For example the teetotal Whittaker family's ownership of the *Scarborough Evening News* group of publications from their foundation in 1882 until purchase by Emap in 1986.

[7] For example the *Manchester Evening News*, Wolverhampton *Express & Star*, *Birmingham Evening Mail*, *Leicester Mercury* etc

[8] In order of current total circulation size: Trinity Mirror, Johnston Press, Newsquest, Northcliffe Media.

[9] See Riley, E., (2006) Life is Local, The History of Johnston Press.

[10] Emap plc annual and interim reports 1990-1995.

[11] Davies, N., (2008). The author has happily credited the term to prolific journalism academic Tony Harcup of Sheffield University, though elsewhere Waseem Zakir is acknowledged as its author. Success has many fathers...

[12] See discussion and industry scepticism around success or otherwise of *The Times* and *Sunday Times* paywalls

[13] The *Financial Times* is the only national newspaper to make any kind of success out of website subscription models, and this is believed to work because of the access it offers to its unique and authoritative data archive.

Note on the author

Tor Clark is Principal Lecturer in Journalism, BA Journalism programme leader and a Teacher Fellow at De Montfort University in Leicester. His main interests are political journalism, the UK regional media, the history of journalism, learning, teaching and the student experience. He was a previously a journalist in the regional press working on free, daily and weekly newspapers, two of which he edited. He is now a regular contributor to BBC Radio Leicester on political and journalistic issues and has also written for *Total Politics* magazine.

Reclaiming the streets? An academic overview of hyper-local journalism

Hyperlocal journalism has become a key battle ground for media organisations searching for a way to re-engage with communities and re-establish lost lines of income. But, as David Baines explains, their approaches have met with mixed results.

Across Britain, the United States and Europe, there is a new intensity about the competition among local media for our attention. Local newspapers, TV channels and radio stations have long come to see themselves as serving towns, cities, even regions. But their attention today, as they transform into media companies delivering their content across a range of platforms, is increasingly adopting a narrower focus: on individual villages, on town and city suburbs. And the competition is often being played out street by street.

Many of the contributors to this section are independents: entrepreneurs, local activists and local champions who are often experimenting with new forms of journalism, new ways of doing journalism, thinking afresh about what journalism is for. They wish to use journalism to support and sustain their communities by providing access to news and information, promoting people's interest in and care for each other and often positioning their communities more prominently in wider communicative networks.

But big media also wants a slice of that ground, and successive governments have come out on their side. Before it lost power in 2010, the Labour government supported the establishment of independently funded news consortia (IFNC) to provide local news across media platforms – and leading local newspaper group Trinity Mirror was among those selected to join pilot projects. The Coalition government dropped that idea, but Culture Secretary Jeremy Hunt still sees local newspaper publishers as integral to his plans to support 'strong local media to nurture a sense of local identity and hold locally-elected politicians to account' and he aims to relax – and even remove - cross-media ownership rules at local level so newspaper companies can own local radio stations and set up local TV stations[1]. The Shott report on Hunt's proposal teases out some of the complexities in these plans. (Shott, 2010). But wider complexities exposed by these developments are yet to be adequately addressed by, and present an important new field of inquiry for, journalism studies. We need better to understand the dynamics of communities; the ways in which those community networks are using and making meaning of both geographical and virtual spaces and places; what we mean by 'local'; the relationships between 'local' and 'global' - and how all these factors are transforming the roles and responsibilities of journalists and the professional processes, practices and values of 'local' journalism.

Hyper-local attractions for local papers

The problems facing local newspaper companies are explored at length elsewhere in this book, but the substantial transformations which they are undergoing along systemic, economic, technological, structural, cultural and social trajectories are of critical relevance to this narrowing of focus to the 'hyper-local' level. The process has been driven for local newspaper publishers in particular by long-term declines in circulation and precipitate declines in profitability.

Some newspaper publishers responded earlier than others by attempting to engage more localised audiences and mine more fine-grained advertising markets by developing internet-based 'hyper-local' news and information websites dedicated to city suburb, small town, village, or post-code (US zip-code) areas. DMGT, owner of Britain's national *Daily Mail* and Northcliffe regional newspapers, launched hyper local sites in 2006 and later expanded their reach (*Press Gazette* 2006; Luft, 2009); UK regionals Trinity Mirror and Newsquest went hyper-local (*Press Gazette* 2007; *Press Gazette* 2009); the *New York Times* launched hyper-local sites in 2009 (Jarvis 2009); Britain's *The Guardian* in 2010 (Pugh, 2011). Hyper-local journalism came to be seen as a vital strategy for major media organisations and was the central theme of the 2010 European Newspaper Congress, which featured a session boldly titled *Hyperlocal news as the key to success*[2]. Enthusiasm was not, and is not, confined to newspaper publishers: In 2009 AOL bought hyper-local news producer *Patch*[3]; MSNBC bought hyper-local aggregator *EveryBlock*[4] and in 2010, Scottish Television (STV) launched six hyper-local sites in Lanarkshire (Media Guardian, 2010) and Amsterdam-based investment firm, PPF Group launched a series of café-based hyper-local sites in the Czech Republic – *Nase Adresa* (Tailleur 2009) The commercial attractions of hyper-local projects, for local-newspaper publishers in particular, are clear. They eliminate many production costs and all distribution costs inherent in print and promise the participation of their audiences in content-production at little or no cost. Indeed, Roger Parry, outgoing chairman of local-newspaper publisher Johnston Press, predicted that journalists' jobs will be done better in future 'by enthusiastic amateurs for next to nothing' (Engel, 2009).

But such ventures into hyper-local journalism by traditional media organisations have met mixed success. *The Guardian* gave up on its sites in 2011

(Pugh 2011); PPF Group shut *Nase Adresa* in 2011 (Heald, 2010). Others persist with their sites but community participation in them is often problematic.

Community concerns

Studies by Baines (2011) and Thurman et al (2011) found a series of structural and cultural factors which hampered companies' abilities to engage audience commitment with their commercially-inspired, hyper-local projects and Baines in particular noted in his study that such 'one-size-fits-all' sites ignored (a) communities' needs to position themselves globally as well as locally and (b) that the diversity brought about by local 'ownership' of the site is critical to its chances for promoting community engagement. But why would a community engage with – visit, contribute to, join discussions on – such a site? I would argue that the main benefits for its 'community of use' and the individuals who make up that community lies in its contribution to community sustainability. Andre Jansson puts forward a useful explanation of what that involves in his study of ICT networks in rural Sweden:

> "The enduring potential of a particular community to maintain the social and cultural interests of its inhabitants, including equal access to various services, good opportunities for political and cultural participation, expression and integration and an enduring sense of community." (Jansson 2010 p180)

Local media play a multifaceted role in building networks and maintaining connectivity, generating and reinforcing representations of place and community and, through dimensions of connectivity and representation, reinforce people's sense of belonging. Such media create a communicative space of civic, social and cultural engagement, which in turn fosters economic interactions. They host spaces for advertising and economic activity, but are also actors in local economies. Local newspapers proclaim themselves to be more than a service provider, but 'part of the community' itself (see the Newspaper Society's Local Newspaper Week 2011 publicity material[5]).

But for commercial organisations providing local media, 'local communities' are also at the same time markets within which their papers are sold and commodities to be sold to advertisers (Smythe, 1977). The conception and identification of a 'community' by media corporations can be determined not by the community's own sense of identity and space it occupies (materially and conceptually), but by the manner in which that community-commodity can be packaged and sold. Many regional newspaper companies and corporations enjoy local monopolies and some refrain from competition with each other within circulation boundaries (Murphy 1998: 82; Franklin and Murphy 1991) in order to efficiently commodify communities. And Weinhold's study of workplace socialisation in a group of US community newspapers found that senior journalists' news-sense was determined primarily by a story's market potential, rather than the interests of the wider communities within which the papers circulated:

> 'The pressure of reporting while meeting newspapers' profit demands seem to intensify reporters' need to condense , and as a result omit, important and illuminating content , and citizens are the losers in the end.' (Weinhold 2008: 485)

Changes in the way we live and work and new technologies bringing new media platforms have shrunk the returns to which papers have become accustomed from local communities-as-markets. New ways to shop and source goods and services have hit local papers' advertising revenue – which has led to conflict as competition for the local community-as-commodity hots up. In contrast to local papers serving towns and cities, Hargreaves and Thomas (2002: 64) noted that in Britain "most television news does not even attempt to focus at the truly local scale". Britain's public-service, publicly-funded broadcaster the BBC (conscious of its duty to serve all who finance it through a compulsory licence fee) planned in 2007 to launch web-based video news services at the local level of town and city. The Newspaper Society, representing regional and local publishers, and the Society of Editors protested about unfair competition and the BBC Trust, the corporation's governing body, ordered executives to withdraw their plans for finer-grained video news serving smaller communities (Linford 2008).

Yet Hargreaves and Thomas (ibid) also noted that newspapers, which can reach small localities do not necessarily engage with all communities which occupy those spaces. They have, for example, "a tenuous hold on young readers and a very weak position among the black and Asian population".[6] Aldridge holds that weekly-papers, usually based in small towns are conceptually "closest to the everyday term 'local paper'. (2007 p27). But many such newspapers have closed (Franklin 2008, p7[7]) and many rural communities have lost access to a local paper (and local papers to rural communities-as-commodities-as-markets) as village shops and post offices have closed.

What do we mean by 'local' media?

The term 'local media', and the assumptions which underlie it, can be contested. Hans Kleinstuber in his research into local cable TV, reminds us that 'local' can be interrogated in other than geographical dimensions. He points to factors relating to technological, legal, economic, programming and access (Kleinstuber, 1992, p144). 'Local' papers bear names linked to geographical areas and carry news about those localities in which the papers circulate, and in many cases have done for a considerable time, but ownership of 'local' titles has migrated and concentrated in national and multinational corporations (Aldridge 2007; McNair 2003; Murphy 1998; Williams and Franklin 2008). Britain's Trinity Mirror publishes more than 130 regional daily and weekly newspapers; Johnston Press, 18 daily newspapers and 245 weekly newspapers; Northcliffe 113 regional newspapers. Gannett has 81 Community Publishing media outlets in the US and its subsidiary, Newsquest, publishes more than 200 local and regional titles in the UK[8]. What are the consequences of this non-local ownership? Until the recession hit advertising revenues in 2007-2008, such groups maintained typical profit margins of around 25-35% on revenue[9] by aggressive strategies put in place to maximise income and minimise costs, primarily by exercising economies of scale and cutting staff. The revenue is drawn from those communities – readers and advertisers - in which the companies operate, the profits go to distant corporate shareholders and to service the debt burden incurred in funding their acquisitions. This represents a substantial net financial loss for the local communities. But because much of the savings have been made through job cuts, those communities suffer further disadvantage. As a result of the converged companies taking advantage of economies of scale, the designing, sub-editing and printing of many local weekly and daily newspapers has been centralised and takes place outside, often far outside, their circulation areas (for example Luft 2011). Local reporters are less likely to be local people than graduates who are working in an occupation 'people pay to enter' and often gain admission to local newspapers through centralised recruitment departments and only after prolonged periods of unpaid 'work experience' or 'internships' (Journalism Training Forum 2002: 25. See also Aldridge 2007: 155; Delano and Henningham 1995).

Of course, there remain local papers which still have teams of reporters who live in and know their local communities intimately and are committed to fairly representing those communities in their journalism and even championing their interests, but there is a case to be made that within traditional 'local newspaper' organisations, local communities are conceptualised in very different ways to those in which they might see themselves. They are regarded as resources to be exploited, and this generates tensions between journalists' professional, public-service' values and their obligations as employees to their employers (Weinhold 2008: 47). Despite the industry discourse proclaiming that such papers are 'part of' the community, the relationships which exist between a 'local' corporately-owned newspaper and the community within which it circulates are fundamentally different to those relationships which might be held to exist between individuals and other non-commercial organisations, civil society groupings within the locality and its interactions with and within the local community are primarily motivated by commercial advantage.

But if a media group sets up hyper-local sites for the community to populate and over which the community has editorial control – such that it can be said they take ownership of the site – need it matter that the virtual space which it occupies is provided by a corporate concern? John Myles, exploring ways in which internet spaces provided by municipal-commercial partnerships can help sustain communities in Manchester (UK), argues that the

"… meaning of community in community networks is the outcome of relations of power and there needs to be critical awareness of this in local authority community telematics policy formation. This critical awareness may well be threatened in partnerships with the commercial sector, and the priority must be … putting the networks more thoroughly in the hands of the community of use." (Myles, 2004 p487)

So if such networks are put "more thoroughly in the hands of the community of use" – the local or hyper-local community – the issues raised by the peculiarities of the relationship between media company and community should be resolved and the sites' value in terms of supporting and sustaining a community would lie in the community's own hands.

But Baines's study (Baines, 2011) found that although editorial control of the content was passed to contributors, the hyper-local news sites' design and architecture limited opportunities of the contributors to showcase their community in the global, as well as local, context which was important to a community which was reliant to a large extent on tourism. The hyper-local sites were visually 'branded' by the media organisation and this limited the community's opportunities to take ownership of them and make them distinctly of that locality. Paradoxically, the handing over of editorial control inhibited contributors who came to the site cold and wanted to work with the professionals to learn some of the relevant skills of journalism that they might apply these to telling the stories of their own community.

Thurman et al (2011) also found that the individual hyper-local sites were designed with branding and the categorisation of subject areas for the hosting of content, using architecture that was clearly determined by print newspaper traditions. The Northcliffe sites did employ people with journalistic skills to supply hyper-local content to the sites, but interactivity and engagement with the community was primarily facilitated through comment streams on stories. And in the age of YouTube, Twitter, Flickr, the ubiquitous camcorder and the smart-phone which can instantly upload text, still and moving images to websites and social media streams, both Baines and Thurman et al found that the print paradigm dominated the local papers' hyper-local sites. Thurman concluded: "print publishers … bring structural and cultural qualities that may hold back the development of hyper-local news as both an empowering medium and a commercial enterprise" (Thurman et al, 2011: 8).

Do the independents do it differently?
Internet-based hyper-local news sites perform local paper functions as 'town criers', informing local communities about local affairs, and this is part of their attraction to local-newspaper companies. But because they are web-based, they inevitably position those addressed communities within globally interconnected perspectives – a process which has been conceptualised as 'glocalization'. This global-local interaction is characterised by a complex range of dynamics. Douglas Kellner, citing Allan and Carmen Luke (2000), points out that these

dynamics are different, and generate different outcomes, in each locality because "every local context involves its own appropriation and reworking of global products and signifiers, thus encouraging difference, otherness, diversity and variety" (Kellner 2002 293).

Mark Deuze has been to the fore in conceptualising media work as essentially made up of collaborative processes and media texts as collaborative artefacts (Deuze, 2007, 48). But the collaboration in producing 'journalism' need not necessarily involve a 'journalist' – or media organisation – and the community-sustaining bit of what is going on might lie as much in the process of collaboration, conversation and discovery as in the product – the story, the text, the image, the video, or the stream of contributions to the social media site. Such social media sites as Twitter, MySpace, Face Book, Linkedin deliver networks of connectivity which allow ordinary citizens collaboratively to produce media artefacts in what Peter Dahlgren conceptualises as a "constellation of communicative spaces". They also facilitate economic interactions – which are also of concern to local communities and might be necessary if the sites are to be sustainable. Such media products chime with Manuel Castells's definition (2010; Vol1, p. xliv) of a network society in which organisational arrangements of humans in relation to everyday life-issues such as production, consumption and experience are made of networks. This does not undervalue proximal, localised and lived interactions – interactions within and beyond the community are complementary. The rural community in Baines's study of hyper-local media wanted to know what was happening in their small town, but they also wanted the wider world to know.

Urry (2007) sets forth a valuable conceptualization of "network capital", which Jansson (2010 p182) applies to explore "how new technological networking resources in countryside regions may contribute not only to network sociality, but also to social capital, a sense of stability and spatial coherence".

Independent hyper-local sites which are neither grounded in the print paradigm, nor hosted in the shadow of a print product which generates more revenue for the owner and which are organisationally smaller, less hierarchical and more entrepreneurial, are also able to be more experimental about the journalism they are doing.

In her review of journalism education, Mensing (2010: 512) identifies the tensions between a "transmission-driven, industry-conceived model of journalism" and "a community-oriented model of journalism" which refocuses "attention on the role that journalism can play in the health of a community". Encouraging students learning to be journalists to embrace the latter model, she argues, offers the prospect of a "laboratory of inquiry, researching how journalism matters and experimenting with ways to practice journalism in a rapidly reconfiguring environment" (2010: 512). Such a laboratory of inquiry is more likely to emerge from diverse bottom-up, community-led hyper-local news sits, rather than top-down industry-led sites and this relates to the vexed question of developing a sustainable business model for the commercial sustainability of hyper-local journalism. A study by a colleague and myself (Baines and Kennedy 2011) suggested that hyper-local news sites offered opportunities for journalists to start their own entrepreneurial and independent media businesses, for journalism students to enhance their employability, experience and reflect on journalism's role and purpose beyond the industrial model and sustain professional practice and values at a time when industrial local journalism was in decline.

Former *Guardian* journalist Ian Wylie launched a hyper-local news site in Newcastle upon Tyne (UK) serving the suburban community of Jesmond. *Jesmond Local*[10] provides news and information to the Newcastle city suburb of Jesmond. His initial concept was similar to that of a traditional local newspaper: to carry news online, of and for that community, funded through advertising from local businesses. The project was supported by Newcastle University journalism students working specific patches (beats): crime, shopping, business, property; community, transport; food and drink, politics; sport; arts and culture; environment. Reflecting on the project two years later, he said:

> "My nervousness about this project was ... can I get excited about reporting on flower arranging? But it's not just about reporting, it's not just about bringing a newspaper out. It's about being woven into the fabric of that community, about being part of that community. You got to know the people behind the flower-arranging feature, the bobby on the beat, and all these stories are important, they are important to me because they are important to people I have got to know as friends." (personal communication with the author)

From the beginning, he and the students approached journalism, not in the highly competitive manner in which it is traditionally engaged – an exercise in getting the byline, the story, self-promotion – but as collaborators in a joint enterprise; reflecting on and exploring new ways to do journalism. This critically reflective, investigatory approach has been a factor in *Jesmond* Local's evolution into a into a hub for new experiments doing journalism and journalism-related activities, while remaining a resource for the hyper-local community which it serves. The team has organised community-based events such as election hustings; informed the development of the university's journalism programmes and is working in schools and the community to pass on journalism skills and extend media literacy and media practice and engage members of the community as collaborators in the process and production of journalism. The team – with freely-given support from other freelance professionals in the region - produced a 'pop-up' magazine in a weekend to mark the Turner Prize exhibition in Gateshead[11]. They produced a documentary on a special school (a school for children with learning difficulties) for the BBC Radio 3 Free Thinking Festival 2011[12], and the team are working on plans to produce a further documentary and explore the possibility of developing online community TV programmes. The project has developed along its own trajectories, uniquely shaped by its *local* context, to support both community sustainability and help to sustain - and develop - the professional practices and values of journalism. It has not produced 'a business model', but drawn in a range of shifting and occasionally opportunistic, revenue streams from advertising to grants from charitable trusts and opened opportunities for the editor to earn an income as a visiting university lecturer. Some of its 'revenue' has been given in kind, rather than cash.

Thurman et al warn that independent hyper-local operations are often precarious and can depend on the enthusiasm and availability of a single person – but can build greater strength and sustainability through networks. They conclude that "a successful commercial model (for hyper-local news) is as likely to come from the independent sector as from as from traditional publishers or broadcasters" (Thurman et al 2011: 8). But as a variety of approaches develop, each embedded in a particular locality, I would argue that a range of sustainable commercial models are likely to emerge, each supporting an independent media operation (or several operations); which supports and sustains a community's need to know what is happening in its world; and which might also help to develop new ways to do journalism and sustain what is valuable in the way good journalism is practised today.

References

Aldridge M. (2007) *Understanding The local Media*. Maidenhead. Open University Press.

Baines, D and Kennedy, C (2010) An Education For Independence: Should entrepreneurial skills be an essential part of the journalist's toolbox? *Journalism Practice*, Vol. 4, No 1, 2010, 97-113

Baines, D. Hyper-local: Glocalized rural news. *International Journal of Sociology and Social Policy* 2010,30 9/10 581-592.

Castells, M. (2010) *The Rise of the Network Society* (2nd ed) Vol 1. The Information Age: Economy, Society and Culture. Oxford. John Wiley & Sons .

Delano, A. and Henningham, J. (1995) *The News Breed: A report on British journalists in the 1990s*. London: London Institute.

Deuze, M. (2007) *Media Work in a Digital Age*. Polity. London

Dahlgren, P. The Internet, Public Spheres and Political Communication: Dispersion and deliberation. *Political Communication*, 22 147-62 (2005).

Engel, M. Local Papers: An obituary. *British Journalism Review*. 20 55-62 (2009)

Franklin B. and Murphy D. (1991) *What News? The Market, Politics and the Local Press*. London. Routledge

Franklin B, ed (2008) *Pulling Newspapers Apart: Analysing Print Journalism*. Sage, London

Hargreavess I and Thomas J (2002) *New News, Old News*, London Broadcasting Standards Commission / Independent Television Commission. Available at: http://legacy.caerdydd.ac.uk/jomec/resources/news.pdf (Accessed May 23, 2011)

Heald, E. (2010) PPF shutters local media project *Naše Adresa? Editors Weblog*. *http://www.editorsweblog.org/multimedia/2010/08/ppf_shutters_local_media_project_nase_ad.php* (Accessed January 20, 2012)

Jarvis, J. The Times and CUNY and Others Go Hyperlocal. Jeff Jarvis blog, posted Feb 28, 2009. http://www.buzzmachine.com/2009/02/28/the-times-cuny-and-others-go-hyperlocal/ (Accessed January 20, 2012)

Jansson, A. (2010) Mediatization, Spacial Coherence and Social Sustainability: The Role of Digital Media Networks in a Swedish Countryside Community. *Culture Unbound: Journal of Current Cultural Research (Thematic Section: Rural Media Spaces)* 2 2010: 177-192.

Journalism Training Forum (2002) Journalists at work: their views on training, recruitment and conditions. London: Publishing NTO/Skillset

Kellner, D. Theorising Globalization. *Sociological Theory* 20(3) (Nov 2002) 285-305

Kleinstuber, H. (1992) The Global Village Stays Local. In In Siune K and Treutzchler W (1992)n *Dynamics of Media Politics: Broadcast and Electronic Media in Western Europe.* Euromedia Research Group. London. Sage.

Linford, P. (2008) BBC Trust rejects local video plan. *Holdthefrontpage*, November 21, 2008. Accessible at: http://www.holdthefrontpage.co.uk/2008/news/bbc-trust-rejects-local-video-plan/ (Accessed March 23, 2011)

Luft O. (2009) Daily Mail owner launches websites aimed at 'hyperlocal' communities. *The Guardian.* July 2, 2009. http://www.guardian.co.uk/media/2009/jul/02/daily-mail-hyperlocal-websites (Accessed January 20, 2012)

Luft O. (2011, February 1) Johnston Press plans 'hub' to sub all its southern titles. *UK Press Gazette*, Available at: http://www.pressgazette.co.uk/story.asp?sectioncode=1&storycode=46625&c=1 (Accessed January 25, 2012)

Luke, A. and Luke, C. (2000)A Situated Perspective on Cultural Globalization, 275-98 in *Globalization and Education* Nicholas Burbukes and Carlos Torres (eds) London. And New York. Routledge.

McNair B. (2003) *News and Journalism in the UK.* Routledge. London

Media Guardian (2010) STV launches move into hyperlocal. (September 13) http://www.guardian.co.uk/media/pda/2010/sep/13/stv-local-hyperlocal (Accessed January 20, 2012)

Mensing, D. (2010): Rethinking (again) the future of journalism education *Journalism Studies*, 11:4, 511-523

Murphy D, (1998) Earthquake undermines structure of local press ownership: many hurt. In Making the Local News, Murphy D and Franklin B eds, *Making the Local News.* Routledge London.

Myles, J. (2004) Community networks and cultural intermediaries: the politics of community net development in Greater Manchester. *Media Culture Society* 26 467-490

Pugh, A. (2011) Guardian Local axed and four jobs in doubt. *Press Gazette* (April 28, 2011) http://www.pressgazette.co.uk/story.asp?sectioncode=1&storycode=47032&c=1 (Accessed January 20, 2012)

Shott N. (2010) Commercially Viable Local Television in the UK. A Review by Sir Nicholas Shott for the Secretary of State for Culture, Olympics, Media and Sport. Department for Culture Media and Sport. Available at: http://www.culture.gov.uk/images/publications/Local-TV-Report-Dec10_FullReport.pdf (Accessed January 22, 2012)

Tailleur J.P. (2009) A new experience in journalism, at multiple levels. Editors Weblog (May 22, 2009) http://www.editorsweblog.org/analysis/2009/05/nase_adresa.php (Accessed January 20, 2012)

Thurman, N., Pascal, J.C., and Bradshaw, P. (2011) 'Can Big Media do 'Big Society?'': A critical case study of commercial, convergent hyperlocal news'. Paper presented to the Future of Journalism Conference, Cardiff University, Wales, September 8-9.

Tunstall, J. (1996) Newspaper Power: the new national press in Britain, Oxford: Oxford University Press.

Press Gazette (2006, August 4) *Associated 'hyperlocal' sites to broaden regional empire* http://www.pressgazette.co.uk/story.asp?sectioncode=1&storycode=35180 (Accessed February 17, 2010)

Press Gazette (2007, August 9) *Trinity Mirror hints at more hyperlocal titles* http://www.pressgazette.co.uk/story.asp?sectioncode=1&storycode=38431 (Accessed January 20, 2012)

Press Gazette (2009, September 4) *Northern Echo to hire 30 non-journalists for ultra-local sites.* http://www.pressgazette.co.uk/story.asp?storycode=44242 (Accessed January 20, 2012)

Urry J. (2007) Social Networks: travel and talk. *British Journal of Sociology*. 54(2) 155-175

Weinhold, W.M. (2008) "Newspaper Negotiations", Journalism Practice 2(3), pp. 476_86.

Williams A. and Franklin B. (2008) *Turning Around the Tanker: Implementing Trinity Mirror's Online Strategy*. Jomec. Cardiff University Press.

Notes

[1] The full text of Jeremy Hunt's speech on June 8, 2010 is available on Britain's Department of Culture Media and Sport website at the following link: http://www.culture.gov.uk/news/ministers_speeches/7132.aspx

[2] European Newspaper Congress 2010, Vienna, Austria. http://enc.newsroom.de/lang/en/enc-2010/lokalinformationen-local_information/ (Accessed January 20 2012)

[3] Patch: http://www.patch.com/

[4] EveryBlock: http://www.everyblock.com/

[5] http://www.newspapersoc.org.uk/local-newspaper-week

[6] Young people are seen a commodity group attractive to advertisers, ethnic minorities have often been seen as less attractive to advertisers and British newspapers have historically done little to engage with them, indicating that commercial utility trumps 'localness'.

[7] The 1,306 paid-for weeklies in the UK in 1948 had fallen to 526 in 2005 (Franklin 2008)

[8] Trinity Mirror PLC website: http://www.trinitymirror.com/our-portfolio/regionals/
Johnston Press: http://www.johnstonpress.co.uk/jpplc/ourbusiness/
Northcliffe: http://www.northcliffemedia.co.uk/
Gannett: http://www.gannett.com/section/BRANDS&template=cover
Newsquest: http://www.newsquest.co.uk/

[9] For example Trinity Mirror Regionals' profit in 2005 was 28.3%, and Johnston Press's was 34.7%. Source company annual reports: (Available at Trinity Mirror:

http://www.trinitymirror.com/pdf/B8B19C7F-F882-D918-BD4A7E9AAF1ED9B0.pdf Johnston Press: http://www.johnstonpress.co.uk/jpplc/mediacentre/pressreleases/?year=2006 Accessed January 22, 2012)

[10] Jesmond Local: http://jesmondlocal.com/

[11] Turner Prize 2011 BALTIC Exhibition http://www.balticmill.com/whatsOn/future/ExhibitionDetail.php?exhibID=148

[12] BBC R3 Free Thinking Festival 2011 http://www.bbc.co.uk/programmes/b0144txn

Note on the author:
David Baines lectures in journalism and the sociology of journalism at Newcastle University and has worked for many years on daily newspapers. He is researching the development of hyperlocal journalism, the changes taking place in the way communities use journalism and ethnic diversity within the news industry workforce.

How Filton's new voice can be a business model for hyperlocal journalism

Richard Coulter left his executive role on a leading evening title and went back to genuine community journalism. His focus on print is already paying dividends, he believes, for him and his readership.

When I left the Cardiff Journalism School in 1992, I knew exactly where I wanted to go in my career. I had the same dreams most journalists have – making a difference, seeking the truth, all that stuff – and having had a taste of newspapers in the USA, I was going to win Pulitzer Prizes for my sparkling copy and insights.

What I didn't expect was that, nearly twenty years later, I would be sitting in the sparse pavilion of Filton Town Council, north of Bristol, on cold Tuesday nights reporting on the minute details of the parish finance committee. My presence usually swells the "public gallery" by around 50%. In the past eight months I have never seen a reporter from any other organisation.

It is the grass roots level of grass roots journalism – discussions on potholes, traffic calming, streetlights and the local podiatry clinic. That's feet, by the way. I will not win a Pulitzer Prize for this work and much of the subject matter I report on would not make the news in brief column of any self respecting regional paper. But...it's relevant for local people. And if you live in Filton, it's interesting.

Relevant, compelling and interesting
A few years ago, when I was assistant editor at the *Bristol Evening Post*, we invited a consultant over from the States. It was one of the most pleasurable weeks of my career. He challenged conventional thinking and he understood that newspaper companies are businesses.

His mantra for a good newspaper was this...the stories must be "relevant, compelling and/or interesting". As a summary of what makes news, I have yet

139

to hear anything better. The view was, if it ticks any or all of those boxes, that it must – by definition – hold the attention of the reader. This has stuck with me. And as savage cuts have made the jobs of journalists in the regional press so incredibly difficult, the ability to remain "relevant, compelling and interesting" has become a real strain.

I was lucky to work with outstanding journalists at the *Post*, from editor to trainee. My time there was very happy, but as the cuts became deeper and deeper, I felt I would not avoid them for much longer.

I left the *Post* in July 2011, not totally sure what I was going to do, but certain that new models for sustainable journalism could be created and, indeed, had to be created. I had never detected any drop in the desire for people to be given information which affected their lives. What I had noticed was a reluctance to go out and seek that news – and pay for it.

The local community
It is important to understand the context of Filton. It is a well-defined "town" within the Bristol conurbation, with around 12,000 residents in a mix of private and social housing. There are three primary schools (four if you count the Catholic school just over the border in Bristol), one large secondary school, three churches, several strips of small shops and two shopping plazas with larger operators.

But it is large industry which has put Filton on the map. It is one of the UK's homes of aero engineering with Airbus, BAE Systems, GKN and Rolls-Royce all providing jobs over the decades. There are fewer jobs now than there once were but it is still a large part of the community. A big news story, currently still rumbling on, is the possible loss of the Filton Airfield and runway, the vast strip which catered for the early flights of Concorde and Airbus. These days, it rarely hosts much more than light aircraft and, with development on the site as part of South Gloucestershire's core strategy, the airfield, as I write, seems doomed after a long and acrimonious battle.

At the other end of the community the large MoD procurement base at Abbeywood is a modern hive of activity. There is a nearby rail station which connects Filton to all parts of the country and, for what is a relatively traditional community, there are several large employers on the doorstep. To what extent Filton people benefit is not so clear. It is defined as a "priority neighbourhood" in the South Gloucestershire Council area, with below average ratings on several measures, although this has to be taken in the context of the district, a relatively affluent part of the South West.

In recent years, the town council has found itself on the radar of larger news organisations, partly due to some highly controversial "leisure" developments including a cycle track, costing £40,000, which no one appears to use. Bitter fallouts among some councillors contributed to this.

What this all means is that Filton is well defined, there is activity in terms of industry and retail, and there are social issues affecting the population. It also has smallscale local political issues while being at the heart of larger regional concerns, such as the airfield.

In short, in my view, it is ideal for hyperlocal news coverage. It also helps, I might add, that I have lived with my family in Filton for 15 years. My eldest son went to a local primary, as will my youngest and we are members of one of the churches.

Competition and advertising

When I left the *Evening Post*, I set up a publication, supported by advertisements, for Filton people - *filtonvoice*. My mission was to report news which would be "relevant and interesting"...compelling would be a bonus. I had very little business knowledge. All my career I had been in the corporate world, working hard and taking my salary each month. For most of that career I had barely given a thought to where the money came from. It was only with the redundancies of recent years that journalists seemed to finally wake up and understand that we were part of a business rather than some airy-fairy mission to seek the truth. Most of us had bills to pay.

I felt I understood the community well enough to set up a magazine, I knew how to report and sub-edit, I could design pages and I believed the community had enough going on to sustain a newsy, monthly magazine which would be delivered to every home and also be available in public places. I also had the added issue of competition.

Across the UK there are numerous publishers, often one-man bands, who produce local magazines of varying quality. Many of these have very little content and often the editorial, such as it is, tends to be somewhat bland..."I was delighted to be invited to the local Scout troop." That sort of thing.

Easy to mock, perhaps often not too relevant, these local magazines would not pass the test of what most of us cynical journalists would call "news" publications. Some are franchises which come with the claim...'you don't need to be a journalist to edit your own local magazine'. And the fact is, they are right. Putting to one side the scoffing, many of these magazines are commercial successes. I collect local magazines everywhere I go now. I have seen small A5 booklets, 64 pages and more, stuffed with local adverts while the editorial is nearly non-existent. The vast majority of these adverts are small businesses or tradesmen, paying perhaps £20-£30 for a business card sized advert each month.

Typically they will book for a year and get a discount, assuring themselves of presence in what is essentially a local directory. And the adverts work.

In issue one of *filtonvoice*, a gardener friend of mine said he would place an advert. It was October, a time when gardening services were not in the greatest of demand and he was perhaps just advertising to help me get things off the ground. He secured three clients right away, giving him guaranteed work for eight weeks with the hope of more beyond. His small advert had paid for itself many times over.

The magazine gave him visibility in front of the very people he is seeking to sign up for jobs. This is hyperlocal at its most obvious, there is nothing clever or scientific about it: small firms getting their message to a niche audience, all of whom could conceivably use his services. For him, advertising in larger publications would be more expensive and the majority of the readers would be unlikely to hire him since he is not local to them.

Editorial stance

I launched *filtonvoice* in October 2011, with a 16-page publication in quarterfold format, which is slightly smaller than A4. As a former chief sub I was struck by how the A5 magazines were unable to display images to any kind of reasonable size, and many publishers would shrink the type size to the point where reading was seriously difficult. Some of these magazines would carry editorial in tiny green fonts, squashing or stretching to fit the available space. There was no evidence of subbing or even proofing in many cases.

I was probably somewhat sniffy about it, but I felt I could create a niche from an editorial point of view, report on the town council and the traffic issues and the schools. Yet I had to accept the magazine would not run on thin air – it had to match or exceed the commercial success of some of the advertising-led booklets.

My editorial stance was clear from the beginning. Using the "relevant, compelling and interesting" mantra, I wanted to offer Filton people stories which would affect their lives or which attracted a spark of recognition, perhaps a child in a play or a neighbour with an issue to raise. I have some fixed features... stories from the local schools, with the cooperation of head teachers, comprehensive coverage of the town council, a column from our MP, what's on in Filton, letters and comments, and a column from the different church leaders.

In many ways I feel like I have returned to the roots of my career. The town council meets roughly twice a month and the issues are often of the bread and butter variety. We had some excitement when Legionella was possibly discovered in the football showers and there is an ongoing and bitter debate about charging policy for the local boules team (run by a former councillor).

There is a danger in being too close to the councillors... some are neighbours, some I know from my days at the *Post* – and one is my brother-in-law! The issues which they debate affect the readers but they also affect me. It's my £2.66 extra I was expected to pay when the precept went up. If I had an opinion, I hope I kept it to myself in my report from the finance committee.

Yet this close knit community has its advantages. When our deliverers had trouble getting in to some blocks of flats, it was a councillor and a local activist who stepped in and offered to sort it out. There is real appreciation in some quarters that the community has a magazine which attempts to bring the issues to the people.

I have been "summoned" by the president of the WI for failing to mention its meetings and I was corrected by a member of the local history society for failing to remove a paragraph about wartime graves in a contributed article about the airfield.

There is no doubt that some people read every word and on more than one occasion I have been alerted by emails to some spending scandal or other by mysterious characters called "Filton Independent Party" and "True Voice of Filton". There are around a dozen regular website commentators who go by such cloak and dagger names, although some appear to be one and the same person. I will idle away moments at the council wondering if the bald gent with the walking stick is "Sally", a regular cynic and reluctant council tax payer.

This is the essence of the community. I can't claim to change people's lives but I try to engage the community. Often it is the same people at meetings, complaining and trying to change things. It is usually well meaning and there is satisfaction at being part of it.

In some of my more fanciful moments, I aspire to be like the small town editors of American literature, at the hub of the community and shaping the debates. There is a responsibility and it is one which needs to be taken seriously. Having gone from a big city daily to a community newspaper, there is the danger that you believe you are somehow "playing" at being a journalist. I have never had that thought. The issues are real – in some ways mundane, perhaps, for the rest of the city – but vital for the twelve thousand people in Filton.

Where I can, I take copy from local people. In terms of editing, I will correct errors but I try to retain the flavour of the original contribution. The fashion page always features shops in or close to Filton.

It is not the most demanding journalism in the world. The difficult part is being editor, reporter, chief sub and commercial manager all in one. There are headaches with finding delivery people and making sure they do their deliveries on time. I had numerous discussions with printers until I found a gem of a firm with exemplary customer service.

I occasionally wake up in the middle of the night, utterly certain that no one will ever advertise again. I am fortunate to have teamed up with two former colleagues on the commercial side, which helps with those fears.

More than anything, my family is incredibly supportive. My wife Bridget writes the fashion page and my eldest son writes a column and delivers. It feels like an old-style, small family business, and that is probably exactly what it is.

Chasing up unpaid bills is hard, I am a novice at accountancy and I often feel like those music hall entertainers spinning plates. Occasionally, some of them fall off but as yet, not all of them at the same time.

Digital or print?
All through my career as a journalist I had been struck by the chaotic approach to digital. At various times it has been:
- "User comments good, user comments bad."
- "User comments moderated, user comments not moderated."
- "Stories from journalists, stories from anyone."
- "Paywalls, no paywalls."

As I write this, I have been reading about one regional newspaper which is introducing a paywall just as another is abandoning the scheme. The overwhelming feeling was one of people making it up as they went along while the brighter journalists and editors paid the penalty for this guesswork. Crucially, I noticed how digital journalists assumed that everyone in the population was like them. So as tablets became more popular, the assumption was everyone had one or would have one in a very short space of time. Likewise for smartphones. As I speak to people in Filton, I detect no great feeling that tablets are omnipresent.

This, for me, has been one of the biggest mistakes of the regional press: the assumption that because one new toy comes long, all the old ones must be thrown out. I am no dinosaur and I am open to any innovation, but I cannot accept, at the moment, that large numbers of people find print an unacceptable method of consuming information.

Some people may not like paying for print publications any more and they may find it more difficult to obtain in some cases but that does not mean the medium itself is flawed.

In time, things will change and possibly new and as yet unimagined gadgets will take over (making tablets, I might add, redundant in the process). But for now, as long as we can get the magazine to everyone in Filton, it works. I have yet to hear anyone say they reject the concept of print, especially if it is free and delivered through their letterbox

filtonvoice has a website which is limited to breaking stories and content which has already been in the magazine. I see no worth in devaluing a publication which is developing a sound business footing. Having worked on this for several months now, I have had just one request from an advertiser to appear on the website.

The future
It is hard, as a journalist in 2012, to predict the future. For the first 12 years or so of my career in journalism, I barely knew what the word redundancy meant. Then the cuts came, with the gap between each shortening. I didn't see it coming, nor did most of the rest of us. There is a lot of discussion in the industry about blame. Easy to do with hindsight.

I am trying to create a model which will go beyond the bounds of Filton. It will not replace the large news gatherers with their still-enormous resources. This model will likely adapt over time but, for now, print will not be abandoned as part of some faddy exploration into the world of new gadgets. When the time is right, if the time is right, I would hope to move to new mediums, perhaps alongside print.

The commercial model is based on offering advertisers certain numbers of magazines being delivered through certain numbers of letterboxes. I'm not sure digital can yet offer such good assurances.

What has been clear to me is that local communities have had a sense of being disengaged over many years now. Yet they crave information and they want it in a format which is delivered to them (and cheap...or free).

This year, I will be launching courses for journalists and possibly citizen journalists who have had some training and experience, to show them that there are alternatives at a time when mainstream jobs are so scarce. And I want to encourage a new kind of entrepreneurial thinking among journalists.

If this can be achieved with the mantra of "relevant, compelling and interesting" there has to be a future for genuine local journalism. And with that, a future for local journalists.

Note on the author

Richard Coulter is the editor and publisher of *filtonvoice*, www.filtonvoice.co.uk. He can be contacted on 0777 555 0607 or Richard@filtonvoice.co.uk. Details of courses in community publishing and local entrepreneurial journalism will be announced this year on trade publications and websites. He is the former assistant editor and chief sub-editor of the *Bristol Evening Post*.

Local reporting: At the heart of the past, present and future

Ross Hawkes knows more about hyperlocal journalism than most, having founded Lichfield Live. He argues that partnerships between traditional media and local start-ups can pay dividends for both.

When did local become a dirty word?

Those at the coal face of reporting might argue that it is anything but dirty. And yet the industry that employs them seems to be embroiled in a centralisation goldrush, an unstoppable charge towards a single newsroom for all journalism output in the UK.

It seems strange for an industry to undermine its own foundations, but that is exactly what it has done by blackening the name of local reporting through the systematic withdrawal of funding and resources.

Patch reporters in the true sense of the word are a dying breed. Gone are those who are known by everyone who is anyone in their local area with a finger firmly on the community's pulse, replaced instead by ever-changing bylines hidden behind an email address.

The harsh fact is that traditional journalists are becoming remote from their audiences who are also – although the terminology is an example of all that is wrong with the industry – the customers. If they are always right, then how can we ignore their needs?

This centralisation culture must surely have had an impact on the ability of journalists to understand and reflect the issues facing their readers. If you do not have your ear to the ground how can you accurately represent the views of the community? That is not to say there is a need for a physical newsroom in the centre of a patch, thanks mainly to the tools that now allow the journalist to set up a newsroom anywhere a Wi-Fi or 3G signal can be found. But utilising this technology requires something that is not readily found in the modern newsroom – trust. Reporters are too often chained to the desk, hamstrung by the theory that if you cannot be seen then you are not working.

Steve Dyson, a former editor of the *Evening Gazette* on Teesside and the Birmingham *Evening Mail*, believes newspaper groups cannot underestimate the need to have boots on the ground.

"I'm not sure that traditional newsrooms know what they need anymore," he said. "But to be successful, any future media business – online or in print – needs people in and around local communities digging up stories of interest."

It is an interesting view from someone who has seen the harsh realities of keeping the plates spinning as declining profit margins compete with the demand for news. News is still the central ingredient in a media business but the difficulty lies getting bodies on the ground in an affordable way.

The media industry is no different to any other, with entrepreneurs identifying gaps in the market ready to be exploited. The rise of the hyperlocal publishers has been testament to the opportunities being presented to those with an understanding of the modern, digital community.

One of the accusations regularly leveled at hyperlocal publishers is that no-one is making significant money from them yet. While this may be true, positive signs are there. In his hyperlocal review of 2011, Damian Radcliffe[1] acknowledged that funding was an ongoing challenge, but recognised that traditional media and start-ups were experimenting. A number of initiatives have come and gone in recent times, including the Guardian's much-vaunted Local project. Despite being wound down because the sites were no longer deemed sustainable, the organisation did admit that "as an experiment in covering local communities in a new way, it has been successful and enlightening"[2].

This struggle by traditional publishers to find a way for the newsgathering benefit to outweigh the associated costs is not a surprise. But according to the man nicknamed 'The Godfather of Hyperlocal', the solution is not to measure the success of such a site in the same way as traditional publishing. Rick Waghorn's idea of making sites 'not-for-loss'[3] as a first step is an important one, but one which is not comfortable for many of the traditional publishers trying to secure a slice of the new market. For former newspaper man Steve Dyson, the odds seem stacked firmly in favour of the new visionaries rather than the old guard – thanks mainly to the issue of centralisation.

He explained: "They [traditional publishers] won't go in the opposite direction, as this is counter-intuitive to the way they are structured and organised. And so this is where real local businesses could develop, because most major news organisations are leaving the marketplace wide open."

And it is a view shared by Nigel Barlow of hyperlocal site *Inside the M60*: "The structure of the media was blown away by the four big players' consolidation of the independents over the last 10-15 years and it will be difficult to untangle that state of affairs. It seems that media groups, in an attempt to cut costs, are trying to do things on a regional scale. By doing this, they are once again making the mistake of being too remote from their audience."

Getting to the roots of local

Part of the growth and perceived success of the new hyperlocal movement is down to passion and knowledge for the communities they serve – and recognising that 'local' is no longer a catch-all term. The idea of 'community' cannot even be described as a purely geographic phenomenon, with many people having a greater empathy and connection to an online social group than to their physical neighbours.

The emotional connection between audience and publisher is particularly important in a society that is used to choice and being able to interact with their media, be it through phone votes, Twitter hashtags or red-button offerings. So for many of the successful hyperlocal sites, the 'one of us' mentality and the open nature of the work has been crucial.

There is also the social currency factor. With many websites being run as voluntary, non-profit enterprises or sapling start-ups, there is a greater goodwill element involved in the support they get. *Lichfield Live* (formerly *The Lichfield Blog*) was able to tap into this network when technical problems threatened the future of the project. Philip John, one of the founders of the site, explained: "We were quite honest about the fact that we were in desperate need of financial assistance and the local community supported us by taking out adverts and allowing us to purchase new equipment to safeguard the site for the future."

This goodwill is also borne out in newsgathering. Eyes on the ground have always been a crucial part of the local journalist's life. But the effect of this network within a community is increased thanks to the ready availability of social media. The opportunity to interact with an audience in real time, all of the time has allowed the new breed of reporters to put themselves firmly at the centre of a local, social circle. By positioning themselves at the heart of their community, hyperlocal journalists can understand the needs and desires of the audience they are serving. In the current, technology-driven and globally-connected society, the journalist has the ability to be at the heart of the community at all times. It is important to recognize the difference between centralised services and centralised reporting. It is possible for a newsroom to exist beyond the realms of bricks and mortar, by utilising the many technological tools available. This ability to put the journalist back into the local setting would surely put the local setting back into the journalist as well.

Who should set the agenda?

If anything, this latest incarnation of entrepreneurial journalism at a local level is merely the industry going full circle to the days of pamphleteers and individual publishers. The only difference is the platform and range of tools now available.

However, Steve Dyson insists the make-up of the community is the key: "When the printing press was first invented, hundreds and thousands of pamphlets were printed by individuals - whether they were politicians, activists, businessmen or quacks. But they quickly disappeared once newspapers were born and organised the content. At this stage of multi-media, there is a tendency for readers to be 'search happy', looking for and finding a multitude of disparate content and enjoying the early days of this online adventure. But still the most popular websites are those that organise the content, editing out the rubbish."

But the argument that society is increasingly looking for openness rather than pre-moderated media cannot be ignored. One of the key issues facing regional journalism is the inability to woo audiences in a defined geographic area. This is because the definition of local to the individual can vary, as can their point of access. Traditionally, local media sprung up around closely-connected communities. But with a more transient and commuter-led society, the issue of how to get the product to market becomes far greater. After all, how can you sell a product to an audience when you do not know where they are to buy it? This is where digital offerings should come to the fore, by providing a universal option for those outside a circulation area to continue to access local information and news which has longevity and ease of access.

If newspapers and other media outlets are struggling to come to terms with the fact that news, particularly at a local level, is now beyond their sole ownership and control, there are many who suggest the horse has already bolted. Media commentator Arif Durrani has claimed[4] that social media has already turned the tide, suggesting "the hold of traditional media outlets like Rupert Murdoch's on setting the news agenda is increasingly being superseded by Twitter". If we are accepting that the national picture is changing, then we can safely assume the local picture will undergo, or already has undergone the change. Much of this change has been powered by the social media giants, with Twitter and Facebook allowing small media to punch above their weight in the marketing of content. This has in turn enabled them to build audiences quickly and effectively and gain support within a defined local community.

The view that news is no longer the sole domain of the journalist was supported by Professor Paul Bradshaw[5] who said: "Traditionally, the media were the gatekeepers. They took information and they decided what went through the gate, what news people got. Now the gates are open, the news is circulating regardless of your decision as a journalist as to what is newsworthy."

Hyperlocals have taken this standpoint and run with it. By utilising openness and information sharing, they have been able to tap into the flow of news thanks to an understanding that they do not control it, but are merely sharing it with like-minded individuals who share common values, ideals and interests.

Content is still king

A wise person once decreed that content was king – but it is not a universally-accepted view. Andrew Odlyzko suggested that the communication element of the internet was more important than the entertainment value of the information it contained[6]. For journalists, fusing the power of communication granted by the internet and its many tools with rich, valuable local content, journalists at a community level will be able to thrive.

The quality of reporting certainly cannot be undervalued, mainly due to the fact that for many local reporters this is the gap in the market they will be attempting to exploit. In terms of the big, headline stories then speed is likely to be the space they are attempting to fill. However, in terms of longevity then it will be going back to basics.

For all the technological breakthroughs and tools now available, no-one has yet replaced the ability of a journalist to get their nose stuck in and dig out a story.

This is where big media's centralisation policy falls down. By not having the staffing levels or funding to make a case for sending a reporter to a parish council meeting or village fete, they are missing events that have real meaning to that particular community. By going back to basics and patch reporting, the hyperlocal journalist can have a steady supply of stories that will appeal to a local populace, as well as raising his or her profile within the community. Physical presence still carries more weight than faceless email.

If centralisation is leading to lack of face-to-face contact, the situation is being compounded by the lack of value placed on communication as a whole within journalism and the wider media industry. Speculative meetings and time spent establishing contacts do not make a mark in the plus column on the balance sheet. But for the smaller, independent organisations who are likely to flourish if Clay Shirky's view[7] that we should allow 1,000 flowers to bloom in place of newspapers is correct, communication will be the central pillar on which their success or failure rests. While traditional media attempts to shoehorn outdated working methods which restrict the creativity of its workers, vibrant forward-thinkers will be busy taking advantage by creating the sort of close-knit community networks which their media forefathers held so close to their hearts.

Is Clay Shirky right? Should we allow the flowers to bloom in the soil left fertile by the demise of newspapers and other media in local communities? Conor Clark argued[8] that they should be "propped up" if they were deemed to have a public worth. But surely if a media organisation has attempted to reinvent its offering a number of times and adopted countless new strategies without success then surely there comes a point to put it out of its misery. The death of those media organisations who are merely holding back the inevitable would stop blocking the sunlight from those who have the green shoots of a new era ready to rise from beneath the soil.

It is a difficult argument to call. Those media groups who are not able to adapt to the shifting face of localism and are not prepared to meet the demands of their consumers should not be allowed to distort the marketplace further. It could be argued that attempts to support and underpin crumbling media businesses are actually acting against the public interest by blocking the rise of viable alternatives.

And the big newspaper groups cannot have their cake and eat it. After lobbying hard to prevent the BBC from offering an improved online offering for local communities, many of these organisations have failed to do anything to support the argument that they even had viable products worthy of protection.

It could further be argued that they are taking the same 'Big Bad Wolf' role when it comes to independent start-ups. Free newspaper entrepreneur Chris Bullivant claimed that the ability of the national groups to throttle local advertising markets would lead to the ultimate demise of the independent publisher[9].

The battle for local audiences

There is no doubt that lessons could be learned from both sides of the battle for local audiences. Traditional media has years of experience behind it, while new start-ups and hyperlocal initiatives have the spirit of adventure within them. However, the barrier between the two is still firmly up in some quarters. The phrase 'citizen journalist' is often trotted out in a derisory manner by many of the old school within the industry as a way of undermining the efforts of some new model journalism enterprises to give greater power to their audience. After all, reader interaction is nothing new. The letters pages of regional newspapers across the country for decades have been the original user-generated content.

Philip John, who also runs his own internet consultancy business, believes the use of the citizen journalist analogy is a dangerous one for modern reporters: "Citizen journalism is a term coined by journalists who needed a label for this new phenomenon that they were struggling to understand. Interestingly, it seems to have become a qualifier for whether or not, as a journalist, you've moved with the times - those using it as a derogatory term showing their inability to adapt to the new way with which they need to interact with their community."

The BBC are one of the big media organisations who have moved towards greater integration of content submitted by the audience. In a 2008 blog[10] Peter Horrocks explained the role user-generated content played in the corporation's newsgathering. Notably, he did not refer to 'stories' posted by the audience, but instead pointed to 'information' being submitted.

Differentiating between journalism and information is crucial in the whole debate over citizen contributions, particularly when working out how to harness community engagement and support in a local arena. Few members of the public actually have any great desire to be a journalist – those who do tend to train professionally. What they do have is a thirst to become involved in the discussion surrounding their community. Often this manifests itself in allowing input into the finished piece, by providing an element of the published article and working with, rather than for, the reporter. Hyperlocals have grasped this concept of partnership as opposed to top-down management of communities and the information and news contained within them.

All of this begs the question: why doesn't closer integration exist? Some efforts, such as Trinity Mirror's Communities project in Birmingham, have sought to bring independent news sites closer to the professional journalists. However, this is the first step on a long road of true integration and partnership

– and many more regional and local publishers are still some distance from even recognising the value or potential business threat that new hyperlocal efforts could pose, especially in the long run.

This is not to say that newspapers should seek to emulate or replace the hyperlocal publishers. The make-up of their organisations will make this virtually impossible and there are no signs that investment to make ultra-local, ultra-niche reporting will be forthcoming any time soon. But it can be argued that what they should be doing is attempting to understand the value of such sites as newsgathering tools and starting points for a wider analysis of local issues and local news. They have the potential to become agencies or specialist reporters in a reworking of the freelance model that would return to the theory of retainers. Most hyperlocal sites will not, at present, have the resources to regularly tackle a wide range of issues in great depth over an extended period of time – but this is the area where traditional media can utilise its knowledge and expertise. Therefore, there is no reason why this new breed of ultra-local sites cannot act as a community news wire, breaking stories for the wider media to delve deeper into. This theory of an almost two-tier journalism, created through partnerships, could lead to a greater sustainability for both traditional media organisations and their newer counterparts, improve the understanding of what local is and inform how best it can be exploited in a journalistic sense.

Notes

[1] Radcliffe, Damian (2012), Hyperlocal review of 2011, Online Journalism Blog, 4 January 2012. Available online at: http://onlinejournalismblog.com/2012/01/04/2011-the-uk-hyper-local-year-in-review/, accessed on 8 January 2012.

[2] Pickard, Meg (2011), Guardian Local – an update on the experiment, The Guardian, 27 April 2011. Available online at:
http://www.guardian.co.uk/help/insideguardian/2011/apr/27/guardian-local-update?CMP=twt_gu, accessed on 12 January 2012.

[3] Williams, Rob (2010), Rick Waghorn: Why the 'Godfather of Hyperlocal' is keeping it simple, The Independent, 31 August 2010. Available online at:
http://blogs.independent.co.uk/2010/08/31/rick-waghorn-why-the-godfather-of-hyperlocal-is-keeping-it-simple/, accessed on 9 January, 2012

[4] Durrani, Arif (2012), Murdoch no longer sets the news agenda, Twitter does, 9 January 2012, MediaWeek. Available online at:
http://arifdurrani.mediaweek.co.uk/2012/01/09/murdoch-no-longer-sets-the-news-agenda-twitter-does/, accessed on 16 January, 2012.

[5] Bradshaw, Paul (2011), Don't be afraid of the future, Coventry Conversations, 8 December 2011. Available online at:
http://coventryuniversity.podbean.com/2011/12/08/dont-be-afraid-of-the-future-professor-paul-bradshaw/, accessed on 20 January 2012.

[6] Odlyzko, Andrew (2001). Content is not king, First Monday, volume 6, number 2. Available online at:
http://firstmonday.org/htbin/cgiwrap/bin/ojs/index.php/fm/article/view/833/742, accessed on 20 January 2012.

[7] Benton, Joshua (2009), Clay Shirky: Let a thousand flowers bloom to replace newspapers; don't build a paywall around a public good, Niemann Lab, 23 September 2009. Available online at: http://www.niemanlab.org/2009/09/clay-shirky-let-a-thousand-flowers-bloom-to-replace-newspapers-dont-build-a-paywall-around-a-public-good/, accessed on 19 January 2012.

[8] Clarke, Conor (2009), Why we shouldn't let newspapers die, The Atlantic, 6 April 2009. Available online at: http://www.theatlantic.com/politics/archive/2009/04/why-we-shouldnt-let-newspapers-die/7260/, accessed on 20 January 2012.

[9] Luft, Oliver (2010), Bullivant withdraws from Birmingham newspaper war, Press Gazette, 11 October 2010. Available online at: http://www.pressgazette.co.uk/story.asp?storycode=46113, accessed on 20 January 2012.

[10] Horrocks, Peter (2008), The value of citizen journalists, BBC Blogs, 7 January 2008. Available online at: http://www.bbc.co.uk/blogs/theeditors/2008/01/value_of_citizen_journalism.html, accessed on 19 January 2012.

About the author

Ross Hawkes is a senior lecturer in Journalism at Staffordshire University and the founder of hyperlocal website LichfieldLive.co.uk. His areas of teaching and research interest are social media, hyperlocal journalism and sustainable local reporting models.

Interviewing the PM with toddler in tow: an experiment in hyperlocal journalism

Richard Jones founded hyperlocal website the Saddleworth News in 2010, and soon found his patch in the national spotlight. But could editorial triumph translate to commercial success?

It's January 2011. The scene is a cramped, upstairs room at a car repair garage in Oldham. I'm sat next to a couple of other local journalists as we interview David Cameron about the Conservatives' prospects in the forthcoming Oldham East and Saddleworth by-election.

A radio reporter begins a question: "Labour are portraying this by-election as a referendum on the coalition..." He's interrupted by giggling. It's my young daughter, who is perched on my knee.

"There we are, you had your answer," says the Prime Minister, turning in her direction. "How old are you?"

"Fifteen months," I say.

"There you are, fifteen months and laughing at that idea!"

So, how did I come to the unusual position of interviewing the Prime Minister with a toddler in tow?

I was covering the by-election for *Saddleworth News*, a hyperlocal website which I started writing in February 2010. A few weeks before that, my wife had gone back to work, leaving me as a stay-at-home dad to our first child.

I'd done various journalism jobs, in TV and radio, staff and freelance, since graduating from university in 2002. I spent the best part of six years at Sky News. But my wife earned more than I did, which made it an obvious decision for me to give up work to become a full-time father.

I set up *Saddleworth News* for two main reasons. The first was pure selfishness. I didn't want to leave journalism forever, and knew it would be harder to get back in with a gaping hole on my CV. I also thought my brain would appreciate

154

something to think about every day that didn't involve nappies, feeding or Heads, Shoulders, Knees and Toes.

The second reason was more public-spirited. We'd only recently moved to Saddleworth, a collection of largely rural Yorkshire villages on the Manchester side of the Pennines. With just one or two articles a day in the Oldham paper, and some monthly freesheets and magazines, there was relatively little news coverage of an area which has a distinct identity. I hoped my skills might be of some use to the local community.

So, instead of talking in worried tones about the future of our trade, I thought the best thing would be to actually do journalism, and experiment with something new. My personal circumstances had given me an opportunity, and I decided to take it.

An evening with Wordpress

It's easy to become a publisher these days. A quick purchase of some web hosting and an evening tinkering with a free WordPress theme, and *Saddleworth News* was ready to go. I got a Twitter account, a Facebook page, some business cards, and started writing stories.

At first I set aside one hour a day to work on the site during my daughter's afternoon nap, and gave myself a target of one post every weekday. The site was established as a blog, as I thought that one daily update would be enough to give regular visitors something new to look at without putting me under too much pressure to constantly come up with new material.

The site hadn't been going long when a teenager sadly killed himself at a nearby railway station. A passenger on the train involved was posting updates and pictures from the scene on Twitter. After getting in touch and asking if I could use his content, I was able to quickly publish it in articles about the incident.

With the local paper not getting anything online about the story until the following day, my site was the only resource for information about why the trains between Huddersfield and Manchester weren't running. The site's hits increased more than fivefold overnight, mostly thanks to Google searches. It was an early lesson in the value of publishing content that other media outlets can't or won't produce.

Over the following weeks, every time the site had a spike in traffic like that, the hit stats always settled back down at a higher level than before, until several hundred unique users became the daily norm rather than the exception.

If publishing stories faster than other media is one service hyperlocal sites can provide, doing issues in more depth is another, and it's surely a more valuable one too.

I've always enjoyed covering politics. In the run-up to the 2005 general election, I spent months on Sky's election unit helping to prepare their coverage. As polling day in 2010 approached, I knew that both the Westminster constituency of Oldham East and Saddleworth, and the local wards being contested on Oldham Council, would be closely fought, particularly between Labour and the Liberal Democrats.

Pondering how to approach the campaign on *Saddleworth News*, I mentioned to a newspaper reporter that I was thinking of doing full interviews with all the candidates. He said he'd had a similar idea, but had been told by his editor that "there wasn't space in the paper" for it.

This was nonsense. The editor could have found space, if not in the paper then certainly online, had he wanted. He just chose not to, and instead the paper's readers were only given prepared statements made by each of the candidates, unchallenged by even basic questioning. It was clear to me that I could use my journalism skills to not only keep myself entertained by covering the campaign, but also put the candidates under a bit of scrutiny that they wouldn't face from anyone else.

This had some surprising effects. When trying to get hold of the UKIP candidate for the neighbouring seat of Colne Valley, I discovered that he'd pulled out at the last minute. After reading about this on my site, a local bookshop owner came forward and replaced him. I jokingly told the Conservative frontrunner that, if he ended up losing by fewer votes than UKIP received, he could blame me personally. He didn't look entirely thrilled at the prospect, so it was perhaps just as well for me that he won comfortably enough in the end.

Along with an article about each candidate, I included a link to the whole interview as an audio file. I soon realised that well-known local councillors were getting dozens of downloads of their full interviews, while some of the Westminster candidates languished in single figures, something which encouraged me to redouble my council coverage after the election was over.

The internet is forever

Defending the marginal seat of Oldham East and Saddleworth was Phil Woolas, then Labour's Immigration Minister. As with all of the interviews, I had my daughter with me when I went to see him in his campaign HQ. His wife agreed to look after her during my chat with her husband, and I left Mrs Woolas getting her rosette chewed by my obviously-hungry daughter as I began asking questions. There were piles of leaflets all around the office, although I didn't realise at the time quite how significant they would turn out to be.

Woolas held the seat narrowly after a couple of recounts, but his Lib Dem opponent Elwyn Watkins mounted a rare and extraordinary legal challenge to the result, on the grounds that Woolas had told lies about his character in those campaign leaflets. Over the weeks ahead, I wrote lots more articles about this, reporting on various small developments in the saga.

By the time the case ended in a shock triumph for Watkins and bitter defeat for Woolas, *Saddleworth News* had by far the largest online archive of material about the story. Checking my web stats, I found that people from Saddleworth and much further afield kept finding old articles I'd written, including my campaign interviews with all the protagonists. They were the interviews which didn't exist anywhere else because nobody else had bothered to do them.

When national journalists arrived to cover the subsequent by-election, clutching printouts of my articles which they'd read on the train, I had evidence I'd been doing something right.

The depth of my coverage of the Woolas saga and by-election helped raise the site's profile, and also taught me another lesson about online journalism. The internet is forever. No longer is a news story tomorrow's fish and chip paper, forgotten about within a day of being written. It can be discovered and read months and even years later by people searching on Google. So if your article is going to have a long life, best make sure it's good.

I've described how speed and depth can be two qualities of good hyperlocal reporting, and I'd add context to that list.

One of the main differences between writing my own site and working as part of a team at a conventional news operation was the lack of an editor. In my experience, editors are full of reasons as to why you shouldn't cover a particular story. Reporters at all levels of journalism will be familiar with responses along the lines of "I'm not interested in that" or "we don't do that kind of story" or "we covered that last week/month/year" before being told to find something else.

If you're the editor as well as the journalist, you don't have to worry about such whims. I had the freedom to stick with ongoing local issues, such as a continuing row over the future of the running track at a playing field.

After a packed public meeting on the issue, the local paper put the issue on its front page. But then rarely covered it again for months, presumably because of an editorial view that the story had been 'done' and little or no following-up was required.

On *Saddleworth News*, I reported on every new angle however small, including petitions started by both sides of the argument, letters giving different views, and discussions at various council meetings. I also used the Freedom of Information Act to obtain a copy of a council report on the fields, bringing significant details into the public domain.

Quickly, I'd built up a mass of material that couldn't be matched anywhere else. In every article I took care to link back to all of my previous coverage of the topic, putting each new development into the proper context.

This meant that if a reader was new to the running track debate, they could easily find lots more information and an assortment of views about it, simply by clicking on the links in my stories. It's the sort of context which is all too often missing from reporting, whether it's the parish council or Israel/Palestine.

Obviously you can't put a hyperlink in a newspaper, but even newspaper websites are often reluctant to include them. This could be because of corporate decisions to try to prevent readers clicking onto other websites, or because journalists simply don't know much about what links are or how to use them.

As with the political coverage, this isn't necessarily a criticism of newspapers. They've got plenty of other things to do every day, often with declining numbers of staff.

But if newspapers can't or won't cover issues quickly, or in reasonable depth, or in the proper context, those are things hyperlocal sites can and should be doing instead, adding value to a local community instead of rehashing what is already available.

To stick it to the snoozing councillor? Or not?
Covering news on a very local basis throws up all kinds of dilemmas. Lest I get too big for my hyperlocal boots, a couple of weeks after all the by-election excitement I found myself at a meeting of Saddleworth Parish Council.

The councillors voted on whether to continue paying for a summer tourist shuttle bus to a local reservoir. Not exactly a huge issue, but worth a few grand of public cash all the same.

With the vote tied at six-all, the councillors noticed that one of their number had dozed off. They all thought it was rather amusing, and prodded him awake. Having slept through the whole discussion this councillor could have decided the future of the scheme one way or the other, but, unsurprisingly a bit confused about what was going on, decided not to vote.

Walking home, I wondered how I should report this. I was tempted to really stick it to the snoozing councillor. After all, his inability to stay awake during the meeting had a direct impact on whether several thousand pounds of local taxpayers' money was spent or not.

If I'd been writing for the paper that's probably what I would have done, because being part of a local institution like that would have afforded me a bit of protection against any backlash from the councillor's colleagues.

But when you're on your own, your own credibility and reputation is all you've got. Having a pop at an elderly gent, who despite illness was still attempting to do the unpaid role he had been elected to, would have been rather mean-spirited. If his colleagues had chosen not to speak to me because of my coverage it would have made my job a lot harder. And it would have been embarrassing when bumping into them at the shops or in the pub, as I regularly did.

So I mentioned the sleeping councillor, but in a straightforward way near the end of my story, rather than taking a more accusing angle. It still got a notable reaction in comments on Saddleworth News, although I was spared too much criticism. Perhaps I was too cautious. But on the other hand, if you're covering a very local area where you also happen to live, perhaps it's in everyone's interests to take a less sensational slant to your reporting.

Hyperlocal sites face a much bigger problem than fretting about councillors, though. It's the same problem exercising managers, bean counters and journalists at news operations around the country and the world. The problem of money.

I'm a journalist, not a salesman. And I found selling ads on *Saddleworth News* difficult. I think this was partly down to my own lack of selling skills, and partly because most business owners weren't used to internet advertising.

Despite my site's reach of more than 20,000 unique users per month, in an area of only 24,000 people, I found it hard to persuade the butcher and the baker of the value of taking out an ad. Much easier for them to do what they've always done, and use the glossy magazines or the daily paper.

Most of the ads I did sell were to people who used the website as readers and had their own small online businesses. But I only ever made £150 a month from ads, a paltry return given I had extended the time I spent writing it to two hours every weekday.

When my daughter turned two and we wanted to start putting her into nursery for at least a couple of days each week, I thought about trying to make *Saddleworth News* my full-time job. Had I been 22 I might have given it a go, but when you've got a family and a mortgage, gambling isn't so attractive.

And a gamble is exactly what it would have been, one with the odds stacked against. I would have needed to increase my income from the site at least tenfold to start to make it viable as a career, which would have meant spending all of my time chasing cash rather than chasing stories.

There was also no guarantee that even if I became financially successful, others wouldn't simply seek to copy me. Partly inspired by the perceived success of *Saddleworth News*, other local people had already established different sites focusing on events listings and Groupon-style daily deals for local shops and restaurants. Not competing with me for content, but certainly competing for advertising money.

That helps explain why it was an easy decision to give it up and get back into more traditional work, including lecturing. I had various options for the site, but all but one would have had me continuing to do *Saddleworth News* for little reward. Most involved bolting on some kind of paid-for business directory to the site, while a freesheet offered me a very small sum to republish my stories. Thanks, but no thanks.

So, I chose the best offer I had, and passed the site to University Campus Oldham, part of the University of Huddersfield. A journalism student is now writing *Saddleworth News* as a final year project. I believe there's a great untapped potential in university journalism departments, both in terms of under-used equipment and talented and enthusiastic students. But that's a discussion for another day.

Hyperlocal websites have a future. Of course they do. As I've explained, it's easy to set up a website nowadays. There's no reason why well-intentioned local residents shouldn't do just that and fill them with details of coffee mornings and church services, much in the same way that people have long been producing parish newsletters.

But I'm sceptical about whether hyperlocal journalism of a professional standard has any more of a future than newspaper journalism. For all the benefits of hyperlocal reporting which I've described, the cash crisis facing other parts of our trade is there too.

I hoped my experiment with *Saddleworth News* might provide some answers. It was fun and frustrating, exciting and boring, illuminating and tedious, just like journalism is. But I'm afraid it didn't get me any closer to a model which will keep reporters in the councils and courtrooms.

Although if journalists start routinely taking their children with them to interview politicians, you'll know who started the trend.

Note on the author

Richard Jones is a freelance journalist and visiting lecturer in online at the University of Leeds. He has a background in national TV and radio, including six years spent working at Sky News. Richard set up hyperlocal site *Saddleworth News* in 2010 after becoming a stay-at-home dad to his first child. The site gained attention for its extensive coverage of the Phil Woolas affair and subsequent Oldham East and Saddleworth by-election. In 2011, it became part of the Digital Journalism course at University Campus Oldham. Richard can be found on Twitter @rlwjones.

Pits 'n' Pots 'n' Stoke-on-Trent

Mike Rawlins isn't a journalist, but he wanted to know more about politics so decided to do something about it. The experiment in political engagement took him further than he could have imagined.

Local can be many things to different people. It can be a few houses on a road, a street, a village, a town or city. All geographically local, of course. Then there is your local hospital, chip shop, library, school or children's centre, which are local, defined by use or need. Local government is by its very nature local and can be split down from the largest city councils in the UK to parish and town councils and then even smaller sections of localness – the ward.

But what of other things that are "local", interests, campaigns and issues for instance?

Interests can be local or indeed can spread much further afield. Taking photography as an example, there are many thousands of local groups on Flickr. People who are possibly connected in real life locally, but more often than not just sharing a space, passing by in close proximity from time to time and never knowing, populate these local groups on-line with their photographs, often many of them being pictures of the same things.

With groups such as the ones on Flickr, people from the wider global community can become part of the local group by just visiting the locality, taking a picture and posting it on to the local group.

Campaigns and issues again are broadly based around geographically local – the campaign to save your local hospital, chip shop, library, school or children's centre.

A dislike of the extreme

Much of my work in my day job is helping people understand how to use the many different freely available and free-to-use tools on the Internet, to help them to amplify their voices to help them to run their campaigns. Although their drive may well be local, campaigners still often need to harness the global power of the Internet to ensure that they are connecting with as many people as they can locally.

For me local is politics. I'm not a big political animal, I don't make my political leanings public and how I vote is between the ballot box and me. I do, however, make no secret of my dislike of extreme politics, both far right and far left. You could argue that a whole city, even a medium sized one like Stoke-on-Trent, isn't really local in the purest form. But if that is the seat of power in the local area, although it may be stretching the definition, it is local.

I am not a member of any political party but I like to know about what is going on politically both locally and nationally. I have to confess that I have even become slightly addicted to watching Prime Minister's Questions every Wednesday, observing the political posturing, barracking and braying from all sides of the House while parties and individuals are trying to score points. No matter what, it is always the fault of the other person or party.

In late 2008 I became involved in a very new political website called *Pits n Pots* that had been set up in Stoke-on-Trent by Tony Walley. He told me it was called *Pits n Pots* because it was a swipe at his old careers teacher, who was infamous for saying "you're only good for t' pits or t' pots" – meaning you were either going to the coal mines, the pits, or the potteries, the pots.

Pits n Pots was set up to fill a gap in the market in Stoke-on-Trent where political commentary and discussion was concerned, the more main stream media were not fulfilling their duties of holding power to account as well as they might. The coverage was quite scant in many cases and the chances of having a discussion about anything political on the mainstream media websites were quite slim.

An attempt at being different

The BBC generally doesn't promote commenting on news on its website and *The Sentinel*, the local paper in Stoke-on-Trent had, for very good legal reasons, a policy of censorship over moderation for comments on their website. If you left a comment on *The Sentinel* website that was deemed to be even slightly near the knuckle, it was removed. This policy made debate impossible in some cases.

Because of this gap in the market for debating political news and ultimately getting people more engaged in local politics, we decided to try to do things differently on *Pits n Pots* and actively encourage debates on local political issues. Trying to keep conversations and discussions lively while treading the right side of the libel line when dealing with any politics is no mean feat. Add in the fact that the BNP had nine councillors in the city and it certainly made for some interesting times moderating comments. Not only were we dealing with the BNP councillors and their supporters from the city, but also the anti fascist movement too from further afield, which was watching what was going on in the city from afar.

In the early days we were taking stories from the local paper, republishing them with attribution and links, allowing people to debate them. We became almost like a third party commenting system for the paper. Understandably it wasn't too happy about this at the time, but thankfully, other than a few snide comments left by reporters every now and then, it didn't make too much noise about it. We were totally open and honest about where the content was coming from and always linked back to it.

After a while we noticed that we were regularly getting more comments on our copies of the articles than *The Sentinel* was on the originals. From the feedback we were getting this was because we were allowing the debates to flow as much as we possibly could by not removing comments because they had a mild swear word in them or called a councillor useless.

We spent a lot of time ensuring that the site was set up to loosely enough to allow people to voice their opinions freely but tight enough that gratuitous swearing and profanity wasn't prevalent. Because we were working in a very small, almost niche market, and on a subject that both Tony and I enjoyed and found interesting, we were able to spend time replying to comments, something that rarely happens on mainstream news website. We could also explain to some of the posters why we were not going to publish their comments, but if they wanted to rewrite them we would happily publish them. Building that relationship with the readers and contributors helped the site to grow.

Writing our own content
The site was growing and becoming more popular so we had to keep feeding it. Therefore we slowly started to write our own content – initially not very much, perhaps one or two pieces each week, when the opportunity arose, and when we got the lead on a story about the council or a councillor. Tony would write a regular opinion piece about what was going on in the city and we were quite surprised when we saw these got as much traffic and as many comments as the articles we were "borrowing" from *The Sentinel*. At that point we began to realise that so we really were on to something, not only writing to feed our own egos but also providing a service by becoming an alternative political news and commentary site for Stoke-on-Trent.

It didn't take very many months until we had stopped borrowing content from *The Sentinel* and we had become pretty much self-sufficient when it came to content. In this respect we were helped greatly by the political make up of the council. There was no overall control in the chamber, although Labour were the biggest party with around twenty six to thirty councillors present at meetings. There were also, in order of size:

- City Independents
- Conservative and Independent Alliance
- British National Party
- Liberal Democrats
- Non -aligned Group
- Libertarian
- Three non-aligned individuals

This mix used to change almost on a weekly basis, with councillors crossing the floor to join a different party or leaving a party and becoming non aligned.

This intermingling of parties in the chamber made for interesting, if somewhat long, full council meetings where bargaining and deal making was rife just to get the most simple of items passed. Every meeting different groupings were joining together to get a majority on a certain item; following this, the next item there would witness a different set of allegiances made. Because of this we were able to get two, three, four or even five different sides to stories to put on the site. Sadly this is no longer the case now that there is an overall Labour majority.

We did notice that with the mainstream media outlets locally there was very little coverage of the British National Party. There would be nothing reported other than the odd campaign that would be fronted by one of their councillors. Tony and I therefore decided that we would talk to all the political parties that held a seat in the chamber, if they would talk to us, and we would report on them openly, honestly and equally with any of the other parties.

We have often been asked why did we give some much column space to the BNP and the answer was simple – they were elected representatives of people in the city and therefore they had the right to have their say. I often pointed out to people that we reported on Labour or Conservatives but that doesn't make us supporters so why should reporting on the BNP be any different?

Many people have tried to tell us that we were wrong for taking this standpoint and that we should have actively ignored them. But by doing that we would surely be no different than the mainstream media which we felt were letting people down. We possibly spent more time with members of the BNP from the local councillors and activists right up to their party leader and MEP Nick Griffin. This was on our part a calculated risk; we wanted to report on them, (Nick Griffin had said that Stoke-on-Trent was the jewel in the BNP's crown and claimed the city would return the party's first BNP MP when he launched its 2010 General Election manifesto) because the only way people can understand the policies, beliefs and workings of any party so they can make an informed decision on who to vote for is by getting close to them and reporting on them.

By giving the BNP this platform, we also gave the public that same platform to question them and their policies, something that no other website has done, as far as we aware. There are plenty of sites that support the BNP and probably five times as many anti fascist sites, but none of them actively encouraged the debate.

Allowing a better informed decision
The people of Stoke-on-Trent never did return the first BNP MP in the 2010 General Election and in the 2011 local elections they didn't return a single BNP councillor. We can't say this is solely down to what *Pits n Pots* did, but I'm sure that by allowing the debate we allowed people to make a better informed decision on where to put their cross.

One of the other big selling points we used when trying to get audio and video interviews with people was that we would never edit the interviews. They would be published from start to finish as recorded. How many times have you watched a television news report and the interviewee fades out to a background shot or they slip slightly to the left or right? This is where the interview has been edited; more often than not this is just down to the time constraints of the news bulletin, but there have been times when people have said that the section of their interview that was broadcast was taken out of context.

We made it quite clear to everyone we interviewed that what they said would be published unedited, putting the ball firmly in their court. We wouldn't try to spin anything by taking sound bites but they had to be careful because if they let something slip it was going to be published. This was probably one of the best decisions we made, gaining us huge amounts of credibility with the councillors, because they knew that what they said would be published and they could capitalise on that.

To this day I can honestly say that every audio or video interview we have done with anyone from any political party has been published as is. If there was ever anything libellous in an interview, and we picked up on it while we were recording, we would delete the whole thing and start again.

After the 2011 local election, politics became very boring; there were boundary changes which meant we went from sixty councillors in twenty three-member wards to a strange mix of forty four councillors in thirty one single member wards, five two-member wards and one three-member ward.

A changed chamber
At the time of writing in March 2012 Labour has a majority of thirty four so there is very little in the way of decent debate and bargaining in the council chamber; it is simply a case of Labour getting what Labour wants.

Long gone are the days when *Pits n Pots* was breaking the latest news from the council, not because we have taken our eye off the ball but simply because there is no breaking news. A former council officer said to me recently: "It is easier to get information out of the Kremlin than it is to get it out of the Civic these days." He is very right but that in itself is a challenge and hopefully a challenge that *Pits n Pots* is up to taking on with the support of the Journalism Foundation.

In November 2011 this newly formed foundation, fronted by Simon Kelner, the former editor of *The Independent*, contacted me at *Pits n Pots* to ask me to go to talk with them about ways in which we could work together to promote *Pits n Pots*, and to give it a kick start in what is now quite a dull political landscape.

This is a potted history of *Pits n Pots*, some self promotion thinly disguised as a book chapter. In some ways it is, but there is a bigger point that needs to be made.

Tony and I did this because we believed in local democracy and getting people to engage with it. More importantly, neither Tony nor I are trained journalists or have any desire to be. Tony is the managing director of a company in Stoke-on-Trent, and I am a social media trainer. So the question is, if we can do it why can't others?

I'm not suggesting people try to create a new version of *Pits n Pots*, although imitation is said to be the sincerest form of flattery, but if people feel that they are not being well served by their local newspaper, whether that be politically or more generally then why don't they have a go at using the free tools and start publishing something themselves? They don't need to be massively technically skilled. If they can send emails and shop online, they have the technical skills. All they need to add to this is a grasp of the English language and the desire to do something good in their local area for the benefit of everyone. They should think of it as an old-style parish magazine, but one going online to give it greater reach.

There are of course some aspects people should be aware of when it comes to publishing. Commonsense usually prevails and a local news site is unlikely to get in to too much trouble, unless it goes looking for it. There are many resources available online to help a local website become established – and then once that has happened there are more on hand about legal dos and don'ts.

Other inspirations

Here are some websites that might inspire readers to look at what local means to them:

- The *Kington Blackboard*, from the small town of Kington in rural Herefordshire, is a digital replacement for a physical blackboard that used to be used in the town square. The Kington Blackboard often used to go missing if someone wrote something on it that wasn't liked by the town council so it created a digital version that couldn't be removed – www.kingtonblackboard.org
- Parwich a small village in the Derbyshire Peak, – http://parwich.org. This is also rumoured to be the inspiration for the Ambridge village website in the BBC radio drama, The Archers.
- *My Tunstall*, one of the six towns of Stoke-on-Trent – http://mytunstall.co.uk.
- *Drimnagh Is Good* from Drimnagh just outside Dublin – www.drimnaghisgood.com.
- *It's Happening In Heeley*, a digital version of the *Heeley Voice* from Heeley in Sheffield – http://heeleyonline.org.
- *WV11*, a community website for the WV11 postcode area of Wolverhampton – www.wv11.co.uk.
- Of course *Pits n Pots*, political news from Stoke-on-Trent – http://pitsnpots.co.uk
- And, finally, *Talk About Local*, which has been supporting the creation of local websites across the country with training seminars and hands-on workshops – http://talkaboutlocal.org.uk.

Note on the author

Mike Rawlins moved from Manchester to Stoke-on-Trent thirteen years ago and now splits his time between Stoke-on-Trent and North East Scotland, where he is hoping to self build to enable him to relocate permanently, with Borris, his Jack Russell, and his wife. He has been using the Internet since 1995 and works with people in disadvantaged areas across the UK helping them to get online and use the many free social media tools that allow them to amplify their voices to try to improve their positions.

Mike often speaks at conferences on subjects such as the benefits of social media, DIY democracy and citizen journalism. Away from the computer Mike is a keen semi professional photographer and part time radio presenter. He is also an enthusiastic Manchester City fan.

For more information see his occasionally updated website – http://michaelrawlins.co.uk or follow him on Twitter @Mike_Rawlins

His long suffering wife has pointed out that he should say how much he enjoys spending time with her as well.

Hyperlocals and the importance of community engagement

Tom O'Brien found local news outlets lacking during the London riots of 2011, so he set up a not-for-profit ad-free site. Here he recounts how it all happened.

Sitting there, pints in hand, a friend and I chewed over a conundrum. It was the time of the 2011 London riots. Violence that started in Tottenham had spread all across the capital. Shops were being looted, livelihoods destroyed and buildings torched. Our neighbouring postcodes had been attacked – Enfield, Camden, Green Lanes – but there was nothing being reported in our local area, Muswell Hill.

We had both spent the previous night frantically searching Twitter, reading the updates from local tweeters. They reported some trouble and apparently with good reason. The following morning the evidence was clear – we had been hit. The shop windows of a number of local businesses had been smashed, but again nothing on the news. There were no cameramen here, no column inches to lend, no coverage. It was a news blackout.

The following evening we hit on the nub of the issue. There was no go-to, sufficiently reactive, hyperlocal news platform that could tell the people of Muswell Hill what was happening on their streets. Traditionally it was the job of the local paper; *The Hornsey Journal* had served the community for decades. Unfortunately in the face of the riots –with no dedicated Muswell Hill reporter and a team already stretched across the whole of North London – it just couldn't cope.

That weekend was spent drumming out a viable working model for something that could fill the vacuum. We decided on a hyperlocal website. Three months later, in December 2011, we launched. It was called *MyMuswell*.

MyMuswell is an ad-free, non-profit online space for Muswell Hill residents. The website is populated by news and features content that has been uploaded by the local community. It also hosts a live Twitter feed, a user-managed events system, business listings, a review application, a photo-feed and a vouchers page. It works in tandem with our Twitter account @MyMuswell.

Re-thinking the hyperlocal

A common mantra amongst start-ups today is "don't be first, be second and be the best". It is a line about learning from the mistakes of your digital precursors. With this in mind, we set about identifying the flaws in Muswell Hill's existing local, online media services. The most prevalent of which was the lack of audience engagement.

It was particularly noticeable in the lacklustre content the sites carried. Many of the websites had no original, long-form contributions, with very few articles written by local people. Instead, the sites acquired content using aggregating tools which would locate, suck-in, then re-publish original work from other web domains – principally, local newspapers. This lucky dip into broad content pools was fraught with problems of its own and many hyperlocals ended up running irrelevant news stories. A Highgate hyperlocal, for example, ran its front page with a story about an assault in Tottenham.

This same lack of engagement was evident in an underwhelming use of Twitter – more specifically, a lack of energy in cultivating or nurturing followers. Many hyperlocals saw Twitter only as a conduit to their website. They used it to bombard their audience with hyperlinks that led back to articles hosted on their webspace. Little attempt was made to interact directly with any of the followers or to construct a relationship between brand and audience.

It was an approach almost certainly governed by commercial obligations. An overreliance on the advertising business model geared their entire online strategy toward page views. Tweeting out click-throughs helped increase website traffic, *ergo* more eyes-on-screens and more money in the bank. To engage followers in conversation-chains had no immediate monetary benefit and therefore, wasn't considered a worthwhile pursuit.

To avoid making the same mistakes we formulated two key aims: to implement a long-form content model that engaged with its audience; and to build an active, extensive Twitter following.

The content model: a digital town square

Creating a working content model was a great challenge. Success meant a steady supply of high-quality articles catering specifically toward the shared local interests of our audience. The answer, we felt, lay in the community itself.

Citizen journalism was a growing phenomenon. The riots, with its plethora of self-shot video had demonstrated this and we discovered a plenitude of bloggers and self-styled reporters living locally. We planned to utilize them for *MyMuswell* under an editorial policy we called the digital town square.

MyMuswell's digital town square was inspired by the idea of the real world town square. To us, this was a space where communities gathered to share news, gossip and opinion. A local hub, where some people listen while others speak. These dynamics are analogous to the workings of a good online community –

with actives posting (speakers) and passives reading (listeners) – a tried and tested model of content generation. The town square was also a universal symbol that cut across the real and the digital domains; an instantly gettable metaphor for what we were trying to achieve.

So how did we apply this idea practically on the website? Essentially, the digital town square is an open, long-form article submissions system. Anybody who wants to write for *MyMuswell* can – they need simply get in touch. By publishing their work, the website can help them reach a targeted local audience. We set only two editorial guidelines: the work must be fewer than 500 words and must touch on an issue within the local community; train tracks designed to ensure the content stays relevant and punchy.

The digital town square has no commercial dimension. The traditional financial infrastructure surrounding hyperlocals never sat comfortably for us. Putting the words profit and community together felt unsavoury. To avoid the issue we made a decision early on to eschew advertising completely and run as an ad-free, non-profit social enterprise. There were many benefits to this. Most obviously it made the navigation experience less cluttered. It also strengthened our credentials as a grassroots, community-spirited project making it easier to recruit journalists. Finally, it ensured the eminence of our writer's voices by muting any competing commercial noise.

The Twitter strategy

Our approach to Twitter was inspired by the way local, independent shops are often taken to heart by the communities they serve. Their intimate knowledge of product and affable, attentive customer service can help them gain the market-edge on bigger, better-funded chain stores. This phenomenon is particularly acute in Muswell Hill, which has a high-street full of thriving independent businesses. We wanted to capture some of this spirit and let it play out through our Twitter account.

Achieving this required us to form an emotional connection with our followers. To find out what connected with them we undertook an extended period of experimentation by tweeting out a variety of message types. The gamut of topics included: listings (dates, times, prices of local classes and clubs), conversational (good nights, good mornings, good days), gossip (uncorroborated reports of local goings-on), exclusives (breaking news from Harringey Council's planning application website) and photographs of local life. We tweeted these out, scattergun, at the rate of roughly five per day. Our metric for success was a re-tweet or a comment from one of our followers.

Interestingly, what proved most popular were minutiae, tittle-tattle and familiar local issues. Photos of a beautiful sunset at Alexandra Palace, the announcement of a new Oliver Bonas store opening on the Broadway, celebrity spots in the neighbourhood – more often than not topics of conversation one might hear on an amble down the high street. They were all issues that touched on people's daily lives, the glue of common interests that defined the local community. Twitter was the perfect platform to facilitate this existing nexus of community communication and map it out virtually, online. The net result was a following that came on in leaps and bounds, in two months, reaching 1,367.

Engaging the community

It's far too early to make any worthwhile evaluation of the success of *MyMuswell*. We've only been in operation for two months, with just 30,402 hits. Something can be said with certainty though – our Twitter account and digital town square could not exist without the high levels of community engagement we enjoy. Without it, there would be no articles, reviews, events or conversations – in fact *MyMuswell* would be hollow. This in itself is the innovation that sets us apart from Muswell Hill's existing local media hubs – our success in engaging the local community in our project; and it is this bottom-up model that I believe offers nascent hyperlocal start-ups their best chance of success.

Engagement is the quickest route toward a supply of regular, relevant content – the bedrock of any successful media enterprise – whether that be from citizen journalists writing long-form articles, or from tweeters using the *MyMuswell* Twitter account as a free classifieds service. Relevant content is what the community coalesces around and utilizing the audience in this way offers a sustainable, cheap and vibrant editorial model to provide it.

Putting the community at the heart of a hyperlocal also establishes a radically pure relationship with the audience. Put simply: who knows what issues matter to the community better than the community themselves? As an editor, one need no longer second guess the tastes and interests of the readers – instead, by letting the locals inhabit your hyperlocal, you act as a digital megaphone, echoing the existing concerns and conversations of the real-world local community, as voiced by the community members themselves.

The London riots were the breaking point for the local press; their rigid editorial structures collapsed in the face of a rapidly evolving and geographically disparate news story. Communities themselves filled the void, heading online to share information on Twitter, Facebook and blogs. There was an explosion of local content, to which the official local media's output paled in comparison. *MyMuswell's* grassroots model was designed to help facilitate this groundswell of community-action, by creating a clearly delineated virtual space hosting citizen journalism and local discussion. That, at least, we've achieved.

Note on the author

Tom O'Brien is a television producer, journalist and media advisor. He has worked with talkbackThames, ITV, Endemol, the BBC, Twofour Broadcast, The Guardian, Vodafone and the Media Trust. He is also the co-founder and editor of hyperlocal website MyMuswell
(www.mymuswell.com, @MyMuswell). More details can be found on
www.tomobrienmedia.com or you can follow him on Twitter @thomasaobrien.

The revival of local community: the case of West Hampstead

Sarah J Johnson examines the growth of *West Hampstead Life*, a hyperlocal community website that began life as a series of posts on Twitter.

In an age where transport links are better than ever before and transient populations move between cities and countries, communities are breaking down. In a city as large as London the problem is even more acute. As rent skyrockets in pockets of the city, people are pushed out and forced to relocate while others who already own a property remain.

In such a climate, how can local news survive? Is there even a need for it when neighbours sometimes don't even know each other to say 'hello' to?

Is it any wonder that local papers are struggling with depleted resources and tumbling readerships?

Roy Greenslade, media commentator and former Fleet Street editor, recognizes that changing demographics are largely to blame for the demise of local newspapers.

He said: "One of the reasons for the collapse in circulations of local newspapers is because of the collapse of community. Geographical mobility has changed everything. Communities have broken down and people are moving all over the place. There is a lack of community involvement and historical continuity. Your local paper is failing for that reason."

Perhaps, in London the situation is at its worst.

Bob Satchwell, Society of Editors executive director, quoted by *Press Gazette* in 2004, said: "The bigger the city - and obviously London's the biggest - the greater the problem is with communities breaking down. The success of weekly papers is because they are very into community news. Because communities in London are less well defined, that is more difficult to achieve. The irony is that it's these areas which need weekly papers most to develop those communities." (Ponsford 2004)

Local papers are struggling to respond to that need, however, often crippled by publishers that are more concerned about the bottom line than investing in digital innovation and good journalism.

We are left in a world where societies are crying out for good, local journalism. As Charlie Beckett, director of media think tank Polis, puts it: "In an age of increasing education and individualism there is a growing demand for more open, accessible and informative news media." (Beckett, 2010)

Some people are taking journalism into their own hands and are prepared to help create it themselves – for free. These efforts often take the form of sites or blogs that utilise social networks to generate an audience, stories and interest.

West Hampstead Life - the birth of a hyperlocal project

Take Jonathan Turton, the face behind hyperlocal blog *West Hampstead Life*, for example. His efforts started through Twitter, the micro blogging site that allows its users to post thoughts, opinions and news in 140 characters or less. "I started to realise that it might be a good way of doing local news. It seemed quite an interesting idea."

At first, his efforts were an experiment with two aims. Turton wanted to see whether the concept of spreading news on Twitter would work and he wanted to meet new people locally.

A resident of the area since 1998, Turton found his friends had begun to scatter. "I was newly single and trying to rebuild a social life. I like West Hampstead - most people like it. There are places to go but if you don't know anyone then how do you do that?"

The blog came about on June 9, 2009 when Turton posted a short entry about local election results that he could not fit into one tweet. It progressed slowly until the Autumn when it started to take off. Page views were largely driven by his Twitter following.

The big turning point for the blog was the general election in 2010. It was then that it started to become a separate entity from Twitter. Turton started doing much more in-depth coverage. He interviewed all the candidates and tried to present a balanced view of what was going on. His efforts did not go unnoticed. *The Guardian* featured him in their Top London Bloggers list in April 2010 and he was the only non-mainstream journalist allowed to attend the election count in his constituency as part of the press.

The peak in readership came in August when the riots took hold of London. Over a week, Turton's Twitter following increased by about 25%, from around 3,000 to 3,800. Although the area was not heavily affected, panic and worry were rife after a *Guardian* tweet said that trouble had spread to Kilburn. Turton spent the evening of Monday 8 August allaying people's fears by tweeting what was happening with the help of trusted sources he knew in the area.

Fast forward to February 2012 and Turton has 4,227 followers on Twitter. Over the same month his blog has around 4,000 unique visitors and 10,500 page views. His Twitter account, meanwhile, has become the hub of a rich and varied news network that provides timely and relevant news for the residents of West Hampstead.

His success proves that people hanker after local news that informs them of what is happening in the community.

It should come as no surprise. "Conventional wisdom has always been that communities form most naturally locally, so surely a kind of journalism based on linking people to gather together at that level should succeed?" (Beckett, 2010)

Rebuilding communities, reforming the local press

Despite all the technological advances and improvements in transport, life is lived locally. In the case of West Hampstead, there are two newspapers that cover the area: the *Camden New Journal* and the *Ham&High*.

Turton said: "West Hampstead is very much on the edge of the *Camden New Journal*'s catchment so although they do publish stories, they cover more of what is happening in Camden itself. The *Ham&High* has been losing staff and seems to be struggling to churn out a newspaper every week that has got harder hitting news.

"There are weeks where their West Hampstead news has come from Twitter, either from me or from people I've retweeted."

Despite this, Turton maintains a good working relationship with both papers which he regards very highly. If he has a story or a lead that he cannot follow up, he will send it to the papers as a tip off.

Greenslade sees a mutual benefit in this kind of collaboration. "If I was a local newspaper publisher I would be encouraging hyperlocal sites. You could link to their sites and then they would give you what they've got. In return you will be each other's best friend. You will be the hub and they will form satellites."

For publishers, however, this brings up a whole host of problems. They would lose control and think that their audience would leak away to the hyperlocal sites where they would get the news first.

For now, *West Hampstead Life* serves its audience in a distinct manner. Turton's "labour of love" may not make money, or employ others, and it may not provide comprehensive coverage, but like all genuine community organizations it has a valuable function.

His blog is a way of facilitating people to meet each other and strengthening the sense of community as well as being a platform to share local news, ideas and thoughts. It is about conversations not broadcasting.

West Hampstead Life is not just about news, though. Turton's efforts have transcended the digital world. He holds social get-togethers called whampgathers, the first of which was in October 2009 with 16 people in attendance. Since then, there have been eight gatherings. The latest one saw between 100 and 120 people turn up to a local pub.

There have been other success stories as well. A couple of football teams started purely from Twitter. In their second season and third seasons, they ended up coming first and second in their league. Over £1000 has been raised for the Winch, a local charity based in Swiss Cottage that helps disadvantaged young people. And, through *West Hampstead Life*, Turton has helped people network professionally as well as socially. There have even been a few romantic relationships that have formed.

This proves that community spirit is not dead.

All Turton has done is to tap into whatever interest is already there and made it easy for people to meet their neighbours. Beyond that, he offers a local news service where local people can connect over micro issues.

He said: "People feel a bit more of an ownership of where they're living, even if they're not going to be here for the long term. I find people are inherently interested in where they live even if they're not invested in it materially in terms of owning property. I don't think it's true that people aren't interested in community, I just don't think there are many opportunities for them to realise it."

Perhaps, then, this is where the future for hyperlocals lies?

Greenslade thinks it will be down to a set of circumstances concerning local finance, enthusiasm, and skills. There will not be a simple formula. Social media will be the basis for the start up of many local enterprises because people are already talking to each other and have shared interests. There will be different models but what will link them in the end is the hunger to know. If you want to know more about the world in which you live, you will get involved.

Meanwhile, Greenslade wonders if hyperlocal sites could be instrumental in re-breeding community. Could disparate groups of people that no longer have a historic connection with each other, be brought together by technology that enables them to communicate with people they did not even know were there?

In the case of West Hampstead Life, it would seem so.

With special thanks to Roy Greenslade, Jonathan Turton and Teodora Beleaga for giving up their time and providing such valuable insights.

Bibliography

Beckett, Charlie (2010) The Value of Networked Journalism, London, LSE

Ponsford, Dominic (2004) Capital gloom as London turns back on local papers. Available online at http://www.pressgazette.co.uk/story.asp?sectioncode=1&storycode=25199 accessed on 25 February 2012

Note on the author

Sarah J Johnson is currently studying for the MA in Newspaper Journalism at City University London. She graduated with a BA (Joint Hons) in Modern Languages from Newcastle University before working for a magazine and national newspaper in Vietnam.

The 100 per cent solution: For innovation in news

It starts with a vision: what if we could cover all of it? When you try to act on that vision, you invariably run into problems. And it's sweating those problems that leads to innovation, or at least to new knowledge.
By Jay Rosen.

Here's a little idea for creating innovation in news coverage: the 100 percent solution. It works like this: First, you set a goal to cover 100 percent of... well, of *something*. In trying to reach the goal you immediately run into problems. To solve those problems you often have to improvise or innovate. And that's the payoff, even if you don't meet your goal.

Got it? Good. For that's the whole idea.

In the rest of this piece I will explain what I mean and why I think it can work. And I will give you some examples. Because the 100 percent solution is not an entirely new idea. It's been tried. My aim is to get more of you to try it in some form.

So let's start with a few imaginary cases

There's going to be a wide open mayor's race in Chicago because the incumbent, Democrat Richard M. Daley, is retiring. Rahm Emanuel is running and he will have plenty of competition. A big city mayoral election generates a lot of events: Candidates appear all over town. Unions and community groups have to decide whom to endorse. Speeches, debates, rallies, fundraisers in living rooms, backyard barbeques, meetings in church basements... Picture them all on a spreadsheet. Now tack that spreadsheet up on a wall.

What if we tried to cover *every* event, big and small, involving every candidate who had a legitimate chance to be the next mayor, but also all the events where the candidates themselves may be missing but the campaign is somehow alive and present in the space between Chicagoans. That would be 100 percent coverage of campaign events.

Of course in their weakened state, the *Chicago Tribune* and the *Sun-Times* couldn't manage it. But the news ecosystem in Chicago has many players: the weeklies, a big public media sector, community newspapers, the ethnic press, any number of news start-ups, lots of local blogs. To cover everything, they'd have to collaborate in a way that hasn't been seen yet in Chicago. And figuring out how to do that would be innovation.

Now I know what you're thinking: who wants *that* much information about a single election? Wouldn't it just overload the voter's circuits and turn people off before the race even got going? Yeah, probably. But I'm just easing you into the idea for now. Aligning supply and demand with experiment and invention is hard, but this is just another way of saying that innovation rarely happens.

All the sermons in all the churches

Every Sunday, in the churches of Philadelphia, the ministers give their sermons. Each in his way is a community leader. But what do these leaders talk about each week? Maybe there should be a way to find out. The system that would permit us to know by Monday what was said in *all* the churches on Sunday… that's the 100 percent solution for the church-going community in Philly. Are you *sure* there would be scant demand for that kind of information? I'm not.

Here's an example that comes from my friend and podcast partner, the technologist Dave Winer. In New York City, Verizon is rolling out its super high speed Internet service, called FIOS. There's no map that tells us which buildings have FIOS, which are in the process of getting it, and which do not have it at all. The company doesn't provide that kind of information. Verizon does allow you to enter your address and find out about your building, but it keeps the big picture to itself.

So Dave and I have been wondering: there's roughly 110 blocks in the coverage area for the *Local East Village* (which is co-produced by NYU and the *New York Times*.) We figure there has to be a way to get good information about the availability of FIOS in every building on every block. And if we *were* able to get it, and map it, and put that data before the users of the site, would there be demand for that information? I think there would be.

Is the 100 percent solution beginning to make some sense? I hope so. It starts with a vision: what if we could cover *all* of it? Then a glimpse into the value proposition that 100 percent coverage presents for a given community of users. When you try to act on that vision, make good on the glimpse, you invariably run into problems. It's sweating those problems that leads to innovation, or at least to new knowledge.

Now to some real life examples of the 100 per cent solution in action.

What if we interview all the bands?

In March 2010, AOL attempted to interview all 2,000 bands appearing at the South by Southwest music festival in Austin[1]. Saul Hansell, the director of AOL's seed.com, a network of freelance writers, explained it this way in a blog post aimed at potential contributors:

"With this project, we're starting to show off how Seed is going to be very different from other sites that offer writing work over the Internet. Seed is an integral part of the new AOL, one of the largest journalistic organizations in the world. And we're asking Seed contributors not simply to regurgitate what they can find searching the Web, but to get on the phone, get out into the world, ask questions, witness events and write what they've discovered.

"You can also see how we are going to evolve the way Seed deals with creators. So far, we have mainly had open assignments, in which any number of people could submit articles. Some have said this seems more like a contest than a job. For SXSW, we are only asking one writer to profile each band. To make this work, we are using e-mail for part of the process. Soon the Seed site will automatically handle this sort of assignment. And it will invite creators to tell us about their professional experience, so we can match the right assignments to the right people.

"Like everything we're doing now at Seed, this is very much an experiment. We don't know how these interviews will turn out. But I'm betting, they will be as lively and varied as the SXSW festival itself."[2]

Right there you can see what I mean by "… In trying to reach the goal you immediately run into problems. To solve those problems you often have to improvise or innovate." Seed.com didn't have the systems in place to handle that many contributors on one project. So they had to do it by email. But what a great way to get a handle on the system you need to build. The spec sheet practically writes itself.

Of course there were problems[3]. I asked Hansell what the goals of the experiment were:

"What we did had internal and external goals. I came up with the idea when I was told that AOL had decided to be a corporate sponsor of the event and would make Seed a major theme. Since the show was about four months after I joined AOL (which was a week after Seed's launch), it seemed a good time to show the world what we wanted to do with it. There had been a lot of discussion about Robocontent, so one main point of our project was to focus on human reporting—in this case telephone interviews with the nearly 2000 bands that play the show.

We also wanted to stress test our very new systems, both people and machines.

"The project achieved my goals with flying colors. We used our platform to create fun and unique content. In many cases, these were the first interviews with these bands ever by a national outlet. We also created enough stress on the system to diagnose many weaknesses we've worked to fix.

"In the end, we did phone interviews with well over half the bands. Some wouldn't call us back. In a few cases there were language problems or reporters who were unreliable. I've said it was a PR mistake to say we would interview all 2000 bands rather than *try* to interview them. But in my mind, that's a footnote."

Would he recommend this method?

"I'm of mixed opinion on the merits of trying to cover 100 percent of something. I think there is a great user benefit to promising to cover everything in a set. A site about cars or movies that has all the models or all the films is far more useful than one that only has some. The risk of wasting your time when you go there looking for something is mitigated by the promise of completeness. And everything is of interest to somebody somewhere, people who we would love to serve.

"On the other hand, there are some fields in which there are so many individual elements that it is very expensive to cover them all equally. There are 2000 times more searches each month for Lady Gaga than for Shar Jackson. We would love to create the best possible page for Shar's still considerable number of fans. But the market is telling us to spend 2000 times more money on the pages we make on Lady Gaga."

Friday night lights

True. It isn't always possible to achieve 100 percent coverage of what Hansell calls a "set." And I'm not recommending it as an "always and everywhere" solution. Just a neat little idea that can sometimes spark innovation.

I'm on the advisory board of a newspaper chain, Journal-Register Company (JRC) that has gone "digital first." John Paton, the CEO, agreed to create an IdeaLab for employees who wanted to experiment with new ways of covering the news[4]. If selected they would get 25 percent of their time to work on their ideas. I urged members of the IdeaLab to try the 100 percent solution and two of them took me up on it.

Chris Stanley, online editor for *The Reporter* in Lansdale, Pennsylvania, tried it with high school sports. JRC has a number of papers in the suburban Philadelphia area but they had rarely worked together.

We wanted to get coverage and scores from not just the high schools in our area, but all the schools in PIAA District 1 (the state High School sports governing organization that covers much of the Philadelphia region). Since we have news organizations in these areas that cover these schools, we needed to find a way to integrate their coverage and live score reporting with our own. But some areas of the district are not covered by us, our own sports staffs work on different deadlines, and posting stories for sharing was usually somewhat of an afterthought.

Some games were double and triple-covered, others got no coverage at all. Scores did not appear on the web sites until late at night, if at all.

For live score coverage of Friday night games we turned to Twitter. Reporters, photographers, editors, readers, fans, whoever is at a game can send us Tweets via @phillyscores. We promote this online and in the print product.

Some editors were concerned about spamming or kids trashing rival teams with this account, so we compromised with a system of re-tweeting scores. One person in the cluster monitors the account and re-tweets anything marked @phillyscores. In addition, that account follows many other media, sports and school Twitter accounts and will also re-tweet relevant score information. A Twitter widget is posted on our HS football page, and relevant local scores are also highlighted on a scroll bar.

So not only do we get the benefit of reports from our own staff, we can also draw on many sources in the community. Other score reporting sites have started re-tweeting our own scores, which is fantastic. We can also embed story links among our scores to draw readers to our web site.

One of the benefits of the project was to get the sports departments of the various newspapers in Journal-Register onto the same page.

Other new efforts include using Google Groups to arrange coverage among sports editors at different properties, to avoid double or triple-covering overlapping games and ensuring every game is covered. In the past, sports staffs at different properties rarely talked. Now we know what each property is covering, and overlap has been eliminated.

Schools, teams, parents groups and others post their own web sites, with game information, stats, rosters, photos, videos and more. We need to link to these resources and arrange to use some of them in our own coverage. We can't be afraid to recognize good information wherever it comes from. The next step will be to integrate all these elements – complete coverage of ALL district games, Twitter, blogs (staff and community), links to those team and school sites, schedules, player and team pages – into a package that will be the ultimate source of information for football (and other sports, as well) in the region. Plans for such a site are in the works on a company-wide level.

Every high school football game in Greater Trenton
Ben Doody is the assistant sports editor of the Trentonian. His Idea Lab project is "live coverage of every high school football game in Greater Trenton."

The goal was to harness the power of Twitter to have reporters — and, ideally, fans as well — send updates from games, then, through hashtags, bring the tweets together in a live blog in which readers can follow along and ask questions.

We unveiled the feature during the first weekend of play in New Jersey and have run the chat every time there are multiple games in the area. (Essentially, any time games are played other than when one or two makeup games are going on and there's not enough content to fill a chat. But even then, we've had reporters tweet updates.)

The readership total still produces a tiny percentage of our daily page views, but it's grown steadily over the first three weeks, and compares extremely favorably to what most sites get for live chats… it's the single-most innovative feature on our site, and the one with the biggest potential.

On the first night, we had 30 readers and two or three games uncovered. Yet this past Saturday, we had every game in the area covered and brought in 150 readers — several of whom chimed in with questions and comments.

I didn't set out with a particular readership goal in mind, both because it's not something we can directly control and because I had little idea what the response would be. But a fair metric to be judged upon is growth, and I'm extremely pleased with how quickly it's caught on.

The one metric I set out to reach was 100 percent coverage — a goal we achieved for the first time in October 2011, but one that we'll have to work hard in order to make every week. One thing I've learned over the past two years is that doing something once is easy. Doing it consistently is the hard part, and that means instead of popping open bottles of champagne, we need to focus on how we're going to do it again every week.

In order to get live coverage of all the games, reporters had to learn new skills. But not all of them are equally ready for that. Ben explains:

"Some reporters needed no prodding and virtually no training. Those were the easy ones. I told them which hashtags to use, and that was it.

"Others already had Twitter accounts or were willing to set them up, but needed a lot of guidance when it came to things like the tone and frequency of tweets we were looking for. I showed them some examples, explained the concept we were working with, and they've done a good job so far.

"We have a third group, though it only has one member: Rich Fisher, a stringer who's been in the business for more than 35 years — including a long tenure as a full-timer at The Trentonian —and who's trying as hard as anyone to learn how to stay as modern as possible.

"Fish is the one veteran journalist I work with who frequently sends text messages. He also publishes a website — Fish4scores.com — dedicated to youth and high school sports in Hamilton Twp. and wants to market his own site on Twitter. I created a Twitter account for him, and he worked his way up to tweeting from his phone — a huge success story, since he's the only member of what I'd call the Old Guard who's now a self-sufficient tweeter.

"The fourth group has given me some encouragement as well, though in different ways: People who I was certain weren't going to tweet their own updates, either because they were unwilling or unable to do so. This is where we need to be honest about how things work and not bite off more than we can chew. We have to recognize situations where we can't run through a wall and figure out a way to walk around it or break it down piece by piece.

"There are a few people in this group, and we've reached the point where all of them are calling me with updates so I can post them. One, legendary Trentonian sportswriter, George O'Gorman, loves what we're doing and is happy to contribute, but is often without a laptop and is unable to see the keys on his cellphone clearly enough to send texts.

"The system is unorthodox, but it works extremely well: George calls with updates. I have The Trentonain's Twitter account open and type the updates as he says them. He's crystal-clear about what's going on and I'm Twitter-savvy enough to convey it in 140 characters. In many ways, it's the best of both worlds

— and it doesn't at all diminish the quality or quantity of information we're giving readers."

Hundreds of small platform meetings
When I worked with Amanda Michel, Marc Cooper and thousands of volunteers on OffTheBus.Net, the citizen journalism wing of the Huffington Post's election coverage in 2007-08, we looked for ways to experiment with distributed reporting and data collection. Here's a simple example[5]:

WANTED: Citizen reporters to help HuffPost's OffTheBus cover the Obama campaign. Over the next two weeks the campaign will be holding hundreds of small platform meetings where the public is invited to help shape the nominee's platform. We need you to be a reporter in your local meeting, and to measure the effectiveness of the campaign. Already planned to attend one? You can report in directly to us. Either way, it's another great way for you to get involved in the presidential race.

In order to execute on this invitation, OffTheBus needed:

- a sign-up form and corresponding database of participants;
- instructions for how to navigate to local events;
- a form to fill out with questions the volunteers were to answer, along with guidelines for the act of reporting;
- a deadline by which to submit reports;
- reminder e-mails, telling people that that OffTheBus was counting on them, including one that went out shortly after the event ended;
- a tracking system that told the editors of OffTheBus if the necessary materials had been downloaded. ("There was always attrition," Amanda Michel told me. Meaning: people who said they would file a report who never took the necessary steps.)
- constant recruitment after the initial call-out, so that whenever OffTheBus mentioned the upcoming platform meetings the invitation to help report on them was repeated. "We never relied on one attempt," Michel said.

These necessary steps are the learning dividend from trying to cover *all* the meetings.

So that's the 100 percent solution. The point of trying it is to jump right into the middle of the innovation puzzle.

But there is another point, which I haven't mentioned. In a time of contraction in the news industry, and of diminished expectations in the workaday world of professional journalism, we need counter-cyclical measures that broaden our ambitions, widen the lens and insist that with new tools and greater participation—what Alan Rusbridger, editor of The Guardian, calls the mutualization of journalism[6] – we can do way more than we were ever able to do before.

Notes

[1] http://paidcontent.org/article/419-aol-tries-to-seed-sxsw-with-coverage-of-2000-bands/
[2] http://blog.seed.com/2010/01/28/seed-sends-reporters-to-interview-2-000-bands-before-sxsw/
[3] http://gawker.com/5494616/deadline-panic-at-aol-over-hipster-contributors
[4] http://jxpaton.wordpress.com/2010/07/11/meet-the-idealab-2/
[5] http://www.huffingtonpost.com/amanda-michel/become-a-citizen-reporter_b_113311.html
[6] http://www.guardian.co.uk/media/2010/jan/25/cudlipp-lecture-alan-rusbridger

Note on the author

Jay Rosen teaches Journalism at New York University, where has been on the faculty since 1986. From 1999 to 2005 he served as chair of the Department. He lives in New York City. He is the author of PressThink, a weblog about journalism and its ordeals (www.pressthink.org). In July 2006 he announced the debut NewAssignment.Net, his experimental site for pro-am, open source reporting projects. A second project is OfftheBus.Net with the Huffington Post. He serves as co-publisher of OffTheBus with Arianna Huffington. A third was introduced in November 2007: beatblogging.org ("Follow along as 13 reporters build social networks into their beats.")

From 1993 to 1997 he was the director of the Project on Public Life and the Press, funded by the Knight Foundation.

As a press critic and reviewer, he has published in The Nation, Columbia Journalism Review, the Chronicle of Higher Education, the New York Times, the Washington Post, the Los Angeles Times, Newsday and others. Online he has written for Salon.com, TomPaine.com and Poynter.org. This is an abridged version of a blog post first published on October 21 2011

Section C. So is the saviour on the airwaves?

John Mair

"Cutting down trees and spreading ink all over them", as I once heard newspaper publication inelegantly described, seems to be rapidly going out of fashion nationally and even more so locally. Print is, if not dead, certainly in the intensive care ward

So what is to fill the void for local information? In the previous section we have seen the proliferation of hyperlocal blogs and other ways of reaching micro audiences. The potential number of those is infinite but the revenue very limited.

What therefore of local broadcasting? Back in the heady days of the 1990s no big town in the UK was complete without at least two local evening news television programmes provided by the BBC and ITV, at least two local radio stations – one BBC, one commercial – plus the local paper or papers. The audiences in Nottingham, Leeds, Birmingham or Bristol were well served – even super served. The local airwaves throbbed, though the quality may have been variable.

No more. In the noughties, ITV beat a regional TV retreat at record speed. Programmes were consolidated and amalgamated. Branch offices in towns like Coventry closed. ITV Central became ITV Birmingham with small presentation studios side by side 'serving' the different parts of the region from Grantham to Gravesend. 'Border News' is now presented from Newcastle, 'Meridian Oxford' from a Hampshire industrial estate. The combination of supine regulators who believed 'light touch' regulation meant 'no touch' regulation with avaricious new ITV bosses from another world – John Cleese famously described chief executive Gerry Robinson as "a f*****g upstart caterer" – saw an end to the regionalism that had been the very foundations of the ITV network back in the 1950s.

ITV became a network not a series of local franchises. 15 to 1 became a motto, not a TV programme.

Local commercial radio has consolidated and rationalised too especially in the recent past. The days of a thousand flowers blooming in local towns went long after the ambition of presenting local dramas and documentaries had vanished. News, inevitably was squeezed. Music and playlists came to dominate. The local stations were taken over by the big boys. Heart, Absolute and Capital now rule the 'local' commercial airwaves nationwide. Presenters have been let go, local news teams broken up, presentation and shared programmes are now transmitted from a network centre, usually in London. Hardly the dream of the founding fathers three decades earlier.

Here and there local stations – like Touch FM in Coventry and other Midlands towns and Jack FM in Oxford – still peep through. They, sadly, are the exception rather than the rule in the world of juggernaut local commercial radio.

What of the huge elephant in the local broadcasting room – the BBC? Its regional TV network and regional TV news and current affairs shows were set up to combat the initial runaway success of the early ITV franchisees. Some – like Birmingham, Manchester, Bristol and Leeds – for a while became quite large and started to offer and make programmes for the BBC network. But their bedrock was always news for 'the local patch' at tea-time. As ITV beat a regional retreat, the BBC simply segmented its news programmes so the local was trailed in the national. The BBC *Six O'Clock News* found itself kicking at an open goal against the impoverished ITV regional shows. Night after night they won matches (and passed on the advantage to their cousins in the regions) they had previously lost. ITV was hardly on the park.

Driven by a desire to please its political masters, the BBC maintained and strengthened a firm out-of-London policy. Broadcasting in Scotland, Wales and Northern Ireland was much enhanced with the coming of political devolution in 1999. It had to be. Some regional centres waned – Birmingham and Leeds spring to mind – some regions went to sub opts to better serve local audiences. In my patch, BBC Oxford developed its own segment within 'South Today' to serve the Oxfordshire region. But, in a true BBC fudge, it was left under-resourced with few journalists. 'South Today, Oxford' soon became 'History Today, Oxford' with a mélange of warmed-up newspaper stories, too many diary stories and much 'churnalism' – PR dressed up as news.

But the biggest statement of intent to local audiences for the BBC was the commissioning and building of BBC North in Salford. That edifice which took whole BBC departments (Sport and Children's), entire channels (Radio Five Live and BBC Three) and thousands of (often unwilling) workers 'up north' opened properly for business in 2012. At the very moment when commercial media were acting centrifugally and heavily concentrating on London, the BBC was acting in exactly the opposite way. Time will tell whether that is a wise strategy.

BBC Local radio and its 40 stations in England, plus two 'nationals' each in Scotland Wales and Ireland, continued to plough their furrows. Like waves, money flows into and out of BBC local radio. One Director General Greg Dyke visits a local radio station – Hereford and Worcester – and is appalled at what he sees. So money for open centres and new buildings is thrown at the local stations. Another Director General, Mark Thompson, is less steeped in localism, cuts back on their services and ambition (but not as much as he might have liked to) and it is back to the battlements for BBC local radio.

Throughout the tide of BBC political economy, the corporation continues to try to find an audience but not always with success. In local markets like Coventry it is always well and truly creamed by the commercial opposition. Its audience too old.

Here, Bill Heine of BBC Radio Oxford puts up a stern defence for the importance of local radio as the heartbeat of a town. When it works and those phones light up, it is as he memorably puts it "like touching the clitoris of the community". On the other side of the street Steve Orchard, who runs a series of local commercial stations from an industrial estate base in Stratford, seems to have come full circle in his philosophy. His recipe for the success of Touch FM in Coventry is back to basics – local news, local documentaries, local outside broadcasts. Getting the community to talk to itself about itself. It works for his station.

What of Local TV – the great white hope of the Coalition Government and Culture Secretary Jeremy Hunt? He even ring fenced £40 million of the BBC Licence fee settlement to pay for his whim and has advertised for 20 franchisees to come forward to serve local audiences from Oxford to Hove to Edinburgh. The first should come onstream later in 2012. But the queue of entrepreneurs wanting to dip their toes into this pond is not very long. Richard Peel and Paul Potts suggest a model which links local insitutions to provide a local service. They say use the state-of-the-art technical facilities of media universities, the skills (real and potential) of students to make a worthwhile service. They are piloting this approach with the University of Sheffield. Will it work? Long university vacations will be the litmus test of that.

Barnie Choudhury of Lincoln University (and latterly of the BBC News parish) too argues strongly that universities should provide the backbone of any local TV service. They have the ideas, the facilities and the people. Lincoln is leading the way with a community radio station – SirenFM – broadcasting right from the heart of the media department on campus throughout the year.

David Hayward of the BBC College of Journalism has been a local broadcaster. He masterminded the BBC Local TV experiment in 2006 which used six local radio stations as a base to broadcast a loop of local programmes via satellite. It was getting into its stride and gaining confidence – there were plans for it to go both national and hyperlocal – when it was strangled at birth by a posse of local newspaper interests through the Newspaper Society and the Society of Editors. They felt it posed even more threats to their declining revenue base and wanted local TV to be theirs. Few have shown any signs of doing anything creative, sensible or profitable with it since. It was a media mugging for muggings sake.

So does the answer to the future of localism lie in the ether of the local airwaves? The market and the audiences will decide.

Where it matters most

Local Radio legend Bill Heine – of Headington Shark and BBC Radio Oxford fame – knows very well what a difference local radio can make to a community. Here he makes a powerful case by recounting stories that have changed listeners' lives.

"I don't listen to national news anymore because I can't affect it. They are talking at me, not with me. I'm a strictly local news person now; on that level I can get involved and make a difference. It's all a question of empowerment." – a former national radio newsreader now living in Oxford

"I always tell Oxfordshire people first because I am a local Oxfordshire MP and I am accountable." – Douglas Hurd , former Home and Foreign Secretary

"Local radio is a ledge where contradictions in a community come out on level ground, a market place where different neighbours, who don't usually meet each other, talk." – an Oxford urban guerrilla.

I am a presenter on BBC Radio Oxford. I got the job after I erected a local icon on my roof, the sculpture of a Shark crashing through the tiles of a modest terraced house. This was a small swish of the tail that made big waves reaching the Oxford City Council, the courts and even the Cabinet, where the Environment Secretary Michael Heseltine gave it planning permission.

This local event went ballistic and was beamed around the world, but it was quintessentially local – one person engaging with his neighbours (mine were horrified) and asking his Councillors (mine were angry) if there was still a space left where artists and architects could meet and create a new view of acceptable, accessible public art.

The BBC reported this incident, took a flyer and invited me to come off the street and onto the airwaves to say what I saw. That was twenty five years ago, and I'm still doing it. What are my credentials? I have none, no training. The only thing I have is a taste and smell for what "local" means. It means the phones light up when you put your finger on the clitoris of the community. It means the politicians of all parties are equally suspicious of you and think you belong to "the other" party. The local thing happens when the Chief Constable won't talk to another presenter because she knows you know "the lie of the land".

I'll give you some examples. Douglas Hurd was elected to Parliament in 1974 to represent the then Mid Oxfordshire constituency. His career took him to the threshold of Number Ten. When he decided to step down in 1995 he didn't go on national television or call a press conference at the Foreign Office. He quietly rang BBC Radio Oxford and asked if he could "have a moment or two to talk to your listeners." That was how he announced his departure from politics and the world stage; and it was the same way he began, by speaking to local people.

The national media didn't get it. They were incensed that they had to take a feed for such an important event from a local radio station. But it was a clear sign of how Douglas Hurd saw the balance of accountability, empowerment and commitment – it's all local, because that's where it matters most.

But is local also provincial; does it pass the "so what" test?

Playing in a wider world

For a generation I've carried on a conversation with people in Oxfordshire about births, deaths, loves and hates. There have been couples that wooed and won each other over the airwaves, and people who lost each other. But how does it play in a wider world? Just how local is local radio? Well, sometimes not very – we occasionally travel as far away as Reading, a full forty miles.

In August 1996, Reading Borough Council hosted an exhibition about the diary of Anne Frank, which I visited and discussed on air. There really was not much to say about it. The story was a very personal and emotional one, giving a moving experience of a different time and place, unimaginable to some, distanced by time to all.

Then Hans from Reading rang the programme. He had a slight accent and explained he was originally from Holland. "I remember those times very well – 1943-45. I was a teenager, thirteen or fourteen, and I worked on a farm outside but quite near to Amsterdam.

"My father sent me to the city on regular evening errands loaded with bags of corn, wheat and barley. It was not easy. The bags were heavy; we tied them to my back and chest under a cape. I walked all the way from the farm into the city to distribute them. It had to be early enough not to attract attention…not too late or I might be caught by the Nazis.

"I remember one night I pitched up with the last sacks at a house by one of the canals, and the owner quickly dragged me in saying I must stay the night because it was late, and if the Gestapo got me, that would destroy a lifeline to more people than I knew.

"He gave me something to eat and a bed, which was hidden away under the stairwell that led to the attic. It was a small space and uncomfortable, but I stayed there that night. At first light he woke me and said I must go immediately. Later the same day I found out that shortly after I left, the Gestapo raided the house, found the door and stairwell where I had been sleeping moments before, marched up to the attic and arrested the family of Anne Frank."

I remember...

Those war years provided other insights and experiences which illuminated small but personal chapters of that epic story.

One hot, lazy summer afternoon I was discussing on air the colours of the evening sky, a peaceful, whimsical enough subject until Eva rang. "I remember..." (always those deceptively detonating words)... "One night the sky went red. I was working the late shift at a hospital in Coventry when the Luftwaffe flew over. The sound of the planes was blotted out by the bomb explosions. When the grey smoke broke, we could see the orange and red fires above.

"I was a nurse so I kept my eyes mostly on the ground. I can tell you exactly what happened when the bombs fell around us. We were almost opposite the Cathedral, and I saw what happened. People say Coventry Cathedral fell. I can tell you it didn't, I was there. I saw it. When the bomb hit, it didn't fall. It rose. The cathedral jumped in the air for a few heart beats, and then it came down."

A different kind of bomb went out over the airwaves when John rang from a village in Buckinghamshire. He was a former Royal Navy man who had served in the South Pacific in the 1950s. "I was a young recruit happy to be sent to a kind of paradise called Christmas Island. The officers didn't tell us much, only that the Air Force was conducting an experiment and we were going to witness something pretty big.

"I remember the day well, 15 May, 1957. It was very early in the morning. We had dug a trench and were told to stay down, turn to the north and close our eyes. On no account were we to look at the explosion. It was good advice. Even with my eyes closed the explosion created a white blast inside my head."

"So you witnessed the first British atomic bomb test?"

"Yes, after a short time we were told it was safe to look; and we saw the mushroom cloud growing."

"Did you have any protection?"

"No, they said we didn't need any because the winds mostly went east and the radioactive problem from the blast, we were told, was very minimal. It was the danger to our eyes from the flash that made it necessary to be in the trench, facing away from the blast, which was thirty miles south of Christmas Island.

"Unfortunately there was some wind shift because of the blast, and we were outside in the trench when this happened. I didn't feel anything in particular, but I knew not everything went to plan. Well, my problem now is that I've been unwell, and my doctor recently told me I've got cancer. My mind keeps going over what happened then. I'm thinking about it, and I'm not exactly sure what to make of it."

Footnotes of history

What remains of these stories from local people who didn't make the footnotes of history? At the time the airwaves were unavailable. Sometimes they had a tale to tell and maybe they didn't get it off their chest – the innocence of Hans, the anger of Eva and the fear of John. Then one day on local radio they have an opportunity and they grab it. So what? Does it mean anything? Does it matter? Does it change things? Probably not. But at least we now know; it adds to the sum of things, and they've unfurled their particular flag.

"Local" is about how to find a voice and connect to other parts of the community. Oxford is not so much one city as many different communities. Some are full of people with initials – MPs, the DG of the BBC, possibly even the KGB – who usually send their children to expensive local private schools and live in the leafy lanes of Summertown. They mostly have money, high cheekbones and instant access to the media.

Others suffer in silence. Wood Farm is one area with a lot of people suffering. But this silent minority in Oxford found its voice to fight fear, intimidation and violence using the airwaves. The fight started with a single anonymous e-mail to me asking for help and snowballed into a debate that pulled in television, the press and even someone with initials, the PM. Entitled "Under Siege", this email lit the torch.

"Bill, I'm writing to you in despair. There is a gang of vicious nasty thugs terrorising shopkeepers, shoppers and anyone else who happens to cross their path in the vicinity of the Atkyns Road shops on the Wood Farm estate. This has been going on for years and the police and authorities appear unable to put a stop to it.

Recently one man has been driven from his home and people pelted with stones. Others do not go to their local shops for fear of intimidation and violence. Buses have been hit with water bombs and other missiles. The bus stop is regularly vandalised. The shops have had to install very expensive security grills after repeated vandalism, and now we have been told the Co-op is to close as a result of the trouble. This is devastating to the many elderly and disabled for whom the local Co-op shop is a lifeline.

We have had to endure this urban terrorism for far too long, but with the police and Oxford City Council seemingly unable to have significant impact, it all looks like continuing until the community is destroyed.

PS You will understand after the content of what I have written that I wish to hide my identity and I will not come on air."

We rang the Oxford, Swindon and Gloucester Co-operative for a statement on whether they were planning to close their store in Wood Farm, and they were quite open: "We share the concerns of local residents and our own store team face abuse and threatening behaviour on a daily basis. We would like to see long-term action to protect residents and traders alike. As a Co-op we have a social responsibility to support estates such as Wood Farm. However, for the safety and well-being of our staff, we are reviewing whether we have a long-term future in this area."

After I read the e-mails on air, there was a pause in the programme as if people were adjusting their radio sets or their take on reality: "We live in Oxford. We know what happens here. People aren't under siege. This can't be true." Then came the cloudburst and roaring thunder of residents' fears and tales of intimidation, about their daily lives being turned upside down, turned into torture. The people who rang the programme did not want to use their names on air, but they all wanted to tell their stories.

Anonymous caller number ten: "I live in the tower block and there are three individuals in here who are being abused all the time. Two days ago I was stood outside the tower block talking to these people and the gang appeared. Two seconds later we were being pelted with stones and bricks and I was hit by a two-penny piece, which I picked up and put in my pocket. They have caused thousands of pounds of damage here. They even put the lifts out of action in the tower block, and we have fourteen floors here. This has been going on for six months, since before Christmas. The police gave us a "unique reference number". So five times I've called about this URN and five times I've had no response from the police."

Anonymous caller number twenty three: "The youths actually broke into the surgery two times in one week. It wasn't a case of breaking in and nicking anything. It was pure wanton vandalism. They didn't just break in; they urinated everywhere and put graffiti all over. After that the police issued a crime number but did not even come out to discuss the matter. They didn't put in an appearance. There are so many decent, law-abiding people living on this estate, and they are worried about not only their own safety but what will happen to their services. What will they do when they lose their surgery?"

Anonymous number twenty nine: "I'm in my thirties with two young children and lived here since I was born basically. I bought my property from the council to get on the ladder and now I want to sell it. The estate agent keeps coming back to me for the last nine months saying people love the property, it's beautifully presented; but they just don't want to live in the area. I grew up here as a little girl, and it was lovely. My mum lives here and she's elderly and now she wouldn't dream of going to the shops after four in the afternoon. I wouldn't want to tackle the gang and I'm young and fit. There is an undercurrent of fear here. The shops are a 'no go' area in the evening. We don't deserve to feel like prisoners in our own homes."

This saga went on for four days. Anonymous caller number thirty five: "After your programme yesterday we're all very grateful. At least today we had cameras, television, newspapers and police around. We feel very sorry for the shopkeepers and the chip-shop owners who feel particularly victimised. The people who run it call one of the councillors to escort them home at night. I believe their lease has been devalued and now they can't even sell up and get away from the problem. This is terrible. And the Co-op, it was originally set up to help out working-class populations and they don't like to pull out of areas like Wood Farm. I can tell you when the staff say they get threats and abuse daily, it is true.

"Everyone here, we're all afraid. Last night after your programme, for the first time I felt, 'Hallelujah.' I've sixty-one and now I thought I can go out to the shops for a bottle of milk. They were all out there but for some reason I could walk among them without the usual shouts and abuse. Just two days ago I was pelted with stones, bottles and cans. They shouted "grass" at me because I talked to the police. We're used to getting water cannons in our gardens, believe me that's nothing. It's chicken feed."

Anonymous caller number 60: "I live in Wood Farm and I don't think people realise what a loss it would be for the community if the Co-op were to go. We've been over there in the evening just before closing and staff have been locked in with a piece of wood between the handles of the shop door. These kids are not thinking of anyone else's welfare. The youths had barricaded the staff in so they could not get out. This is great how all this has happened, how everyone has reacted to the programme because we are all fed up with it. The fact that we're all going anonymous explains how we all feel."

But one person didn't mind giving me his name – Sidney: "I'm disgusted and ashamed of all this, but there's not much we can do if the council won't help us. Joyriding, kiddies giving people a boot when they go to the shops, piddling on the landing of the tower block…they are using the place as a toilet; it's downright disgusting.

"If I go round the corner they shout at me. 'You nonce, you nonce.' I'm no nonce. I have to use a wheelchair when I go outside. I was taking my little dog for a walk one night. There are flats above the shops, and there were nine of the gang shouting at me from the balcony – 'You nonce, you nonce'. So I turned the wheelchair around, put on the brakes and looked at them and told them, "Come down here and say that." And they wouldn't come down, nine of them against one old cripple, eh! You know they never had the guts to come down."

Every part of BBC Oxford, not only radio but television and the web pages too, ran with the story. These stories stunned the police, the press and the public. The media descended on the area and Wood Farm went in at number one that week on the agenda of Oxford City Council and Thames Valley Police whom we invited to respond to the callers. The police claimed they were too busy with other media pressures for interviews, which is the answer to one e-mail question I received from Chris the following day:

> "To the casual listener it sounds as if the very fabric of society is starting to fall apart for the poor souls living at Wood Farm. I find it astounding that the police have not accepted the BBC's invitation to comment on the situation. I'm sure it cannot be the case, but to someone like myself with no first-hand knowledge of the situation at all, it sounds like the police have just given up on the place and are expending their resources

elsewhere. Did the police give any reason at all for not participating in the phone-in? If not, why not?"

The debate sent ripples that lapped at the front door of Ten Downing Street. Two weeks later I interviewed Tony Blair and asked him three times before I got any focused answer about how such a thing as the Wood Farm failure could happen and the Prime Minister finally promised: "I'll look into the problem of Wood Farm myself."

What's changed? Well, people's sense of value and power and hope has changed. The idea that we-will-be-listened-to has taken hold. There have been regular, sustained high-profile policing, media monitoring and political strategy to remove the gang leaders and disperse the members. The leader was served with an Ant-Social Behaviour Order, banned from the area and finally landed in prison.

Things are different. Wood Farm is changing because the residents decided that the first step is to describe things using the local airwaves so the events can't be ignored, to blow the whistle – and then they can change things, slowly.

"Local" means listening. Margaret Thatcher once famously said – "Home is a place where they have to take you in". Local radio, when it works like in Wood Farm, is a place where they want to take you in.

Note on the author
Bill Heine has written articles for *The Sunday Times, The Observer* and the *Daily Telegraph*. He has broadcast on BBC Radio Oxford for the past 25 years and written a book about the experience – *Heinstein of the Airwaves*. Bill has also written *The Hunting of the Shark* delineating the funny yet frightening battles he had with Oxford City Council planners to retain Oxford's famous and much-loved landmark, the Headington Shark.

What is local in commercial radio?

Steve Orchard, chief executive of Quidem, who run local commercial stations in the Midlands, argues that poor management and heavy-handed regulation have taken the 'local' out of local commercial radio. But there is a way back.

The radio landscape has shifted so fundamentally that there are times when the local content in local radio is barely noticeable.

When commercial radio launched in 1973 it was intended to be a purely local medium. In its first iteration it fulfilled this brief supremely well. Throughout the 1970s local shareholders from the metropolitan areas of the United Kingdom erected impressive radio businesses whose point of difference with the BBC national music services on offer, was local content. Well staffed newsrooms, local output 24/7, radio cars, even the odd orchestra thrown in for good measure. If you seek to understand local in the context of local commercial radio it's very easy if you look at the period 1973 to 1990.

By 2012 economics and technology have changed what was known as Independent Local Radio (or ILR for short) to such an extent that answering the question "What is local" has become somewhat difficult.

Capital, LBC, Clyde, BRMB, Piccadilly, Forth, Metro, Tees, Invicta, Trent, Mercia – the very names of commercial radio's first wave signified redoubtable local intent. It is true that despite incredible listening figures, a number of these local behemoths struggled financially – but that was never to do with lack of audience; it was to do with bonkers regulation under the STASI- style scrutiny of the Independent Broadcasting Authority and its consequent lead weight of redundant costs. It was also due in a number of cases to the dubious quality of managers in control, or not, of the radio business purse strings.

The beginnings of local radio had a visceral impact on me. Cutting-edge technology in those days was the solid-state transistor radio. For the first time, the smaller radio set could be smuggled under the bedclothes. This was the era of the tranny. Radio, the best medium of all at creating colour pictures, transported me one moment to the Pleasure Palace of Fab 208 and the next to

Radio Tirana where I wondered at a modern day Lord Haw Haw denouncing American intervention in Vietnam.

From time to time I'd catch a snip of a ship's Morse signal, or some French chanteuse. Even the static had a compelling romance to it. Then on 2 April 1974, Piccadilly Radio came along, beaming out across Manchester and its satellite towns. Most of the DJs spoke like me, the listeners came from "round here", their sense of humour was just like mine. I heard that there was a traffic jam on Broadway by the Boat and Horses, where I caught the school bus: and I was hooked. We had our own radio station. Eventually the DJs became genuine bona fide stars – James Stannage, Mike Sweeney and Phil Woods were for us at that time and in that place bigger than the national radio celebrities of the day.

Fast forward 35 years and the questions I ask myself now as a local radio operator are: "Does anyone give a toss about local? Was that just a different, simpler, naive time? Has life moved on?" In order to survive the revenue impact of the internet's voracious and disruptive appetite, coupled with a wholesale shift of the BBC's radio services into hitherto unchallenged commercial radio demographics, Commercial Radio is becoming less local hero and more aspiring national media brand.

My neighbour Orion is the latest to lower its heritage colours down the company flagpole. BRMB, Mercia, and Beacon are out, a new national wannabe brand Free Radio is in. Why? National revenue is not what it should be and could be at those particular heritage stations. BRMB means nothing in Soho where the airtime is purchased – Heart, Capital, and Smooth are big, available in many locations and easy to understand.

Despite its gigantic heritage BRMB has been reduced to the role of Oliver Twist – not able to survive on the revenue crumbs left over when the top table stations have had their fill. Suddenly for commercial radio, local doesn't seem that important anymore. Orion's management will not for one second accept that a change of name represents a diminution of localism. Actually – they are right, BRMB *is* just a name. The real question though is this – can BRMB, Mercia and Beacon drop their local name because actually much (although not all) of the real local content went some time ago.

In order to understand what's happening to local in commercial radio we need to differentiate between its various component parts. Firstly, there's a list of functional local information that represents the *sine qua non* for any local commercial radio station. This includes weather, traffic and travel, local news stories and at least a basic coverage of 'What's On' information. Whilst listeners expect a local service to fulfil the function of local information provider, they do not get so excited about this functional service so as to switch their allegiance from Scott Mills on Radio 1 or Steve Wright on Radio 2.

In order to compete, the local commercial radio station also has to differentiate its music offering to represent an improved choice in the listener's mind whilst labouring under the handicap of commercial ad breaks. Finally, in order to build a dominant share of listening in any market, the local commercial station must elevate its local position beyond that of provision of functional local info, and grab the mantle of 'local hero'. We do this by highlighting local campaigns and giving a voice to all sides of the story.

For the Quidem stations that I run, a good example of going beyond functional and perfunctory is our coverage of the HS2 rail debate about which people are concerned and passionate. We also create platforms such as The Pride of Stratford Awards which celebrate on-air and off, the achievements of local individuals, businesses and communities.

We are currently enjoying the title of Arqiva Commercial Radio Station of the Year for our station Touch fm in Coventry. When we acquired the Touch fm Group from Cumbrian Newspapers in 2009 I needed some persuading that the Coventry service should be included in the deal. The owners had announced to local advertisers that the station was unviable and soon to be shut down, and I couldn't make any sense of including what looked like a classic basket case in the deal. At the eleventh hour I changed my mind: I could see the potential.

Two short years later our Coventry team was at a major awards ceremony in London picking up the gong. I have no doubt how we earned this wonderful accolade – we adopted a strategy of "aggressive localism". Whilst others were backing off or paying lip service to genuine localism we could see an opportunity to differentiate in the market. We created space for the stuff that local radio had abandoned. Things like documentaries, news specials, listener polls, local unsigned music - even a short radio play about the impact of the Coventry Blitz on a couple of local youngsters.

For our radio stations local is the only point of difference we have. Our music mix is a bit older than Heart fm's and a bit younger than Radio 2's – but honestly not so much that it's very noticeable, not sufficiently different for us to exist. Because local is our reason for being we find new ways to deliver it. In 2011our Coventry breakfast team broadcast from a different location in the Sky Blue City across 24 consecutive hours for no reason other than to find a different way of getting local characters on air. The entire Outside Broadcast was executed using an iPhone and a 59p app.

The challenge we face is that our competitors have been in the market for thirty years and have earned a position in listeners' minds as the local player. No matter how much they water down their local content, their heritage remains strong. In radio, listening habits and opinions once formed can last a generation. That's why portly, balding, middle-aged men continue to be found in sizeable numbers amongst Radio 1's wider demographic spectrum. Despite the music the station plays, these old blokes can't contemplate switching over, because they've always listened, and that's that.

So what is local? There's a sliding scale of value in localism. At the low value end is the functional stuff that is a cost of entry to the local radio game – traffic and travel, weather, news: stuff that people expect. At the high value end is the programming stuff that identifies a tribal feeling in a market and creates content from that dynamic: stuff that people don't expect. When I ran the programming of GWR and then GCap, then the UK's biggest radio groups, out of the sixty or seventy stations in our portfolio two of the most fiercely tribal markets were paradoxically and surprisingly Milton Keynes and Swindon. These two towns have been the butt of comedians' jokes for decades, and because of that a mountain stronghold mentality had taken hold– a protective and defensive urge.

I once observed a comment in a listener feedback group "No-one is allowed to take the piss out of our concrete cows... unless it's us". All local communities have some version of this "it might not be the best place to live, but it's our place" mentality. Proper, valuable local content emerges when a radio station absorbs that tribalism and finds ways to reflect it on air. We took it to an extreme some 10 years ago now when Trent fm declared "Nottingham – World's Best City". Imagine that! Rio? New York? Paris? None of them compares to our City. The attitude of the station's award winning breakfast duo Jo and Twiggy was "If you don't agree that this is the world's Best City – go and listen to someone else." Now that's high-value localism.

During the GWR era I found myself constantly at odds with the Radio Authority and then Ofcom from the mid 1990s probably for a period of ten years or so. The nub of the problem was that the regulator has to focus on the low-value end of localism – how many news bulletins do you broadcast, where are your studios based, how many hours of programme sharing do you do? These things are measurable, quantifiable, and wholly irrelevant.

I remember Feargal Sharkey seeking me out when he first joined the Radio Authority. He'd obviously been primed that I had strong views on the matter. We met at the old Trent fm buildings in Castle Gate Nottingham and I held forth on the subject of the impossibility of regulating localism at the micro level. He punctured my diplomacy by proffering "So what you are saying Steve is all this regulation – it's just complete b****cks". Put like that, especially by the lead singer of The Undertones, how could I disagree? The conflict occurred because as a local radio programmer my focus was entirely different from that of the regulator – what I (and actually the listeners) consider important is a type of local that is entirely unquantifiable, it is about tribalism. "Don't give me grief about programme sharing – our breakfast show has just declared Nottingham to be the World's Best City!"

The biggest thing I've learned after nigh on 30 years of crafting local radio content is this – when it comes to local, the emotion is more important than the function. To win you need both.

You cannot win with weather and traffic alone.

Create a tribe.

Note on the author
Grammy Award winning radio entrepreneur Steve Orchard runs six TouchFM stations in the Midlands.

Making Jeremy Hunt's dream a reality

Paul Potts and Richard Peel are proposing to develop a network of local media operations providing news and information online by tapping into the willingness and nascent expertise of student journalists at universities across the country. Here they explain their business and editorial proposition.

Molly Ivins, an author and renowned columnist for the *Dallas Times Herald*, perhaps summed up the situation best when she said: "I don't so much mind that newspapers are dying – it's watching them commit suicide that pisses me off."[1]

Five years after her untimely death, the situation is becoming serious. So serious, that the Annenberg School of Southern California has predicted that only four US daily newspapers will be in print by 2017 – *The New York Times*, *USA Today*, *The Washington Post* and the *Wall Street Journal*. At the other extreme, local weekly newspapers may still survive, according to the school's Director of the Center for the Digital Future.[2]

Following this prediction, with great interest, are the doom-ridden writers of a US online site called *Newspaper Death Watch* which claims to chronicle the decline of newspapers and the re-birth of journalism. It suggests that in the States, circulation declines, which have been running at 8% to 10% annually, will accelerate and that the "whole print model will fall apart...within the next 10 years".[3] Although it is pessimistic it doesn't quite endorse the cataclysmic expectation of Annenburg.

So what's the good news? *Newspaper Death Watch* reports that New York Times Co released its first earnings report since it instituted a pay wall earlier this year and digital revenue exceeded its editorial costs[4]. This, it claims, is a first sign that newspapers are crossing the divide between print and digital.

The general situation outlined above is mirrored in the UK where national and local newspaper circulations are in decline and managers anxiously look for increases in online traffic to allay their broader fears.

Cantankerous news editors

For those of us who trained on local newspapers in the Seventies when reporters wet behind the ears trudged off to cover Crown Court cases and coroners' courts and were expected by cantankerous news editors with gout to produce five stories a day or get fired, the world has changed beyond recognition.

In those days, giant Remington typewriters with sticky keys were the tools for production, and newsrooms buzzed with the sound of constant telephone conversations, whoops of delight when someone secured a scoop and the bark of seasoned sub-editors challenging the quality of the copy.

These days many local newspapers rely on news releases to fill their pages, don't have the resources to cover council meetings and courts and will often have one senior journalist whose byline appears on everything from the latest controversy over a new development to the paucity of Christmas street decorations.

Discussions have been going on for some years about how to bridge the democratic deficit and provide people in communities with relevant news and information so that they can make judgments about local politics, find about local activity and understand what is going on in their community.

A changing landscape

The communication landscape has changed forever. There was a surge of interest in citizen journalism, which has not really turned into the force originally predicted. Before that, out of the blue, texting became a vehicle for instant communication and has been followed by the mighty surge of social media. Twitter was suddenly the way to break news and even to incite revolution. Bloggers starting breaking stories before broadcast and newspaper journalists.

Now, with the circulation of national newspapers in decline proprietors are keener to boast about their millions of monthly web browsers, with the *Mail*, *Telegraph* and *Guardian* at the head of the pack in the new world.[5]

The online site *socialmediatoday* takes it a step further saying the Guardian describes itself as a digital organization, even though most of its revenue comes from print. It says that if a story lives online, in social media, it can develop organically quickly. "It's a new way of working for journalists but it's clearly more effective in meeting the needs of the readers. This concept of social journalism... allows journalists to involve the people – the audience.

"You see things like live reporting a developing story to a broad audience, allowing them to interact and engage. A story becomes more expansive because it is open to outside, real-time influence."[6]

Some online news sources are already well established. According to the *Financial Times* the news and commentary site *Huffington Post* is looking to launch in another 10 markets during 2012 through web partnerships with traditional newspapers[7]. It also says a revenue-sharing alliance with *Le Monde* for the French launch in 2012 will provide a template for the site's international expansion by AOL Huffington Post Media Group.

The Huffington Post launched regional editions in the UK and Canada during 2011 and has a total of 40m monthly visitors.

Meanwhile, at a local level, newspaper management has been in denial, while ITV wound back its regional commitment because of commercial pressures and because Ofcom allowed it to. Competition always enriches performance. It is vital to have two or three sources of news but even the BBC, historically always strongly committed to regional and local news, has had to address its priorities and local radio has suffered as a result.

The right dream?

So, while local news provision has declined, the way people get their news – whether national or local – has significantly changed, which is why Media Secretary State Jeremy Hunt's dream of a national local television network doesn't quite add up. Why go down a traditional route to deliver a local news service through local television when there are a multitude of ways to serve the needs of the audience and when there is a new generation of digitally-savvy people who can find new ways of interacting with communities at a low cost? We'll come back to this later.

Jeremy Hunt's solution would seem, on the face of it, to be one dimensional, costly and difficult to execute and his idea has not exactly won accolades from the leading media commentators.

Steve Hewlett commented: "Wherever he goes in the country Jeremy Hunt finds enthusiastic people keen to develop local TV for their communities, towns and cities. And with the availability of relatively cheap kit and internet distribution, lots of them are already doing it. But whether any of them will ever achieve the scale and impact – or commercial viability – necessary to supersede the old, declining ITV services, provide much-needed competition for the BBC, and play the key role in local democracy Jeremy Hunt envisages must at best seem doubtful."[8]

Cost is a major concern for commentator Maggie Brown, who focused on the creation of a single supplier – Muxco - in a Media Guardian piece, and highlighted the complaints of a group of 40 interested parties who put their signatures to a letter critical of the proposals.

"They are asking for a rethink of a critical element of Jeremy Hunt's local TV plan, the method of organising the transmission, via licences for small pockets of digital terrestrial spectrum," wrote Brown. "Under the plans now advanced by Ofcom, the public subsidy of £25m, to be taken from the BBC licence fee, will be handed over to a single supplier, Muxco, without the new operators getting their hands on it."

She pointed out that the engineering costs of creating local TV services in big urban areas such as London are expected to absorb a lion's share of the funding. Costs are critical, Brown explained, since the aim is to bring the costs of running of a local TV station down to that of a small newspaper. The signatories, she said, were deeply concerned that local TV policy was being disproportionately influenced by the interests of big business.[9]

So how could Jeremy Hunt's dream to deliver relevant local news to communities be turned into a reality – both economically and editorially?

A student revolution

At the University of Sheffield, the journalism faculty, supported by us, has been working on a concept called *The Sheffield Record*. The intention is that there would be a multi-media service that would produce factual reportage about the city of Sheffield and cover areas and issues that are currently neglected by the mainstream media and their local news provision (particularly council, court, education, health and lifestyle reporting).

The *Record* would use material that the Department of Journalism Studies' students gather during their course work or in their own time. This material would be derived from all aspects of life in Sheffield, it would be edited and sub-edited by professional reporter(s) to the highest standards and then made available to everyone in Sheffield.

It is not proposed that *The Sheffield Record* be a student views paper, or a simply a hyperlocal news and gossip platform, or a 'ranters' platform. It is work in progress and would change and develop over time as different possibilities are pursued and accepted or rejected.

The concept is an attempt to both redesign and rethink local news provision and to play a clearly-needed civic role.

The *Sheffield Record* would be an outreach project designed to fit into the University's longstanding commitment to civic engagement and to serving and working with its local communities. It would connect with the community by covering little-reported but important daily issues, and is hoping to secure bi-lateral relationships with the City Council, South Yorkshire Police and the Crown Prosecution Service. It is currently investigating other bi-lateral arrangements with other potential stakeholders/funders but has had difficulty becoming operational because of lack of investment. There is clearly a need for Universities to be more commercially dynamic but this, of course, takes time.

The *Sheffield Record* would provide students with an ongoing opportunity to further practice the new skills required of multi-platform digital news journalists and to develop a portfolio of bylines that can act as an electronic CV.

Students would be given the opportunity to acquire editorial, business and enterprise skills, develop more real-time experience in newsgathering and production and the use of social media, and have input into the research, critique and development of local news journalism. All of which combined would help their transition into the job market and provide them with a competitive edge when seeking employment.

The *Sheffield Record* would provide an important platform for research into a diverse range of areas:

- the engagement of young people with local information flows and the local news media
- political engagement
- the role of the local in experiences of everyday life
- deliberative democracy
- changing perceptions of the role of the journalist as an agent within local affairs
- an incubator to develop new models of public service reportage for the digital era.
- a laboratory for the development of new business models and forms of online journalism.
- host vital research often neglected by the news industry
- oral histories of local journalists and local residents[10]

Spreading the word

There are some powerful arguments for this approach and there is no reason why it shouldn't be applied – using core principles – across many of the hundred or so universities across the country that run relevant media courses.

To reiterate, the local media model for newspapers and television has become unsustainable and is undergoing significant structural change because of the growth the internet. The failure of the model is exacerbated by a number of factors: the cost of generating content; the speed of the internet – instant publishing; free content, available immediately; the decline of local advertising revenue and the decline of regional television as a result of audience fragmentation.

As a result, traditional media organisations are facing structural change driven mainly by the expansion of the internet. The old media business is based on resourcing expensive content by means of a professional and unproductive workforce. The position of these traditional content providers is undermined by the speed and instantaneous delivery of on-line content.

And the traditional content provider is also disadvantaged because, while it depends on paying extravagantly for its content, the on-line supplier almost always gets content from free sources. So much so that the online audience expects to receive even high-grade content, particularly news content, for free.

Local content is the life-blood of any community. Communities cannot function without a continuous and free flow of information, from the most trivial gossip to the vital piece of information about chemist opening hours and the occasional major crime or political scandal. For a local media business the good news is that Google, Yahoo and AOL are unlikely to set up in cities around the UK to supply such content. The bad news is that traditional local news organisations are failing to reform their model to exploit their local content monopoly.

Publishers are attempting to meet these challenges through structural change leading to a reduction in services and significant job losses.

But the solution can only be the introduction of a new model for local media.

We obviously share Jeremy Hunt's desire to ensure that local media is reinvigorated. It is a crucial ingredient for democracy because it enables people to make informed judgments about their community; it provides cohesion and a sense of place and it gives them essential background on everything from council activity and court judgments to the latest road works.

The Business Strategy

Our proposal is to establish a network of local media operations providing information online by utilising the student journalists at universities across the country.

The stories generated by the students would be supplemented from free and contributed sources and the overall editorial control exerted by senior journalists or content managers. Each university would be part of a network working to the same editorial guidelines and adopting the pioneering model cited earlier in this paper.

Universities would raise revenue for their online publications through advertising and sponsorship and include the practical experience of working on the new media publication as part of the journalism course curricula.

In addition, local councils would be able to utilise the sites to provide information to the community and make significant savings. Public service information from the police, hospitals and schools could be disseminated through the local publication. Contributions would be accepted from members of the community, creating an ongoing dialogue, and local businesses would be able to promote their activities through advertising, online links and dedicated pages clearly labeled as partial material.

We would expect local companies and other organizations to want to be associated with these new local media sites because they would appeal to their community and civic pride. It would echo the motivation of the original founders of the regional press.

Once a network has been established, then further revenue could be generated through national advertising sales. The result would be a rich and comprehensive service bringing together all strands of local content from information to news, from culture to sport, from business to social networks, with a cost that is a fraction of traditional media.

The pioneering model

By going down this route, everyone is a winner. Universities would be able to advertise attractive courses that would equip students for immediate employment and they, in turn, would have the opportunity to practise further the new skill-sets required of multi-platform digital news.

The community would benefit from its news supply, ability to be engaged in a discourse with other citizens and to be trained in communication skills. Local Councils would be able to use the university sites for marketing and information services instead of employing expensive media specialists and publications.

Public service information, including police, hospitals and schools could be disseminated through the sites and local businesses would be able to promote their products and services.

Most importantly, students would be able to acquire editorial, business and enterprise skills. They would get more real time experience in newsgathering and production and in the use of social media. Also, crucially, they could be involved in the research, critique and development of local news journalism.

Universities who adopt this model would give students a competitive edge when seeking employment. Students would be involved in oral histories of local journalists and local residents. They would be part of political engagement and deliberative democracy, the changing perceptions of the role of the journalist as an agent within local affairs and the investigation of how new models of public service reportage for the digital era can be improved.

Universities would be able to act as incubators to develop new models of public service reportage for the digital era and act as an attempt to both redesign and rethink local news provision with both a civic role and a – clearly needed – civic place.

Sheffield is one of a number of Universities who are taking this experimental course. Lincoln University has an excellent community website. Coventry University is examining ways of making local provision and the University of Westminster in Harrow has taken steps along the ultra local route. All of these Universities have excellent facilities for news production.

Let's leave the last few words to Alex Connock, who has launched a TV/online formats company called Pretend and is a visiting fellow at Oxford University's Reuters Institute. Writing in the Royal Television Society's Television magazine he said the media elite should check out the strides that wired universities are making or risk being left behind.

"Visit Salford's classy new facility on the BBC campus at MediaCity or the HD studios at Sunderland or Middlesborough or Bournemouth's amazing all-digital studio – and be surprised how high-spec they are," he said.

What Connock found interesting was how far down the road the students, and the colleges, were already. "Of 200 students none had not been on Facebook in the past day. Most said they had watched TV the night before while also on their laptop...I requested that anyone who wanted to send ideas should tweet me and gained over 100 Twitter followers during the class."

He added: "Universities have a challenge with recession and tuition fees: to provide a useful service, and turn their recruits (or 'customers') into employees within six months of exit, which is the pointlessly early stage at which official figures are measured. That means teaching to self-start and re-writing the statistical rules so that those entrepreneurially self-employed in TV production start-ups are marked 'employed' and not as they are now, 'unemployed'".

Connock concludes by saying: "If you haven't visited a university this year, your country needs you."[11]

We agree, and we also believe our country needs the universities as the stimulus to drive a new era in local media which, at a sensible and realistic cost, can inspire and deliver a new breed of journalists equipped to work in the ever changing world of communication and help to deliver Jeremy Hunt's dream.

Notes

[1] Molly Ivins column *The Free Press*, 23 March, 2006, availabe at: http://freepress.org/columns/display/1/2006/1338, accessed January 11, 2012

[2] Is America at a Digital Turning Point? USC Anenberg School, available at: http://annenberg.usc.edu/News%20and%20Events/News/111214CDF.aspx , accessed 13 February 2012

[3] Can 1,400 Dailies Die in Five Years? Yes, *Newspaper Death Watch*, available at: http://newspaperdeathwatch.com/can-1400-dailies-die-in-5-years-yes/ - accessed 20 December, 2011

[4] *New York Times* gains confidence in digital, Newspaper Deathwatch Available at: http://newspaperdeathwatch.com/ny-times-gains-confidence-in-digital/

[5] Circulation of national newspapers. *Press Gazette*, September, 2011. www.pressgazette.co.uk accessed January 6, 2012

[6] *Social Media Today*, PR, Communications and Marketing Trends 2012, Part 1. www.socialmediatoday.com/mynewsdesk accessed 6 January, 2012

[7] *Huffington Post* targets global expansion, Financial Times, 4 January, 2012, available at: http://www.ft.com/cms/s/0/e04d1a74-2d8d-11e1-b985-00144feabdc0.html#axzz1mHGrLvId, accessed 6 January 2012

[8] Steve Hewlett, *The Guardian*, August 21st, 2011, www.guardian.co.uk/politics/2011/aug/21/local-tv-jeremy-hunt-big-vision accessed 20 December 20, 2011

[9] Maggie Brown, *The Guardian*, October 21st, 2011, www.guardian.co.uk/media/2011/oct/jeremy-hunt-local-tv, accessed 20 December, 2011

[10] *Sheffield Record* overview document

[11] Royal Television Society magazine, *Television*, October, 2011. 'Our Friend in the North' column

Notes on the authors

Paul Potts is the visiting professor of journalism at the dept of journalism studies, Sheffield University. He was formerly Chief Executive of the PA media group and editor in chief of the Press Association. He is currently a member of the board of Channel 4 and a specialist adviser to the joint Parliamentary Committee on Privacy and Injunctions. In 2008 he was awarded the CBE for his services to journalism

Richard Peel is the managing director of RPPR. He has held Corporate Affairs Directorships and other key communication roles at the Independent Television Commission, the England and Wales Cricket Board, Camelot and BBC News. Richard is a fellow of the Royal Television Society. He started his career in communication as a journalist on the *Northampton Chronicle and Echo*.

Local news is dead, long live local news

Barnie Choudhury makes the case for innovative thinking in the face of cuts that could otherwise signal the beginning of the end for local broadcast news.

On 23 May 1980 Coventry and Warwickshire got their very own local radio station. It was called Mercia Sound. I remember it because I was 15 years old and it was *the* most exciting news event to happen in my city for what seemed like decades. Local news, if you could call it that, was transmitted from Birmingham – a city that may have been only 20-odd miles away but in news terms could have been in, say, Birmingham, Alabama.

I didn't know it at the time, but Mercia would later provide me with my first real foray into professional broadcasting. Jim Lee, now at Radio 4 and Radio 4 Extra, mentored me to success, and my experiences helped me become a BBC Local Radio Trainee, along with other luminaries such as Sian Williams, Clive Myrie and Carolyn Quinn.

A decade after Mercia Sound's launch, in January 1990, the BBC opened CWR [Coventry & Warwickshire Radio]. It was a proud moment for me because I was part of the launch team. Five years later it was closed down...only to be re-opened again in September 2005. Today, it's once again facing cuts under the BBC's Delivering Quality First Agenda.[1]

Meanwhile Mercia Sound has moved away from Coventry...to, erm, Birmingham.

By 2016-17 Local Radio will have its budget cut by £5.3 million. During my eight years in BBC Local Radio, it had already been pared to the bone. Now bosses have started to hack off limbs.

Plus ça change, plus c'est la même chose.

Read DQF, as it's known, and the repercussions are set out in black and white. More shows will be shared between neighbouring local radio stations yet, at the same time, they'll be expected to work more closely with Five Live. The implication is that BBC Local Radio will be doing a lot more for a lot less and that can only be done if the most expensive part of any radio station – news content – is cut.

As for Independent Local Radio…well with all the mergers, we can forget the very notion of local radio for the independent sector.

The price of a cup of coffee
In broadcast terms, the fate of local news is inextricably linked to the survival of local radio. When ever I bang on about diversity, I always remember that I need to make a business case for selling the desire in all of us to be fair and equal regardless of race, religion, disability, gender, sexual orientation, social class or age. To think that I need to justify equality is rather shameful.

It feels the same when fighting to save local news.

So let's make the business case. The price for this wonderful facility is quite cheap when it comes to the BBC's English Regions: £2.83 per listener (Plunkett 2011). So it costs the price of a small cup of coffee for every listener for BBC bosses to fund local radio stations.

But the *real* business case to save local news can be summed up in one simple phrase: local accountability, local democracy and local engagement. Here's how one BBC insider described it to me:

"The cuts will undermine the service Local Radio provides to the broader BBC news machine in terms of newsgathering. It will also limit its ability to hold local and regional decision makers to account, and represent local views and perspectives to those in positions of power. This is an increasingly important role as many local paper newsrooms have shrunk in recent years."

When we think about local accountability there are few better examples than Radio Nottingham's Andy Whittaker taking on the formidable leader of Nottinghamshire County Council, Kay Cutts. When she refused to answer his questions on his breakfast show in 2010, Andy shut her microphone. He made the brave decision to do this on behalf of his listener. This is also the radio station which put people power on top of its agenda with its Big Night Out campaign[2]. The idea of this yearly event is to reclaim the streets from the killers who ran riot several years ago. The high profile murders meant that for a while the city was dubbed 'Shottingham'.[3]

BBC Radio Leeds concentrated recently on "citizenship, local democracy and outreach". Its programmes with Bradford Community Broadcasting show how public money can be used to give invisible and visible minorities a local voice. Anyone who heard Liz Green's programmes on Auschwitz, with Fabian Hamilton MP and students from Leeds, would have been moved to tears[4]. History matters in news; it adds context by reminding us where we've been, where we are and where we're heading. Twenty percent cuts to its budget will mean these types of projects are nice-to-have rather than essential.

There remains loyalty and a real connection between local news and its audience. So much so that the courageous staff of BBC Radio Merseyside penned a letter to the BBC's in-house magazine, *Ariel*[5]. They pointed out how local radio primarily served:

"C2/D/Es – i.e. the poor, the working class, the elderly and, largely, those living away from the South East."

They described the BBC's defence of the cuts as a fraud:

"When the BBC diminishes that with words like regional or national it perpetrates a not very clever fraud upon our listeners who want and expect BBC to reflect their lives, their communities, their voice, where they live."

In a way bosses, BBC and independents know that there's very little hue and cry for the minnows of broadcasting, until it's too late and the decision's been made. The satirical novelist, Joseph Heller, is attributed as saying:

"In democracy you get the government you deserve. Alternately you deserve the government you got."

By diminishing local news we will get the local democracy we deserve.

The Jeremy Hunt Solution:

Only two things stop something from ever succeeding in business: politics and money. But saving local news is an idea which has come of age. I say that because it's been on the mind of the current Secretary of State for Culture Media and Sport long before the last General Election. When I spoke to him a year before the May 2010 elections about Community Radio, Jeremy Hunt's message was clear:

"Barnie, it's local TV that you should be concentrating on; look to the European and American models."

And in office, Jeremy Hunt has been as good as his word (Sweney 2011). During one of his road shows which I attended, Mr Hunt was evangelical about promoting local TV. He tackled questions head-on and did not obfuscate. His case centred on local television being at the heart of local democracy and local accountability. His vision was that local television would have MP-candidates' debates based along the same lines as the Prime Ministerial debates during the last election. Yes, he's now dropped plans for a national network "spine" because it's too expensive a start-up cost (Halliday 2011). But he has never veered from his theory that local television stations will need £500,000 per year, with a one-hour per day local news output and £10,000 advertising revenue per week. Neither has he shied away from insisting that the BBC give up £25m of its Licence Fee in 2013-14 and £5m every year after for a further three years to help local TV with local content. We already know the twenty areas where the first tranche of local TV will appear.[6]

I have every admiration for Mr Hunt, despite his dreadful Hillsborough gaffe (Walker 2010), because he has dared to push through something he believes in. The Minister is, in this respect, a conviction politician and I don't think there are many of them about. Now, he may have been in publishing but even he realises that in broadcasting terms he's a novice. And here's Mr Hunt's saving grace: he admits that he can't be too prescriptive. I applaud this, because no one-size-model fits all. One weakness is advertising revenue. I cannot believe that in this age of economic cutbacks, a local television station will get anywhere near £500,000 in advertising earnings a year.

Hard-headed businesses will be asking local TV stations: "Show us your reach, market share and penetration". At least, that's what I'd expect if I were spending, say, £1,000 per week on advertising. Not only that, I'd be asking what's in it for me because I'm not entirely convinced local TV will take off or be as popular as politicians like to believe.

It's the Economy Stupid:

Local TV is nothing new in the UK. Jim Lee, remembers an experiment in Coventry which started in 1985:

"It was a joint exercise with Mercia providing the journalism for Coventry Cable TV. When a Mercia reporter went out on a job, the Uher [tape recorder] would be plugged into the camera. At end of job they'd go their separate ways and treat the material accordingly. There was a Mercia person attached to Coventry Cable as news editor. Every evening presenters, like me, would go down to present a Midlands Today type programme live using all the material collected by and with Mercia during the day. It was pretty raw stuff at times but was the first set up of its kind ever. It only lasted a few years as it obviously was costly and generated little or no income apart from a little bit of local advertising."

And generating income is the biggest problem, as others have found to their cost. In 2007, Solent TV, based on the Isle of Wight, provided wonderful local television news. But it had to close after five years. Finally, even on the internet, Kent's experiment with local IPTV failed. It was an online service funded by Kent County Council for two years and ended on 31 March 2010. The words used by an unnamed journalism student reporting its demise seems somewhat prophetic:

"The closure represents a very sad admission that online only community TV channels are not a viable business proposition."[7]

No, local TV needs a sustainable business plan, and foresight enough to realise that it won't make you money. It is a public service and needs funding in other ways.

Television news, like all TV, has to be based on the premise of "an appointment to watch". That's because we lead such busy lives, we have so many distractions and we have numerous ways of getting our news, that sitting in front of a television screen every evening is a big ask.

Yet if you want influence then you can do no better than local TV – or so says an American study. Gillam's and Iyengar's 2000 study suggested that crime coverage by US local TV "heightens negative attitudes of African-Americans among white, but not black, viewers" (Gillam and Iyengar 2000). Their reasoning is set out in the first sentence of their American Journal of Political Science paper:

"Local television news is America's principal window on the world."

It's a sentence that also highlights Jeremy Hunt's error. The UK is not the same as the US. Local television news is NOT Britain's principal window on the world. We're not only separated by water and language; we're also separated by culture. America has a culture of Breakfast *TV* shows whose audiences are fought over tooth and nail. Ratings are king.

If anything, in Britain, it's the *radio* breakfast presenters who're the most well known and deliver the biggest audiences.

We get our news from several sources and I'd suggest that increasingly we've turned to the Net to find what interests us. In other words, our news running order depends on our interests rather than those of a newspaper or broadcast editor

Higher Education rides to the rescue?
The paradox is quite simple: if the content isn't there then we, society, won't be able to access it. And this is the beauty of my suggestion. If we accept that local TV news is a public service rather than a core business, then there is a glimmer of hope.

My argument is that seriously local content – possibly hyperlocal, with a high quality threshold – can be delivered by Higher Education institutions. I'm not alone. The Broadcast Journalism Training Council's Steve Harris has formed CULT, Colleges and Universities for Local Television. And just look at the signatories on an open letter to the Secretary of State sent in October 2011.

I have to declare an interest because I'd like a local TV station to be based at the University of Lincoln.

My argument is that every university or college with a journalism course should be able to find enough volunteers to provide a local news service. The quality threshold will be maintained because their tutors are all former or current practitioners. The news team can find local stories. As their reputations grow, as test runs are done, as low-cost marketing campaign are run, people will begin ringing in with stories. Now these stories would NOT find themselves on regional television but are perfect for local TV because of their local interest.

For example, the opening of a new science block at a school may not be regional television. But what if the guest of honour is Professor Brian Cox? A school sports' day happens every year. But what if Dame Kelly Holmes could be persuaded to attend? The local secondary school has an old pupil back. Not really newsworthy, is it? But what if that former alumnus was the Hollywood star, Clive Owen? I'd argue that each is the stuff of local television but, depending on the news day, it may not make it as a full item on *regional* television.

Universities are also, in my view, a perfect place to find stories. Every department has an expert in something, doing some interesting research in something, attracting someone with a worldwide reputation. I'm talking art, fashion, entertainment, performance as well as the panoply of other subjects. Isn't a university a perfect place to hold local chiefs accountable? The University of Sheffield appears to have begun its experiment with local news with Forge TV.

So where might the money come from to turn this into a reality? The University is part of the city's local consortium bid to produce local TV. The only danger is over a conflict of interest. If the local council is part of the consortium, then broadcasters need to ensure complete impartiality and ensure there is no undue influence when investigating controversial stories.

That said, with the proper funding my idea would be to have a local version of *Question Time* and *Hardtalk* every week, holding people to account, as well as having local people contributing local content. Even though colleges and universities are content rich, like BBC 3 and BBC 4, there would have to be repeats. To bring in extra revenue, stations would have to sell off-air space.

Just like local radio, I'd expect local TV to be the nursery slope for wannabe broadcasters. My guess is that listeners are more likely to know the presenters on their local radio station than name the politicians in the Cabinet. And so it will be with local TV, I suspect. The era of the citizen journalist and hyperlocal news is now and has been promoted and discussed widely. Let's not forget that every college and university should have as its remit a mission to engage with its community. So, as part of their submission to the Department of Culture, Media and Sport, they should provide evidence of how they intend to truly engage with their local citizens.

It's the community, stupid

Another solution neatly presents itself: community radio stations. If Frank Gillard, the founding father of BBC local radio were alive today he'd probably wince. For all its efforts, local radio isn't really that local. For example how local can you be in London? What have the people in Manchester got in common with the folk of Glossop? How can Hertfordshire, Bedfordshire and Buckinghamshire ever be considered to be served by one local radio station? The case for "hyperlocal radio" has never been stronger.

Most community radio stations come under the umbrella of the Community Media Association [CMA]. According to its new Chairman, Andrew David, there are more than 200 licences, and more than 170 stations actually on air. David runs Siren FM, based in the heart of the University of Lincoln, and partly funded by the institution. He doesn't think that local news should be in the hands of one supplier. He argues that this would lead to bias and he's right. News needs to be competitive, but in the absence of a news source my fear is that we will end up with PR and propaganda – the mirage of news. David acknowledges that, once again, resources are the major factor when it comes to providing local news:

"Community Radio is very healthy in terms of volunteer commitment and enthusiasm but struggling in the area of funding. But for Siren, localness and local news are absolutely fundamental to what the station's about."

A Welsh community radio station, Afan FM, closed recently and there were some other casualties last year because of a lack of funding. Yet because Community Radio is SO cost efficient and cost effective it makes a great deal of sense in this harsh economic climate. Politicians have begun to take an interest in Community Radio and the CMA has secured Culture Minister Ed Vaizey as its keynote speaker at its Annual General Meeting in June 2012 in Bath. If HE institutions understood the power and relevance of community radio on its campuses, the way it trains students to become more employable and ultimately become a tool for engagement and retentions, then more would adopt the Siren model of localness.

The Love of Inertia

The philosopher and soap salesman, Elbert Hubbard, got it right when he said:

"The reason men oppose progress is not that they hate progress, but that they love inertia."

It was progress when Samuel Pepys started to write in Shelton's shorthand. It was progress when 8MK in Detroit, Michigan broadcast the 1920 US Elections. It was progress when Richard Baker read his first television news script on the 5th July 1954. At the time the then BBC Director-General, Sir Ian Jacob, said:

"News is not at all an easy thing to do on television. A good many of the main news items are not easily made visual - therefore we have the problem of giving news with the same standards that the corporation has built up in sound...

"This is a start on something we regard as extremely significant for the future."

There is something precious about local news. Its demise in all forms is forever predicted. We would be the poorer for it. Local news is where every story begins. If we accept the fact that people make stories then it's axiomatic that ordinary local people have extraordinary tales to tell. As journalists we are nothing more than storytellers and all the while we remain such, then local news will always find an audience. So it must be allowed, and helped, to survive. It's only inertia and a failure of our imaginations that are stopping us from finding a way to make this happen.

References

Plunkett, John (2011) BBC local radio stations gain more than 250,000 listeners, The Guardian 27 October 2011. Available online at
http://www.guardian.co.uk/media/2011/oct/27/bbc-local-radio-stations-gain-listeners?newsfeed=true accessed 12 January 2012

Halliday, Josh (2011) Jeremy Hunt defends decision to ditch national network for local TV services. Guardian online, Wednesday 14 September 2011; available at
http://www.guardian.co.uk/media/2011/sep/14/jeremy-hunt-national-tv-network - accessed 18 January 2012

Gillam, FD and Iyndgar, S. (2000) Prime Suspects: The Influence of Local Television News on the Viewing Public; American Journal of Political Science, Vol 44, No 3. Aviailable online at http://www.unc.edu/~fbaum/teaching/POLI891_Sp11/articles/Gilliam_Iyengar_AJP S_2000.pdf - accessed 18 January 2012

Walker, Tim (2010). Jeremy Hunt: Rough ride for the smooth operator, The Independent, Saturday 3 July 2010; available online at: http://www.independent.co.uk/news/people/profiles/jeremy-hunt-rough-ride-for-the-smooth-operator-2017277.html - accessed 18 January 2012

Sweney, Mark (2011)Jeremy Hunt unveils plan for new national television channel, Guardian Online, Wednesday 19 January 2011; Available online at: http://www.guardian.co.uk/media/2011/jan/19/jeremy-hunt-new-television-channel accessed 18th January 2012

Notes

[1] Delivering Quality First http://www.bbc.co.uk/aboutthebbc/insidethebbc/howwework/reports/deliveringqualityfirst.html - accessed 15th January 2012

[2] Big Night Out http://www.bbc.co.uk/nottingham/content/articles/2009/06/29/big_night_out_feature.shtml - accessed 15th January 2012

[3] Gun Crime http://www.bbc.co.uk/insideout/eastmidlands/series7/gun_crime.shtml - accessed 15th January 2012

[4] Auschwitz: BBC Film project; http://www.leedsne.co.uk/auschwitz_bbc_film.htm - accessed 15th January 2012

[5] Latest Ariel Letters, 11th October 2011 http://www.bbc.co.uk/ariel/15257653 - accessed 13th January

[6] LOCAL TV: MAKING THE VISION HAPPEN published by the DCMS, December 2011. Available at: http://www.culture.gov.uk/images/consultation_responses/local-tv_making-the-vision-happen.pdf - accessed 18 January 2012

[7] Kent TV fails; http://tvsheffield.org/kenttv-fails/ - accessed 18th January 2012

Note on the author

Barnie Choudhury has been a broadcaster for more than thirty years and a BBC Correspondent for national television, radio and online. He has won several industry awards. He is a Principal Lecturer in journalism at the University of Lincoln where he leads the teaching television news production and long form film. His specialisms include racial diversity, home affairs and social affairs. Barnie runs his own production company where he makes radio features, television films and documentaries as well as training in effective presentations, leadership and media crisis management. He is a lay advisor for the Department of Health and is Chairman of AWAAZ, a South Asian mental health charity.

Can universities save local journalism?

David Hayward believes that universities hold the key to a brighter future for local journalism. But we need a more co-ordinated approach, and should look to the US for inspiration.

The Secretary of State for Culture Media and Sport (DCMS), Jeremy Hunt is advocating the greatest change in the local media landscape for a generation. His proposals for a network of local TV stations have been much debated since he outlined his vision at the Oxford Media Convention in 2011.

"For consumers, what this will mean is a new channel dedicated to the provision of local news and content........one that will sit alongside other public service broadcasters, offering a new voice for local communities with local perspectives that are directly relevant to them."

.........People in Barnham don't want to watch what is going on in Southampton. People in Helmsford aren't interested in what's happening in Watford. That is the system we currently have at the moment, so that is what we are trying to rethink."[1]

The plans are well underway, with the first 20 licences to be awarded in 2012. So is this the saviour of local media, or a costly white elephant, delivering a service on an out-of-date platform, to an audience which doesn't exist?

The first question is over money. Can local TV finance itself on the budget it's been given? There are serious concerns about this. Sir Nicholas Shott, the investment banker asked to look into the initial proposals, raised a number of points in his 2010 report.

"Local TV is unlikely to be viable if it is dependent on local advertising revenues alone. The agreement already in place with the BBC will be helpful in both providing an additional source of revenue and ensuring an adequate level of quality. In addition, the Government may need to help facilitate access to national advertising revenue through an existing agency that has a significant existing inventory – for example a national PSB. An underwritten national advertising contract of £15m per annum for at least the first three years will be required to have confidence in commercial viability"[2]

These concerns remain in 2012 as the BBC's Torin Douglas outlines:

216

"Jeremy Hunt has found it hard to convince established media companies that local TV is viable without Government funding - but groups in these 20 cities think it can be made to work.....Some set-up costs will be paid for out of the licence fee - £40m was earmarked for local TV in the latest settlement with the BBC....But beyond this, Mr Hunt has made it clear the services must be self-sustaining, funded by advertising."[3]

The second question is the method of delivery. At the moment the plans are to start broadcasting on Digital Terrestrial Television (DTT), with the channels having a prominent position on the Electronic Programme Guide (EPG). There are again many concerns about this; the cost of set up and broadcasting, the quality needed to compete with other channels and the onset of Internet Protocol Television (IPTV). Almost all commentators believe IPTV can be part of the future for local TV, but at the moment are there enough people watching this platform to make it viable?

I have some experience of setting up just this type of service. I helped to run the BBC Local TV pilot in the West Midlands in 2005/2006.

Six TV stations were established; in Birmingham, Herefordshire and Worcestershire, Staffordshire, Shropshire, Coventry and Warwickshire and the Black Country. We put a team of video-journalists and content producers into each local BBC radio station in the region. They were an integral part of the news team, producing video content for the local area. We broadcast on two platforms; online and on digital satellite.

One of the things we realised at a very early stage was the future was not on satellite, it was online.

Many of the problems we faced were tied into producing the daily news bulletins for the satellite loop. It was far from ideal. We had the six stations on a continuous, hour long loop. Each service had to provide a news bulletin every day of exactly ten minutes. This caused obvious problems. Sometimes there was too much news, sometimes too little; either way it rarely fitted into the prescribed ten minute slot. It also meant the audience had to tune in at a specific time to watch their news. They wanted it on demand, when they wanted to watch, not when we decided to broadcast.

The simple fact was the content we produced - local, interactive material - fitted more elegantly as a multimedia, online offering, which people could read, see and listen to when it suited them.

There is still a great deal the current bids for local TV can learn from the BBC pilot.

Central to the idea is the need for a strong robust local media, holding power to account, acting as a genuine local fourth estate. BBC local radio and local and regional papers continue to do this largely, but it does need to be supported. The effect of falling revenues and tighter budgets inevitably mean the traditional forms of local journalism are under pressure.

The local TV pilot added another level to local news coverage. It was new, exciting and did a fantastic job. News was at the heart of everything we did and we made it a key point to cover local politics on TV to a greater extent than the BBC had done before.

On the night of the May council elections in 2006, we had reporters at every count, reporting on all the stories as they came in. Because of the format we were able to react to stories, and get them on air faster and more effectively than traditional TV. We had the freedom to put content on air and online around the clock, providing the audience with the very latest news in a multimedia format.

We didn't have the constraints faced by existing TV teams. We didn't have to work towards a deadline or bulletin. People were able to access our output 24 hours a day seven days a week.

On the night of the elections we were able to put the first video report online just after 1am, five-and-a-half hours before the first *Midlands Today* bulletin. By 6am we had a full roundup of the main events of the election, and reports from every count in the region. This was a comprehensive service which couldn't have been done before and hasn't been done since. For the first time BBC TV was able to report on the most important events at the grassroots of local democracy. And there was a demand for this service too. That night we recorded the highest audience figures of the pilot, evidence there was a need and demand.

As well as championing local democracy, media literacy was a key focus. Each service had a content producer. It was their job to work with local communities, allowing new voices the chance to be heard. By the end of the project they were producing a quarter of the output. This was an ambitious target, but one that was achieved. It gave under-served communities access to the BBC and a far wider audience.

All of this is central to the ethos behind the current push for local TV; media literacy, connecting communities, serving local audiences in a digital age, and the scrutiny of local democracy.

The pilot proved to be just that, a pilot project. For a number of reasons it wasn't pursued by the BBC. It became the focus of a well orchestrated campaign by the local and regional papers and other media organisations. They claimed the BBC was encroaching on their fast-decreasing market. The area of local, multimedia news online was their future and they didn't want the BBC parking its metaphorical tanks on their lawns.

After a long period of consultation and analysis, the BBC Trust decided not to go ahead.

Six and a half years after the pilot began we are still to see a comprehensive network providing high quality, multimedia coverage of local news.

Obviously if the plans outlined by Jeremy Hunt can be funded and run appropriately this will meet the need. But are we missing an opportunity to create a plural local media using expertise, talent and resources which already exist?

Journalism schools at Universities across the country are already working - albeit individually and on a relatively small scale - with local blogs and communities. Staff and students at Newcastle University help run Jesmondlocal

"*While most hyperlocal services are run by enthusiastic amateurs, JesmondLoca is edited by Ian Wylie, a professional journalist with more than 20 years' experience in national newspapers and magazines, supported by journalism students from Newcastle University and local "citizen reporters" from the Jesmond community.*"[4]

Students and staff at Goldsmiths' College, University of London have been running EastLondonLines since 2009.

The University of Huddersfield's journalism department at its Oldham Campus has just taken over running the widely-renowned *Saddleworth News*. This is the handover blog by its creator Richard Jones. (See also Section B of this book, page 154)

"I announced a few weeks ago that Saddleworth News was going to become part of the Digital Journalism course at University Campus Oldham, part of the University of Huddersfield. Well, it's now time for the handover to take place.

Articles by the students will begin to appear here in the coming days and weeks. I hope you'll show them the same courtesy and encouragement that you've shown me!'[5]

Blog Preston was set up by a student at the University of Central Lancashire, and is a fantastic illustration of how local blogs can evolve and live longer than the passion of one person.

"It is owned by Ed Walker, who now lives and works in London. It was edited between January 2010 – May 2010 by Lisa McManus. It was edited by Andy Halls and Joseph Stashko between May 2010 and May 2011.

Andy has now left Preston but Joseph keeps the Blog Preston flame burning. The editorial team currently consists of Ed Walker and Joseph Stashko.

Plus there are a whole host of guest bloggers, photographers and interested members of the community who contribute to the site."[6]

The community radio station Siren Radio operates in conjunction with the University of Lincoln, one of many such community radio stations in the UK.

"Siren FM is proud to be Lincoln's first community radio station and has been broadcasting since 11th August 2007. We aim to make radio accessible to all and especially those aged between 9 – 25 in the Lincoln area. We've developed a wide range of programmes and we broadcast something like 60 hours of locally produced material a week.

We have a full time licence from Ofcom and therefore we're a proper radio station broadcasting on 107.3 FM and sirenonline.co.uk

Although we're based at the University, who have provided some of the best studio facilities in the area, we are not a student radio station; we are very much a community station and our doors are open to all."[7]

Salford University is launching a multimedia local news service called *Quay News* and Grimsby TV, the longest running local TV station in the UK operates from studios at Grimsby College. There are many more examples, as well as the numerous student TV and radio stations at Universities and Colleges throughout the country.

The theory is nothing new. Many people have already seen the potential of linking up with Universities. Channel 6, the body bidding to run a number of the local TV services, announced a partnership with journalism schools in 2011.

"Channel 6 has signed agreements with Sunderland and Cardiff universities which could see their journalism students working on local TV services launched in the cities.

Under the deal, the universities' studios and production facilities could be used to create local TV programmes, while Channel 6 is also in talks with Skillset Media Academies about partnerships with more than 20 other colleges and universities."[8]

The examples and proof are there. University-supported local media can thrive, but to really work on a wide and sustainable level it needs to be done in a more concerted and co-ordinated manner. The plans by Channel 6 appear to be something close to this, but they rely on the structure of local TV set out by the DCMS, an expensive network of conventional TV channels.

Why does this network need that? Why is it not already being done?

We can take the lead, as so often in this field, from across the pond. I've long admired the way in which journalism schools in the United States have combined teaching, with practical and often groundbreaking journalism. Just look at the work of Jay Rosen at New York University and Emily Bell at Columbia University in New York.

Now journalism schools in the states are leading the way again, in local news. Like the examples I've mentioned above there are already close links between the journalism schools in the states and local news organisations. But unlike the UK there is a concerted and financially supported attempt to do this in a more structured way.

A report by the New America Foundation has called for Journalism Schools in the States to fill the void of local news by engaging with the communities which already exist, to provide a new form of news and information. It sets out the ways this can be done and how it can be properly resourced and funded.

"1. Journalism education programs at universities and colleges should increase coverage of local communities outside the university or college in conjunction with local media.
2. The media industry should make a stronger financial commitment to supporting innovative thinking, research, and curriculum development in the journalism field;
3. Local community foundations should engage by providing funds to support community media outlets through journalism programs; and
4. The federal government should consider the myriad of ways, both monetary and policy-wise, that it can encourage journalism programs to take on this

role especially through grants from Corporation for Public Broadcasting to support journalism schools producing local content.....["]9

So why is this approach happening in the states and not here? Martin Moore of the Media Standards Trust thinks it's down to a different, more innovative and imaginative attitude to local news. He believes US local news is leagues ahead of the UK, due to a traditional of experimentation there and conservatism here.

He cites a number of examples, including the work of the respective universities.

"Role of universities in hothousing and nourishing start-ups.....

Many US universities have, for many years, published highly professional local newspapers and news outlets. This has broadened and deepened since the crisis in local news kicked in. Some college news outlets, like the University of Miami's Grand Avenue News, have formed partnerships with commercial newspapers (in this case the Miami Herald). Some have developed news outlets and then sold them off to outside news companies (as with Montana University's Dutton County Courier to the Choteau Acantha newspaper). Others have won awards for their investigative journalism (like ChicagoTalks.org from Chicago's Columbia College). All these examples are taken from J-Lab's excellent research on What Works. There are many more."

Introverted universities

Similarly, though most universities have a university newspaper (and sometimes more than one), most of these are for and about the university, rather than for the wider community. Nor have many journalism departments sought to incubate, or launch, actual news startups. There are exceptions, of course. Goldsmiths' College in London launched eastlondonlines.co.uk, an independent news website serving Hackney, Tower Hamlets, Lewisham and Croydon. But there is nothing on the scale or ambition of media ventures at US universities."10

There have already been calls for universities save local media. Prof David Chittick of Lincoln University argued in 2009 that universities had a significant role to play. He said that with revenues falling at local newspapers, they had a duty to ensure that a strong local media survives by supporting them.

"We wouldn't want to fetter editorial. The danger is that the medium might disappear. It's not just a matter of influencing the local population, but ensuring that there is the ability to debate issues locally.

"We don't always have a good press, but it is absolutely crucial to have a local press."11

There's little doubt a strong, successful, vibrant and diverse local media can thrive in the UK. The examples are already there, shown by the success of a whole range of grassroots local blogs. (You can see the full spectrum on Paul Bradshaw's Online Journalism Blog.)12 But they need support and there is a fairly simple solution.

If you can combine hyperlocal blogs with journalism schools you can have a formidable network. Local blogs would get the means to add a whole new dimension to the local media landscape. Teams of student journalists, able to cover the local news online in text, video and audio. The most fantastic resources; cameras, editing facilities and studios and databases are available. Why not use them to become a key part of the local media, broadcasting to a far wider audience than classmates or the rest of the university?

As well as daily news, listings and information, live events could be covered; festivals, local sport and concerts streamed online. The opportunities are huge.

It would give students the invaluable experience of working in a real life news environment, a showcase for their material and the chance to put into practice what they're learning in the classroom.

There are hundreds of journalism and media courses at colleges across the UK with thousands of students, more than enough to create a sustainable service, in and out of term time. If you add this to existing services, local media's future could look very bright indeed.

Journalism continues to be at the heart of BBC local radio, even in the face of tighter budgets, there has been investment in local political reporters and plans to introduce chief news reporters. Albeit far reduced from its heyday, there remains a strong network of regional and local papers, providing news and journalism.

So with all of this potential, is there really a need for the government's vision of Local TV? Why risk tens of millions of pounds setting up expensive TV stations which may or may not have an audience?

We know that grassroots local journalism is working. Why not invest the money in services we know can work, creating a platform and network that people can easily access, where and when they want, using new technology to develop it on desktop, IPTV, mobiles and tablets, and making sure the content is relevant, questioning and of a high quality?

By using the skills, enthusiasm and resources already there, surely that vibrant, strong, plural local media can emerge with Universities playing a central role.

References

[1] Jeremy Hunt, speaking at the Oxford Media Convention, January 2011

[2] Commercially Viable Local Television in the UK, A review by Nicholas Shott for the Secretary of State for Culture Media and Sport

[3] Ofcom earmarks 20 local TV stations, BBC News Website. Available at: http://www.bbc.co.uk/news/entertainment-arts-16157352, accessed February 10 2012

[4] http://jesmondlocal.com/

[5] From The (Old) Editor: *Saddleworth News* Under New Management, Saddleworth News, 10 October 2011, http://www.saddleworthnews.com/?p=11284 accessed February 10 2012

[6] http://blogpreston.co.uk/

[7] http://www.sirenonline.co.uk/

[8] Two Universities join forces with local TV bidder, Holdthefrontpage. http://www.holdthefrontpage.co.uk/2011/news/two-universities-join-forces-with-local-tv-bidder/ Accessed February 10 2012

[9] Knight Foundation report, 28th October 2011, Journalism Schools Must Fill the Void For Local Communities

[10] Martin Moore, Media Standards Trust, 4th February 2011, US Local News Experiments Leagues Ahead Of The UK

[11] Universities must fight for local newspapers, *The Guardian*, 3 April 2009. Available at: http://www.guardian.co.uk/education/2009/apr/03/universities-must-save-local-newspapers, accessed 10 February 2012

[12] http://onlinejournalismblog.com/?s=hyperlocal+voices

Note on the author

David Hayward runs the BBC College of Journalism's Journalism Programme, a series of events, masterclasses, debates and discussions on all issues surrounding journalism. He has spent 17 years working as a journalist at the BBC, beginning his career at BBC Radio Leicester. He has since worked across the BBC as a reporting, presenter and editor in network radio, regional TV and for the BBC World Service Trust in eastern Europe.

Section D. The bigger picture: The death of local democracy?

John Mair

Local journalism in the UK and USA has faced and is facing the perfect storm of losing both audience and revenue simultaneously. It has not always coped well.

What of the future, how will it face that? Will it ever bounce back or will too many papers pass soon from the intensive care ward to the graveyard? In this section we attempt to answer some of those questions.

Has the rapid decline of the local press resulted in a diminution in local democracy? Are citizens being short changed through the decline in information available to them? We examine it from two sides. In one city, Coventry. Les Reid is the poacher, Fran Collingham the gamekeeper. He is the political editor of the *Coventry Telegraph* whose staff has more than halved in the last decade and which has shifted from evening to morning publication(despite what the signage outside its large and increasingly empty City Centre offices says) Circulation has still declined. He sees hope in journalism, in stories, in digging and in making waves. The 'Tele' can still do that sometimes. Fran Collingham is the Flack to his Hack – the provider or denier of those stories on behalf of Coventry City Council. She sees the local papers as the bulwark of local democracy, but the local papers defined broadly to now include new and social media. Twitter use during meetings caused a massive row in Coventry Council last year. How long before Coventry councillors set up a Facebook group to replace their face to face surgeries?

The English riots in the summer of 2011 were said to be at least inflamed by the use of one social media tool – the Blackberry Messenger service which rioters used to pass on information without the authorities being able to monitor them. Academics Ben McConville and Kate Smith argue that the current decline of local weekly and daily newspapers is having a negative impact on the political public sphere, skewing political discourse and democratic representation. Does less local media lead to less civic virtue and participation? Is public disorder such as the 2011 riots one of the symptoms of this?

So to the remedies .What is to be done to come out of this perfect storm in some form of order? Is the future still local? Yes: it's where everything begins says Lynne Anderson of the Newspaper Society. The irony in this changed market is that more people than ever are seeing local and regional news but, alas, not reading it on those chopped down trees with ink on them. News has moved from print to screens of various sorts.

Bob Satchwell is the 'editors' advocate' – he is Executive Director of the Society of Editors. He is paid to be optimisitic. The future may be tough, but it is not all gloomy he says. Reports of the death of local newspapers are seriously flawed. Times are very hard, he acknowledges, but believes they still have many years of life left in them. At least he hopes they have.

Finally, Neil Fowler, who spent a year in the Oxford cloisters thinking about the present and future of local journalism as the Guardian Research Fellow at Nuffield College in 2010-2011, argues for drastic and radical action. Long-term management failure has brought the local newspaper industry to edge of the precipice, he says. Now it's time not just for innovation – but for radical thinking, economically and politically. The way to the future may be back to the past and the rebirth of truly local 'paper'. We've seen the evidence of some of these on the streets or on screens in the thirty three contributions to this "hackademic' volume.

To be re-born, local journalism has to re-invent itself. It simply has no alternative.

A bad journalist regurgitates; a good journalist challenges

**There is still scope for the regional and local journalist to make waves.
Les Reid outlines his case.**

As a professional insider writing about the decline of local journalism in its imperfect role as the "fourth estate" holding power to account, a central question must be: Is there a case for the defence? Further, are there reasons for optimism?

I work as a multimedia political correspondent on a daily regional newspaper, covering local and national politics, and as a contributor to the British national "broadsheets". Now 20 years on from when I entered journalism, the view on the horizon is foggy, with more storms brewing after a fundamental sea change.

The great tsunami of course was a revolution in information technology from the mid-1990s, which no-one could have foreseen just a few years before, when I was a postgraduate journalism student at City University, London. As things transpired, I had unwittingly entered newspaper journalism in the dying embers of more than a century of press power fuelled by a mass-market for newspapers.

Seismic shifts

Even in the first years of the Internet, nobody seemed to anticipate just how seismic the technological shift would be. I remember in the mid-1990s when I was political correspondent at the *Coventry Telegraph* – a position to which I returned after working for London newspapers – how one computer stood in the corner where journalists could surf the "information superhighway". Not many bothered, as a cacophony of phones rang, journalists waded through piles of paper correspondence and agendas, and giant metal spikes stood dangerously on desks - the equivalent of the email "trash" bin.

Arguably, reality has only recently fully dawned on professional journalists, after rounds of staff cuts exacerbated by the late 2000s economic downturn further hitting advertising revenue. The industry's ongoing failure to identify how to make sufficient profit from the Internet to sustain already vastly reduced staffing levels signals more anxiety ahead. I do not doubt there will be more job cuts, and more lost local titles too.

But technological change must be embraced. With national newspaper groups like the Scott Trust running *The Guardian*, for which I am a contributor, shifting towards 80 per cent staffing levels on its website, the direction ahead is clear.

As long as local newspaper titles can survive as multi-media operations in some form, and if local media companies and individuals can operate in increasingly fragmented and diversified markets, the technology itself presents opportunities for good journalism, and cause for some optimism.

The need to survive

In 2012, it is clear to journalists working in traditional newspaper groups that websites offer the space for quality, depth and analysis increasingly unavailable in print – with declining pagination and editorial/advertising page ratios tipping in favour of the latter.

Whatever their flaws, it is crucial that media organisations with clout and trained journalists survive in communities. The alternative is a world of unchallenged PR-spun website information from public organisations and businesses, and the work of a volunteer army of "citizen journalists".

Where does all this leave local journalism's ability to perform a democratic function in holding power to account? The question has even more significance because of the current "hacking scandal" climate, with the Leveson inquiry set to introduce new forms of press regulation.

It is easy to forget that the 1990s when I entered journalism also witnessed a clash in the tense relationship between politics and journalism. Then Culture Secretary and Business Secretary David Mellor in John Major's Conservative government had announced the press was in the "last chance saloon". Step out of line again and it would lose the right to so-called "self-regulation". Yet the myth of self-regulation was highlighted by ex-cabinet minister Jonathan Aitken's use of the libel laws to counter-productively take on "the cancer of bent and twisted journalism" – even if in his case it was utterly counter-productive and landed him in jail.

Fighting old battles

Today, it seems to me there are some politicians across the mainstream political parties who are using "hacking" to fight an old battle against an old media. As I have stated in my newspaper columns and blogs for the *Coventry Telegraph*, "we are all publishers now". I have highlighted examples of how certain politicians, in writing for their blogs and social networking sites, do not practise what they preach by publishing corrections or apologies regarding their own inaccuracies and provable falsehoods – let alone by allowing a right of reply by authorising reply comments.

I have argued any serious attempt to strike a balance between the power of political institutions and the press, or between freedom of expression and protecting people's privacy, must address the wider use of digital media, not just the output of traditional newspaper organisations.

The vile instances of tabloid excess, a world away from what happens in the local press, must be addressed. Yet it seems some politicians are seizing the moment, with a press economically weakened by digital technology and the humbling of the Murdoch empire, to settle old scores and address what they see as a necessary rebalancing of power.

These are issues which local as well as national journalists as commentators must, and are, responding to and challenging. It provides one example of how the local press is not simply waving a white flag to economic difficulties and politicians' circling advance.

Journalistic writing in local and national newspapers on the issues raised by hacking/Leveson also serves as a poignant challenge to the modern notion that journalism has been replaced with ubiquitous "churnalism". The argument is made by national journalist Nick Davies in his book *Flat Earth News*, and is discussed at university journalism schools across the country. So-called churnalism uncritically regurgitates the messages, spin and propaganda from those in power, who we in the media are supposed to be holding to account.

In the 1990s as a postgraduate, academic discussions about newspaper practices centred on old neo-Marxist notions of the "ownership and control" model – that journalistic output could only be understood according to the will and political views of newspaper proprietors. Back then, it was also fashionable in the era of post-structuralism to examine how the language of newspapers allegedly subsumed a journalists' consciousness and concepts of "what is news?".

It soon became clear to me in experiencing regional newsrooms that, while both paradigms had their obvious merits, neither came close to explaining the autonomy, independence and intelligence of many ethical and educated hard-working journalists. That remains the case today, just as the concept of "churnalism" only takes us so far in understanding what actually happens in newsrooms.

Scrutinising roles

In a talk at Coventry University in 2012, I urged first-year journalism undergraduates to consider that, despite the economic challenges and pressure on staffing, they could decide if they wanted to be a good or bad journalist. A bad journalist regurgitates; a good journalist challenges.

In my view, many journalists in the local media remain serious about their scrutinising role. They know they are there to challenge what they are told. They know deadlines or staff shortages often require them to simply and quickly attribute views from all sides, however distorting that might be – just as you will hear any night on national BBC television and radio coverage. Yet, just as on the BBC, there remains much scope for local newspaper journalists to challenge, to comment, to criticise. Again, the good news is that the Internet offers a vast space to do so.

It offers, for example, far more space for journalistic comment and opinion through blogging than was ever possible in print. Journalists can use live blogs to put politicians on the spot in the run up to elections, or provide live coverage from public debates hosted by newspapers.

In recent months alone, I have posted on the *Coventry Telegraph's* website research-based critical audio or video interviews with not just local council leaders, but leading national Labour figures Ed Miliband and Chuka Umunna over their alternative plans for the economy; the then Lib Dem Energy and Climate Change Secretary Chris Huhne on the economy and environmental policy; and interviews with Tony Benn and ex-CBI president Sir Richard Lambert inviting comparisons between today's austerity and the early 1980s.

In the last two years, I have interviewed more than thirty of the nation's biggest political beasts as a *Coventry Telegraph* journalist, including two Prime Ministers. It should not be forgotten that national government policy remains the main driver of local policy affecting the lives of readers in local communities – despite the government's stated commitment to "localism". (NB Professors George Jones and John Stewart highlighted how the Localism Bill had contained 142 clauses which cede more power for Westminster and Whitehall to intervene in local council affairs.)

Opportunity remains
So the opportunity remains in local newspaper organisations to critically interview national politicians, particularly when they visit localities. There is potential scope, even in a ten-minute interview for writing and website broadcast, to challenge way beyond the prevailing national media discourse of rolling twenty-four hour news. In my experience, no questioning has been out of bounds, even if politicians' media advisors might seek to bring a critical interview to a close.

While politicians put much thought into how to control the media message, it is the job of PR professionals to advise them. In my view, some of them have an obvious vested interest in overstating the power and influence they hold over the local media.

The centralisation of "openness" and information processing at public bodies through communications departments has made things worse for journalists since the 1990s. Back then, expert council officers were readily available for specialist newspaper journalists to interview and grill. Now, all too often responses to questions come back in email format, with little scope within deadline for supplementary questions.

Yet local journalism continues to put pressure on the flow of information, and can use its power to expose when local authorities fail to meet their constitutional commitment to "openness" and "transparency".

Just as young journalists are being trained in using the Freedom of Information Act, they are also being schooled by more senior colleagues in the old skills of the specialist journalist, which I learned in the 1990s from my predecessors.

Those tried and tested skills include building up knowledge not just about local councils or NHS trusts for example, but central government policy which, as stated, continues to shape local policy and services to people. The skill of a political journalist remains partly to get to know political insiders, particularly the wags who calculate they have a political motive for delivering off-record briefings about manoeuvrings in the so-called corridors of power.

Through the application of these skills, anybody can see how much coverage on the *Coventry Telegraph* website differs greatly from the spin and PR put out in press releases you might find, for example, on Coventry City Council's website. Recent examples include exclusives and critical coverage on plans to close Sure Start Children's Centres, on inspection regimes amid failures at private elderly care homes to meet legal standards, on council budget plans, on the total earnings of top council executives, or on expenses and allowances claims made by councillors and officers.

One more light-hearted story exposed that senior council executives had threatened to ban a leading Conservative councillor who had defied a mobile-phone switch-off ban by tweeting one hundred and three times during one three-hour council meeting. Amid the humour and satire, it raised questions also debated in Parliament about whether use of social networking sites can distract politicians from properly carrying out debates and votes on their electorate's behalf. Even the right-wing *Daily Mail* – picking up our story – avoided a "Loony Left council censorship" angle as its readers lambasted the hapless and affable Tory opposition councillor in question.

Jittery politicians

Twitter is a fast-moving source of opinion and information which can be useful to journalists. It has also provided another new theatre for the playing out of age-old jostling between journalists and politicians. Politicians use it to heavily spin and indulge in one-upmanship with each other, using the distorting narratives of party politics.

Yet local politicians regularly explicitly and implicitly make clear to me they remain very concerned about coverage in local newspapers and websites. Despite circulation decline, they worry. They get jittery. It is why many continue to brief me on a regular basis, and why they continue to employ PR professionals to help guide them.

On more serious matters, there is much scope to hold to account local MPs – just as with Westminster frontbenchers. My work during the MPs' expenses scandal in 2009 involved me using the still powerful lever of a regional newspaper to request of nine MPs in Coventry and Warwickshire that they hand over to me their unedited expenses files.

It was in the weeks when the *Daily Telegraph* was publishing its investigation, after gaining sole access to the leaked unedited expenses files of every MP. (NB Those advocating a new form of "independent" press regulation with statutory guidelines, while eulogising about the importance of a free press, should remember the *Daily Telegraph* obtained those files through criminal activity. The leak was criminality at source, yet who could deny it was in the public interest?)

That leak, and the admirable efforts of Freedom of Information campaigner Heather Brooke to force Parliament to release MPs' expenses, gave me further leverage in making my request to all local MPs. What came back was material that would have otherwise been redacted with the censorial big black marker pen following Parliament's interpretation of the High Court and Information Tribunal rulings of what should be released.

My simple request to the nine MPs amounted to an unspoken yet obvious straight choice – hand over your full expenses files, or face accusations in the local press of covering up. Eight of nine MPs agreed to my request and I set about a forensic auditing process of every line of thousands of expenses claims, files and supporting documents. Only the then defence secretary Bob Ainsworth (Labour, Coventry North East) refused. He had earlier voted in the Commons to completely block the release of MPs' expenses.

What became immediately apparent to me in scrutinising the files was the severity of the Commons authorities' censorship proposals - which MPs had at that stage been asked to check and approve. Red crosses and highlighted markings indicated what deletions they were suggesting would comply, perversely, with the Freedom of Information rulings.

One of the barristers acting for Ms Brooke and other campaigners – Hugh Tomlinson QC – who had challenged Commons Speaker Michael Martin's attempts to block MPs' expenses being released, told me that, in his view, the suggested redactions I revealed to him went well beyond what the High Court ruling allowed.

Proposed redactions included not just sensitive personal data such as MPs' addresses and bank account details, but emails and other correspondence between MPs and Commons' fees office officials which revealed controversial claims and over-claims, some of which had been declined.

It became one focus of my MPs' expenses investigation and campaign in the *Coventry Telegraph*. We put pressure on the Commons' authorities, with support from some local MPs, in calling for them to be less censorial in the public interest. Our campaign provoked personal responses from then Prime Minister Gordon Brown and then opposition Conservative leader David Cameron. Much of my work was also published in *The Guardian*.

My work also uncovered overclaims made by several MPs which they told me they had been previously unaware of. They agreed to pay the money back immediately. The Commons auditor Sir Thomas Legg later agreed with those findings.

I performed this entirely independent work before the *Daily Telegraph* published its own reports on some of those individual MPs' expenses claims. Whereas Meriden Conservative MP Caroline Spelman – now a cabinet minister – appeared in the *Daily Telegraph's* "saints list" because of her relative low "second homes" expenses claims, I was able to exclusively report to her constituents that she was claiming around £10,000 a year just for council tax, utility bills and cleaning for her country mansion.

It was one of three expensive properties owned by her and management consultant husband Mark Spelman, whom I revealed had used the same address as his main residence when standing to become a Conservative MEP. Again, this work, first published in the local press, was picked up by several national newspapers. Much original and scrutinising work by local press journalists remains a source of much national media coverage.

While no clear wrongdoing within the flawed and previously clandestine MPs' expenses system was alleged in Mrs Spelman's case – give or take minor double claims I was able to spot – my work raised questions about whether MPs were really making claims, or choosing lifestyles, in line with the Green Book rules. These stipulated expenses should only be incurred "wholly, exclusively and necessarily in the course of their parliamentary duties".

The answer for many lay somewhere in the murky grey area of moral interpretation about this particular expenditure of taxpayers' money. A letter from one of her constituents published days later in the *Coventry Telegraph* attacking our "scurrilous" journalism probably indicated we had done something right.

Reporting major issues
As I write, in February 2012, one major issue involving local politics is the impending mayoral referenda in May, enforced by the government on ten cities including Coventry and Birmingham. The referenda will ask if those cities want an executive elected mayor to replace the traditional "leader and cabinet" system at local authorities.

The pro-mayor government's propaganda was well represented in a front-page news story by *The Times* newspaper in January. The claim was highlighted that elected mayors would be drivers of economic growth in city regions, and boost local democracy, with new powers under the government's "localism" agenda to help drive inward investment.

As political correspondent on the *Coventry Telegraph*, I had spent several months researching the issue at the local and national level. My work included me challenging the key national proponents of elected mayors – Conservative Cities minister Greg Clark and former Labour minister Lord Andrew Adonis, of the think-tank the Institute for Government.

Its key researcher on mayors, Sam Sims, accepted under questioning from me that there was no empirical evidence either way that elected mayors had driven economic growth in thirteen places outside the London mayoralty held by Boris

Johnson. Much evidence in fact pointed the other way – that mayors had failed to make inroads in economically challenged towns and cities including Doncaster, Stoke, Middlesborough and Hartlepool – some of which retained some of the worst pockets of deprivation in the country.

Mr Sims also accepted under questioning that those elected mayors had not stimulated voter interest as measured by average council election turnout at those mayoral authorities. This formed the basis of questions I put to Mr Clark and Lord Adonis in front of the television cameras at a national launch at the Birmingham Chamber of Commerce in January.

Further, amid the rumbling propaganda war, I invited Mr Clark to clarify that relatively limited powers to be devolved to local authorities – under proposed new "City Deals" and the wider "localism" agenda – would not be dependent on cities voting for elected mayors.

My challenge to the likes of Mr Clark and Lord Adonis, including in my newspaper column/blog, focused not just on the lack of empirical evidence to support their claims, but on the "elephant in the room". By this, I mean that central government will continue with its financial stranglehold on councils amid disproportionate 27% funding cuts, and will continue to wield power over town hall decision-making across vast areas of policy including schools and health – irrespective of whether cities vote for elected mayors.

Summarising, local journalism is far from perfect. Yes, technological and economic changes have put close to unsustainable pressure on staffing levels, and threaten further instability and uncertainty. However, I hope the few examples I have given from my own experience illustrate the flaws in any polarised assumption that local journalism already no longer has the power, skill or will to hold political and other power to account, on behalf of people.

Whether this type of journalism has commercial viability in future, alongside other forms of community-based news, will partly depend on the extent to which it is valued in communities.

In the digital age, it will not only be professional journalists working for traditional media organisations who are doing this important work. At the local level, there will continue to be far fewer professional journalists than in the 1990s, more reliance on reader contributions, and those of the amateur "citizen journalist".

Yet it is an important role that will continue as long as there are those working and investing in local journalism who want it to. Professional journalists have never been luddites. The Internet has been (perhaps belatedly) embraced in the new era of multi-media. It provides a platform to be expansive, investigative and analytical, and it is there for anyone to use.

To the journalists of the future, from trained professionals to "citizen journalists", I say: It's over to you.

Les Reid

Note on the author

Les Reid works full-time for the *Coventry Telegraph* as its political correspondent, covering local and national politics. He was a postgraduate at the Centre for Journalism at City University, London, and has written for local and national newspapers for twenty years. As a contributor to *The Guardian*, his published work includes a detailed, independent investigation into MPs' expenses, which scrutinised unedited expenses files and challenged the Commons' redaction/censorship proposals.

Other published work includes a lengthy interview for the *New Statesman* with professor of political economy Lord Robert Skidelsky, publisher of respected biographies on John Maynard Keynes, and a key national critic of governments' austerity programmes.

The future is still local

**Despite all the advances in social media, local politicians universally
recognise the importance of a thriving newspaper industry, says Fran
Collingham, even if they don't always see eye to eye with the journalists
who hold them to account.**

Meetings in the Council Chamber at Coventry don't often make the national
news. They're important – of course – to our councillors; an opportunity for
every one of the 54 elected members of the Council to gather in one place once
a month and discuss the issues that affect our city.

But while they often provide the political editor of our local paper, the
Coventry Telegraph, with stories that will make several page leads over the coming
days, that's usually the extent of the coverage. Not so, though, a few months ago
when a clash between the new communications tools of the 21st Century and
the traditional ways councils have done business for decades neatly illustrated
the changing relationship between big public organisations like the Council and
the media.

The decision taken by the controlling group on the Council to ban councillors
tweeting in the Council Chamber in order for councillors to focus on the debate
and discussions taking place during the meeting was a controversial one. While
journalists (and council officials) attending the meeting were free to tweet, and
the ban applied only to monthly Full Council meetings (which we webcast live),
some councillors took a dim view of the decision and shared their views with
the world.

When one councillor expressed his opposition to the decision by tweeting
103 times during a Full Council meeting his actions attracted the national media.
But it was the initial coverage in the *Coventry Telegraph* that got the story into the
Daily Mail and the *Sun*. The tweets about the issue were there for the world to
see, but it took a local reporter's eye for a story, contacts with the key figures
involved and the ability to turn an amendment to the Council's constitution into
a front page lead that the nationals thought worth following up.

When local goes social

It's easy to argue that the growth of social media has turned us all into citizen journalists with the ability to make the news whoever and wherever we are. What's simpler than taking a picture of something exciting on your mobile phone and emailing it to the local paper? Why not share your frustrations with the failings of a big organisation by blogging about their woeful service and lack of customer care? And Twitter gives us all an instant platform to tell hundreds of people in a moment what's going on in our world.

So why bother buying a local newspaper (or listening to the local radio station) when the news is out there in the digital world for us all to share and contribute to, updated constantly, and without a cover price?

The best local newspapers are embracing this challenge, and proving that in a world where there are a million views and interpretations of the news at the touch of a button residents, more than ever, need their local media to make sense of the digital cacophony around them.

Circulation figures may make gloomy reading for the management of regional newspapers, but when there's a big story about the Council in our local paper every single man, woman and child in Coventry appears to have read the article, and usually has a loudly voiced view about it.

It takes experience to see a story and analyse its potential. No matter what it is – a cat up a tree or a murder most foul – there's no substitute for the keen eye that has been taught and shown how to make the most of the story. Citizen journalism is little more than gossip, often passed on without a thought or without reflection on its truthfulness. Nothing wrong with gossip – after all, it's what news is and always has been – but there's definitely something wrong with gossip that has little or no foundation in fact.

Just the facts

And that's what it all boils down to. Just give me the facts, as they used to say in that old TV crime show, and they were right. Too often now, we get opinion first and the facts later, often so that the facts outweigh the opinion.

Get it right. Check, check and double check is the way I was taught and so was every other newspaper reporter and, I would hope, they still are. While there's no doubt that many of the traditional news gathering skills I was taught nearly three decades ago are disappearing, it's also true that the basic tenets are still there. They have to be. Not many editors these days can afford to send their reporters to an all-day planning meeting that may only provide a few pars about planning permission for a new home in a small village, but it's what I used to do on a regular basis. And while I was there, I would make sure that whatever I reported was correct. If it's in the newspaper, then it matters to somebody somewhere.

It's so important to retain this sense of community, this sense of belonging. What was the first thing Gandhi would suggest for a village? Setting up a newspaper, a central point through which all the news is filtered and which brings the people together. It may be he didn't have to deal with Twitter in those days but even so, he saw the careful and controlled dissemination of local news as being vital to the thriving heart of any society.

I may be looking back on those days with something of a rose-tinted hue but I can remember fondly visiting the homes of many a couple home for a golden or diamond wedding celebration. It called for a leisurely visit from a reporter and a photographer (and usually a glass of sweet sherry in the happy couple's home at eleven in the morning) just to end up with the useful tip that to survive 50 years in a marriage one should never go to sleep on a quarrel but it was important to them, to their family and their friends.

Every Friday morning I'd disappear from the newsroom to wander the streets of a nearby town, having tea with the vicar and talking to the local Chamber of Commerce president in his shop - all in pursuit of the off diary story. Often I came back with nothing (it was a very sleepy town), but my editor still kept sending me out.

These days, there's nothing I like better than to stand in the corner at a party with a group of like-minded hacks and ex-hacks and bemoan the current state of journalism. We hark back to the glory days of local newspapers before new technology, when we worked our contacts, hung out with coppers and brought in the stories that sold thousands of newspapers every day.

It's different, now, for reporters on local papers. The slimming down of newsrooms, with fewer people around who have less time to spend on stories, has had an impact – there's no escaping that fact. Centralised subbing operations, now the norm in many regional newspaper groups, mean that sub-editors and news editors work less closely together. Ever since I've worked in local government, councillors and council officers have complained to me that while they're happy with the facts in the story about them, the headline hasn't reflected the story accurately; this complaint seems to be more common these days.

We're lucky, in Coventry, to have a political editor on the *Coventry Telegraph*, Les Reid, who spends a lot of time at the Council House talking to officers and councillors and covering council meetings. It doesn't happen any more in many other places. Specialist reporters, whether political, health or business, are seen increasingly as a luxury in the local and regional press, and as a result the quality of coverage in these important (but often not glamorous) areas is suffering.

I also mourn the loss of same-day printing. The newspaper where I worked as a sub-editor once had a print deadline of 10.30 in the morning for the last edition – and you could still get breaking news in the stop press section right up to midday, just before the final edition went to press and was out on the streets an hour or so later. Not as immediate as Twitter, of course, but it still meant that a big story breaking that morning could get the coverage it deserved. These days a story can be more than a day old before a local paper can cover it, and readers are likely to have seen the story across regional broadcast media well before the next day's paper comes out.

So it's pretty hard work, running a successful local newspaper these days. But while the simple economics of the newspaper industry means that editors these days are faced with a huge set of challenges – ranging from simply having fewer reporters around to do the work to the need to edit several weeklies at the same time when once they just had one to worry about – the need for local newspapers has never been stronger. I don't believe for a moment this is old-fashioned and I will continue to defend the printed media. I see no reason why it can't sit happily alongside the internet and phone versions of news delivery but my greatest fear is that the economics of the business will prove to be too daunting for owners to keep on putting up the money. There is still profit to be made, but is there enough? I really hope so. I hope there can be a way for young people to discover that the printed page is as great as a web screen. I don't think it's just that this is my background; I firmly believe that properly trained and questioning reporters are vital and, while I have no doubt they exist on other more modern media, the best ones have grown up on newspapers.

Doing things differently

Ironically, it's the very abundance of information and news now available to us all that makes the role of the local newspaper even more important.

These days councils like mine publish every item of expenditure over £500 on our websites for anyone to examine. There's no ignoring a request for detailed information about a decision or policy; if it comes in as a Freedom of Information request it's logged and replied to. We webcast council meetings and we Tweet results from planning committee meetings. All our agendas, reports and minutes are available online. At the same time residents with a view about our services can share these views to an eagerly waiting world through websites, blogs, the discussion forums on local news websites and (of course) via Twitter. We put out our own magazines. We embrace every kind of news channel there is because we want everyone to know everything. It is public, it is transparent and it is honest.

So the raw data is there in a way it's never been before. And while there are people around in every town and city making sense of this data and using it to prompt questions and debate about policies and initiatives, local journalists are the most important in interpreting what's really going on in their communities and explaining it to their readers.

That means making sense of a huge range of differing views about an issue, doing it quickly and knowing the right questions to ask of the right people at the right time. That's what decent reporters have always done, of course, but now a lot of their work is as transparent and accessible as the data public organisations like councils routinely publish.

It's likely that a tweet that's worthy of a follow-up by a reporter has been seen by hundreds of us at the same time as the reporter first spotted it. So readers of the next day's paper may not be surprised by the story born from the original tweet, but they do want to know if it was really true and, if so, what it means for them.

A question of trust

Local people do, on the whole, still trust their local newspaper (more than they trust the national media) to tell them what's really going on in their neighbourhood, and at a time when they can choose hundreds of different sources that can give them a version of what's going locally, the role of a local newspaper in sorting out the nonsense from the real story is absolutely vital.

That's as much of a challenge for councils like mine as it is for the local media. Despite the occasional fallings-outs and tussles that go on when a feisty newspaper takes the biggest organisation in town to task (that's usually the council), I've never met a councillor who hasn't recognised the importance the local media plays in ensuring local democracy is alive and well in the community. They know reporting of their actions and decisions in the local media will be replayed and questioned in their wards and on the doorsteps of their constituents at election time, and they're up for the public scrutiny that goes with making decisions that affect the people who voted them into power.

Many local politicians are embracing social media as a different way of connecting with their voters, and understand this is much more than a two-way conversation with individual residents. Views in a tweet, or on a local councillor's blog probably aren't worthy of a press release, but knowing that a reporter is keeping an eye on all your interactions with the public on Twitter or online should – and often does – focus the mind pretty sharply.

Councils around the country are seeing social media as a new way of having honest conversations with citizens, but it would be a foolish council that believes this will replace the scrutiny offered by a decent local newspaper. In Coventry we've won national awards for our use of Facebook and Twitter. More than 20,000 people like our Facebook pages and we know that when it comes to putting out urgent direct messages (your school is closed because of the snow, we're gritting the roads tonight because it's icy) we're reaching more people more quickly than ever before.

We've also experimented with using online, live debate forums as a way of gathering opinions on the future of our city. But we did this with our local media; BBC Coventry and Warwickshire covered the launch of the first online debate and the *Coventry Telegraph*'s editor took part in it. And we knew the experiment was a success when the newspaper took an interest in one of the issues and turned it into a story.

We're keen to continue innovating in social media, but it's hard to see how it could replace the role of a local newspaper in holding us to account, questioning our decisions and helping its readers understand our policies.

Like every ex-journalist I mourn the passing of the days when everyone had the local paper delivered through their letterbox at teatime. I'd rather read my news in a paper than online, and I think the NIBs at the back of the paper about a WI raffle are as much to be treasured as the violent crime story that's made the front page. That world is fast disappearing – if it hasn't already – and I think towns and cities are poorer places as a result. But while there are still local newspapers around trying to make sense of the places they cover then, tweet it quietly, there's still life in the old newshounds yet.

Note on the author
Fran Collingham is an Assistant Director with responsibility for the communications service at Coventry City Council. She's worked in local government PR since the mid 1990s, joining Coventry from Birmingham City Council in 2003. She began her career as a journalist, working as a reporter and sub-editor on local weekly and daily newspapers in the Midlands.

The local media's role in civic responsibility

The current decline of local weekly and daily newspapers is having a negative impact on the political public sphere, skewing political discourse and democratic representation, say Ben McConville and Kate Smith. They ask if public disorder such as the 2011 riots in England is one of the symptoms of this? Does less local media lead to less civic virtue and participation?

Local media in the UK has a proud and historic tradition from the early *Weekley Newes* style of newsbooks of the 1640s and the pamphleteering polemics of the 1690s onwards to the hyperlocal editions of digital newspaper (such as *The Guardian's* late, lamented "beatblogger") and current television opt-out segments. Their content included the ubiquitous celebrity trials, mercantile gossip and oppositional tracts on government trade policies and sometimes even the sexual orientation of senior members of the aristocracy. *Plus ça change, plus c'est la même chose?*

Even in times of great austerity people paid for printed local media, including serialised fiction such as the work of Charles Dickens, because it reflected the world around them and resonated in the moment. It was also entertainment. The printing press that created profits was a heady and successful business model – Benedict Anderson coined it "print capitalism" (1983/2006) and this leads to Anderson's concept of "imagined communities". Rather than being based on face-to-face contact and family knowledge, these imagined communities came about from an assumed imagined idea of affinity. The media could create a community and local media could create an even more strongly bonded imagined community because it was easier to find shared areas of interest in local groups such as market prices, harvests, weather and well known local characters.

Lives of the non-aristocracy were mostly lived locally and local media was as close to individual media as it could get. The media could address a local audience on local issues with ease and its resonance can be measured by its sales and vitality in the community. Even the letters pages became areas of contestation. The role of printed local media is, Anderson believes, a strong factor in nationalism. These socially constructed imagined communities with similar issues could discuss common political objectives too. Reflecting on the emerging communities of North America in the eighteenth century, Anderson noted they used vernacular or shared indigenous identity and these imagined communities could define and form a nation-state rather than persist as subjects.

With the move from feudal to mass society the local media was both cause and effect to the shaping of the "public sphere". Jurgen Habermas identified the coffee houses of Europe as the early forum for this public sphere, or the area in social life where individuals came together to freely discuss and identify societal problems, and through that discussion attempted to influence political action.

Placed between the private sphere, which tended to be dominated by the world of private correspondence and bills, chits and cheques, and the "sphere of public authority" with its print culture of an emerging bureaucracy, court circulars and London-based newspapers such as *The Times*, the public sphere through the local media, could discuss issues, policies, politics and from the tell tales of public opinion. Local politicians knew what to campaign on, how to address the electorate and how to take the temperature of local polities, groups and issues. The electorate could communicate through the local newspaper on issues. Drawing on the eighteenth century enlightenment such as the works of David Hume, Habermas painted the public sphere as fundamentally a rationalist ideal of Western liberal democracy. In this optimistic view of a post-feudal world, the discourse was based on emancipation, the human capacity for reason and rational-critical communication.

As suffrage expanded so local media proliferated. As mass society developed in turn so did mass media, including a burgeoning local media. Direct action such as the General Strike of 1926 and the Jarrow March of 1936 still occurred but was reported on in detail by the local press, often sympathetically (Newcastle *Evening Chronicle*, 5 October 1936, "Start of Jarrow's Great Work Pilgrimage: Town gives rousing send off to men").

Political, artisan and issue-based groups still published their own newsletters and magazines to communicate with their members and prospective members; party political meetings still had robust debate and there remained the oratory of Speaker's Corner and other soapbox rhetoricians, but it was the local media which carried the main narratives of political debate in all its disparate and diverse aspects. This may or may not have led to more political unrest and direct action but the print capitalism of the local media, by mediating, by carrying the narratives of the political public sphere, formed a key role of participative democracy – that of representation, encouraging participation and integration of the citizens.

"In modern societies, one particular social space, namely the political public sphere of a democratic community, plays an especially important role in the integration of citizens.

For complex societies can be normatively held together solely by civic solidarity – the abstract, legally mediated form of solidarity among citizens...

"For this reason, the critical state of a democracy can be measured by taking the pulse of the life of its political public sphere." (Habermas, Kyoto lecture 2004).

The recent decline of local newspapers across the UK has an impact not only on the staff writing for them but the communities they serve. Definite records are not available but *The Guardian* estimates that in 2009 alone, fifty three closed across the UK. These included the *Aberdeen and District Independent*, the *Belper Bugle* and the *Huddersfield Express and Chronicle*. Some of these papers had known distributions of more than 70,000. The previously reported events, campaigns and good works of individuals in these communities now go unreported and unknown.

The boundedness of imagined communities becomes more permeable, realigning along other, perhaps less inclusive or less local lines. Those on the kinetic side of the digital divide form imagined communities through social media, and self-select news items through their smartphones. Local news is often limited to just sports news with home news perhaps being ignored all together. Political news will be selected if scandalised or pertinent to individual financial interests – the American idea of "pocketbook politics". International news selection tends to be purely phenomenological or obsessed with news deviance – driven by the visual of natural disasters, acts of terrorism, major election wins and the quirky. What is deemed proximate has changed for some to exclude the local – so stories from America are perceived as proximate to UK consumers whilst those from the neighbourhood are not. These are networked digital imagined communities which are mediated by trans national companies such as Facebook, Google and Twitter. These organisations promote and encourage individuated media use through their benign and personalised interactions with customers or users.

The impact on users is a loss of understanding that they are dealing with multi-billion dollar businesses while they interface with frenetic, ever changing and constantly updated information. They are encouraged to take up ideas and issues or drop them when the next idea or outrage comes along. All the while the individual has willingly or unwittingly surrendered content and privacy. Social media encourages narcissism in the user by asking them to emote and tell the world what they are thinking, feeling or consuming. This is a seismic change from the coffee house ideal of the public sphere where rational enquiry and discourse was centred not only on the individual, but on the collective good and the belief that differences could be settled on the basis of those discussions.

Another impact on the user is a loss of understanding of their locale and the people who live in it. The social awkwardness of meeting strangers is dissipated not by small talk and a discussion of what was in the local newspaper this week, but by bringing out the smartphone and perhaps "checking in" to the area so that your social media "friends" can see where you are. It is a way to be present but absent which keeps strangers unknown and communities atrophying.

For all, living in the community becomes a more anonymised globalised existence. For those on the static side of the digital divide, those who may have taken the local newspaper and especially the elderly, the local information is diluted and their print culture severely depleted. Political parties still produce leaflets around election time but in areas where newspapers have closed, most local information is now provided through social groups, religious affiliations, or television. The closures of local libraries compound this trajectory of declining print culture.

What is lost is the mediation of the imagined community and the journalists who had a central role in this. Local reporters perform vital functions as a quasi actor in civil society, working as part of the community. Their role is that of activist, social commentator, humourist and satirist, record-taker and potentially a force for community cohesion and sub-groups adhesion. Good local newspapers are poly-vocal. The local reporter is an important and privileged role within a community, one that can be carried out by trainees. The policing of this role occurred through the interaction of the reader and community so the standard of their journalistic practices had local accountability. The reader, for their part, may principally use local media for the classified advertisements, but do engage with local issues, local politics and community via the pages of a newspaper.

This anonymised atomised existence affects all age groups and triggers a declining sense of community, forming a downward spiral of people disinvesting in their community and using the poor state of the community – the neglect and disharmony – as a reason to disinvest further.

The loss of local reporting – coverage of local authorities, local courts and public bodies – means access to the political public sphere, previously mediated by local newspapers, is inhibited or closed off completely so one of the main ingredients in participative democracy is lost. This lack of representation injures democracy and so, when issues such as poverty and availability of public services arise, this means there is no access to the political public sphere; as a result little interest in the political process through lack of cognisance and atrophying personal investment in the local area form a perfect storm for rioting, looting and direct action, organised by anonymous instant messaging on smartphones. Torching the local store is easier when you do not know the owner. Not knowing the people and with no possible sanction of knowing someone who might know them, makes it easier to be disloyal to your locale – "dislocal". Dehumanisation is a step towards collective violence and being disconnected from your locality and neighbours also makes it easier to dehumanise them further with violent acts.

In the wake of the 2011 riots there was much soul-searching in the UK national media about this issue. The national media characterised the rioters primarily as looters, a view that was seemingly borne out by images of looters casually trying on trainers for size before taking them and removing goods in branded carrier bags. Amid such images, underlying socio-economic reasons for the riots such as recession, unemployment and the growing misery of the working poor were obscured and discounted, particularly by right wing media. The looters targeted major sportswear shops and electrical retailers, but they also displayed a reckless disregard for local shops, community or the safety of local residents, particularly in arson attacks in London. Not only were the rioters disengaged from compassion for the personal tragedy of the victims of the riots, they were also removed from the restitutional and social censure function which the local media of a community can levy. While national news organisations did run pictures of suspects, it is likely that the rioters had little or no engagement with local media and therefore had no fear of embarrassment or social control at a local level.

The local newspaper is integral to peace and local media drives civic virtue and peaceful democratic participation because there is better representation and stimulation of political discourse. The lessons to be learned from the new expressions of "dislocality" – violent public disorder – also apply to national politics. After all, in the words of Tip O'Neill, former Speaker of the United States House of Representatives, "All politics is local".

Bibliography

Anderson, B. (2006) *Imagined Communities: Reflections on the origins and spread of nationalism.* London, Verso

Greenslade, R. (2009) Britain's Vanishing Newspapers. http://www.guardian.co.uk/media/greenslade/2009/feb/19/local-newspapers-newspapers#start-of-comments

Habermas, J. (1991) *The Structural Transformation of the Public Sphere.* Cambridge, MIT Press

Habermas, J. (2004) Kyoto Speech (on receiving the Kyoto Prize Laureate in Arts and Philosophy).

Note on the authors

Ben McConville is a principal lecturer in journalism at Northumbria University. He is a regular contributor to the Associated Press news agency, former New York correspondent for *The Scotsman* and former Foreign Editor of *Scotland on Sunday*.

Kate Smith is programme leader of the BA Journalism at Edinburgh Napier University and is an award-winning writer.

The future may be tough, but it is not all gloomy

Reports of the death of local newspapers are seriously flawed, argues Bob Satchwell. Times are very hard, he acknowledges, but believes they still have many years of life left in them. Here he explains why.

Hundreds and thousands of words have been written in obituaries of local newspapers but reports of their death are seriously flawed. I cannot understand why so many words are being squandered by an awful lot of usually knowledgeable and sensible people who do not often have time to waste.

Yes, the economic climate is dire and the outlook is not much better. Yes, local and regional editors and journalists are struggling. There seems to be no sign of light at the end of an extremely long tunnel for them. Yes, a clutch of good, experienced, dedicated editors have opted for new lives away from their grim coalfaces. Yes, they have had to trim their staffs to the bone, losing experienced journalists on the way.

But wait a minute. What happened to that doom and gloom prediction that half of our regional press would have closed by now? Why is it that more than two-thirds of the adult population is still reading its local news mountain every week?

And where have all those lucrative advertising pounds that gave local papers a licence to print money for decades been transferred? It has not all gone online or elsewhere so who is to say at least some of it could not be retrieved so long as the still-powerful case for the regional press is delivered properly?

The economy will move.

If thousands of cuts are about to prove fatal, how come the boss of one of the biggest regional groups, Ashley Highfield, the relatively new chief executive of Johnston Press was reported talking satisfyingly about local papers that can still maintain 20% margins in the depths of this economic winter?

Where are all the new digital media moguls who should be lapping up the revenue? Google, Facebook and Twitter maybe – but before long, and when people are clearly confident enough, the economy will start moving again. Then the penny will drop. Websites and searches alone will not bring all the business in. Advertising popping up on mobiles every few yards while you're walking down the high street will become intrusive.

Some advertising is of course perfectly suited to digital platforms. Local papers, as much as any other media outlet, are belatedly playing catch up. But has the traditional appeal of newspapers really vanished altogether? I think not. Whether we are waiting for a friend, sitting in the dentist's waiting room, waiting for the train to stop, sitting in a traffic jam, watching a movie with clever product placement, we are suckers for advertising…and just might buy as the result of it.

Call it what you like, subliminal or the browse factor, it is part of the package that has always been part of traditional media.

Purchasing decisions

Last time I replaced my car I spent hours researching on the web. I got it down to three models after road tests. I was still not convinced. I came home from an early doors pint on a Friday evening, picked up and flicked through the local paper. Something stopped me in the motoring section – part of the paper to which I gave little attention. There was a display ad offering a substantial discount for a direct replacement for the model I was swapping at the dealership which serviced my car. By lunchtime the next day I had signed the lease and the shiny new charger was set for delivery three days later.

Am I so different from the rest of the population? We make purchasing decisions based on conservative comfort, whims, research, opportunity, and availability – a whole range of factors. But we have to be told what we should look for, what will suit our brand inertia most, where the best deals are to be found. Most people simply do not have the time for endless mind-boggling research; we need a bit of help from the advertising industry and the media platforms it requires.

And that's where local newspapers – traditional media – come into their own. They are relatively easy to access and relatively cheap and available. They provide a package to suit a wide range of people. They are there to inform and entertain and to make our lives easier.

We all still want to know if a new block of flats or factory is planned for the bottom of the garden, whether a pub we use occasionally is still open, which local firms are doing well and how our kids or grandchildren played at the weekend. We also want to know where the best bargains are to be had – whether it's a car, TV, or washing machine, and we don't want to travel to buy them.

The keyword is and always has been "package". When I edited a regional evening paper we made sure we carried at least one hundred local stories every day, mentioned a dozen sports each day (and, shock horror, women played sport seriously too!) plus a digest of national news that had relevance for our region.

We worked hard to get what is now called ultra local news to every community and we slaved to print on time in order to get copies through the traffic in time for people to buy casual copies or to read the paper between getting home and going out for the evening.

At an average adult reading speed it would take two hours forty minutes to read the whole package, but we knew that on average most spent only twenty minutes on the paper. They read only about one fifth or one sixth of the paper and they buy it, or pick up their free copy, for a huge variety of reasons.

More leisure time

Has anything really changed? Over my career there was huge economic and social change that affected sales of newspapers. Competition for everyone's time – their twenty minutes – has grown dramatically. People have more to do with their increased leisure time and, despite the recession, more income to pay for it. But we all need help to make the most of the opportunities and the ability to make the best of them if we know where they are.

The opportunity for local newspapers is as clear as it always was. It is only the effort and methods of delivery required that are different.

The second keyword is "platforms". The Internet and the explosion of broadcast channels may have dissipated audiences for traditional media of all kinds but look at the figures. Radio, television and, yes, newspapers, are still mass media, appealing to millions of people. Examine readership as opposed to circulation stats and there is a clue. Cheer the worldwide, soar away success of Mail Online in just three or four years and the picture is clear.

There is a future and it may not be just online. The World Wide Web is an ancient old hat, mobile on phones and tablets are the present. Someone is already working on next week and next month and we need to keep up with them. Every newspaper needs a digital correspondent to annoy us with the relentless pace of innovation. Some of his or her output will be terminally boring but we need to know about the spark that will light next year's trend. We need trained communicators to ensure readers, viewers, listeners, surfers and, above all, editors know what is coming.

The job cannot be left to the techies in the IT department or whoever is in charge of "production", whatever that might mean these days. It is a job for journalists who will see the possibilities for themselves and for their audiences.

Creative journalists

That surely is the message of the last decade. While some media companies wring their hands increasingly desperate about how or if they will ever be able to make money again, journalists aided by clever techies have been amazingly creative and adaptive. Those of us old enough to remember green eye shields and the closed minds and strict demarcation in newsrooms can marvel at how today's journalists, tweet, blog, video, snap and, oh yes, write reports and features, all in a day's work.

Editorial departments used to be criticised for failing to think about how they did the job and how they should change. Editors were charged with the lack of commercialism – despite the fact that we were driven by circulation figures.

The last decade has seen a new kind of editor and new kinds of journalism. Freed from old restrictions and given the prospect of communicating with their audiences faster and in so many different ways, they have grasped the opportunities with relish. More people are coming up behind them on the best college training courses. The National Council for the Training of Journalists (NCTJ) realised some time ago that the whole industry needed a different breed of technically savvy journalists.

It is certainly not easy, especially in current economic conditions, but commercial managers have got to show similar enthusiasm and initiative. If they don't believe it how will potential advertisers? They must forget the good old days when ads and revenue flowed in without huge sales effort. One very senior executive who came up the advertising route told me some years ago that for most of his career it was not a matter of selling newspapers but of managing accounts for advertisers who had nowhere else to go.

Regional newspapers must not suggest they are on their last legs. Intimating that they are "managing decline" is the quickest route to oblivion.

Digital literacy

I was asked recently if it mattered that gaps were appearing in the local and regional newspaper map. Of course it does, for democracy rather than merely the industry and journalists' jobs. And I added that every gap left by a closed-down newspaper was an opportunity. Already journalists and former editors are filling those gaps especially with ultra local websites. More should grasp the nettle, as should local entrepreneurs who want to make a mark in their communities.

The Victorians did it – that's when many local and regional papers were founded on the back of improving literacy following the 1870 Education Act. Now is the time to build on increasing digital literacy that is spanning all generations. And there is that old adage that the best time to start a new business is at the bottom of a recession.

There is some force in the idea promulgated by Neil Fowler in this book and elsewhere that the big regional groups should get out of the way if they no longer want to publish local papers themselves. While consolidation has been the watchword over the past couple of decades, and may still have a place, so does a resurgence of localism in terms of ownership.

Little local papers with a proprietor who is also the editor, who sells ads and subscriptions and prints or delivers the news, do not have to create as much revenue as that demanded by big groups with high costs, hefty bank loans and demanding shareholders. Look to North America where editor/proprietors with one man and a dog to help them still seem capable of bucking the trend.

The big groups could help and benefit at the same time by printing local papers that might start as websites. They could also help support local television initiatives to create local media hubs. It requires some creative thought but it is quite clear that the explosion of digital media also creates new appetites for information – globally, nationally and locally.

But above all local newspaper owners big or small must also get back to basics. They are in the news business and they have to focus on that if they want to stay in the advertising or delivery businesses that can and will produce revenue.

Gathering news is expensive but it is also essential. Ask Lord Rothermere about Mail Online, The Guardian about its website, the BBC or Rupert Murdoch. They are the investors in journalism because they know that whatever the platform, any news business is useless without content that is lively and relevant to its chosen market. Content requires journalists and editors who are highly skilled and motivated to use their inquiring minds and in-built determination to find ways to uncover and deliver their stories.

Note on the author

Bob Satchwell has been executive director of the Society of Editors, the UK's leading media lobbying body, since its foundation in 1999. He is also a member of the Defence Press and Broadcasting Advisory Committee and a non executive director of the National Council for the Training of Journalists. He started his career with the *Lancashire Evening Post* in 1970 becoming Journalist of the Year in the British Press Awards for 1977. He went to Fleet Street as assistant editor of the *News of the World* before returning to regional newspapers as editor of the *Cambridge Evening News* in 1984, a post he held until 1998.

Local: it's where everything begins

Life is local, says Lynne Anderson, and the irony in this changed market is that more people than ever are seeing local and regional news.

In today's hyper-connected world of 24-hour global news, instant messaging and the blogosphere, while high streets spiral into decline and post offices and pubs close down, we could be forgiven for thinking that localness is all but dead.

But being part of a community is a basic human need which remains hugely important to British people. Its significance in our lives has if anything increased as a result of the economic downturn, fuelled by local pride and a growing need for a sense of place and belonging.

The adage "life is local" has never been more true. Most of us continue to live our lives locally – working, relaxing with family and friends, eating, shopping, and playing sport. Indeed, research has found that 80% of us spend at least half our time and money within just five miles of home and we have a growing appetite for local news and information to help us navigate our lives locally.

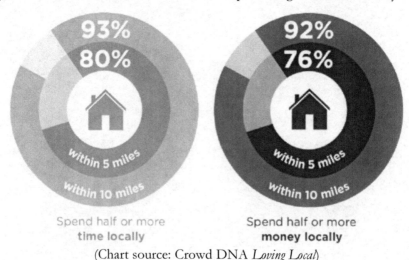

Spend half or more
time locally

Spend half or more
money locally

(Chart source: Crowd DNA *Loving Local*)

People are taking more pride in their community and recognising its importance to their lives. Local newspapers support this increasing sense of local pride because they help people to feel part of their community and spur them to act for its benefit. No other medium can deliver a sense of community and belonging like the local press. According to Ofcom, people regard regional TV and regional and local newspapers as the most important of all media to society.

Growing audiences across multimedia platforms

Local newspapers continue to evolve into local media businesses delivering local news and information across print, online, mobile and broadcast platforms. Britain's local media comprises eleven hundred core newspapers – ranging from large metropolitan dailies to small weekly titles – as well as sixteen hundred companion websites, hundreds of niche and ultra local publications and a range of other digital and broadcast channels.

But the regional and local media sector, with local newspapers at its heart, has been experiencing one of the most severe and prolonged advertising downturns in living memory. The picture remains challenging but publishers believe they are well placed to come through the downturn provided they are given the freedom to continue to innovate and develop their print and multimedia businesses.

It is important to remember that local newspapers are essentially profitable businesses: the sector currently takes around £1.5bn a year in print advertising revenue, accounting for 9.3% of all UK advertising revenue (Advertising Association, Moving Annual Total (MAT) to Q3 2011). Online recruitment advertising in the regional press accounts for another £55.2m. Total print advertising spend in the regional press is three and a half times the adspend on radio, and equivalent to the combined total for radio, outdoor and cinema.

There has been much comment about local newspapers closing down and towns being left "without a collective voice". The reality is that no part of the UK is bereft of any local newspaper coverage. The worst year for closures was 2009 which saw a net reduction of sixty titles. Ofcom has pointed out that most of those closures were marginal free titles occupying second or third position in the local market, and should be considered in the context of the significant expansion of free titles in 1980s. Over the past ten years (2002-2012), the number of paid for titles within the sector has dropped by 1.1% while the number of free titles has dropped by 24.6%.

Ironically, at a time when its primary revenue source – advertising – has been under such challenge, the local media is reaching bigger audiences than ever before across its print, online and broadcast platforms. It delivers valued and trusted local news and information to 33m print readers a week and 42m web users a month. The local media increased its monthly online audience by nearly a third over the past year (Source: ABC 2010-11).

The industry's investment in new platforms, converged multimedia newsrooms, video journalism, user-generated content, mobile sites, smartphone apps and other digital and print innovations means that local papers are now reaching more of the population as well as attracting new online advertising revenues. The industry is finding new ways to cover council meetings and open up public bodies to scrutiny using, for example, live webcams, blogging and Twitter.

Despite massive growth in local media's digital audiences, print remains at the heart of the industry. Independent studies, such as those from KPMG, Ofcom and Deloitte, confirm the relevance and power of the printed newspaper as an editorial and advertising medium and go some way to explaining the resilience local media has shown in the face of the economic downturn.

A major annual study into media usage by Ofcom in 2010 revealed that traditional forms of media such as print remain extremely important to consumers who are consuming more media than ever before.

Its Communications Market Report into the UK's TV, radio, telecoms and internet industries shows that consumers are more likely to use different types of media simultaneously than ever before.

Reading print media such as newspapers, magazines or books was deemed to be a very important media activity by respondents, scoring higher than activities such as social networking, listening to the radio, and playing games on and offline.

The study found that, unlike some new media, traditional media such as print or television holds people's attention even when it is used concurrently with other media.

Consumer appetite for regional and local news

People live most of their lives within a relatively small geographic location. They are increasingly interested in local news and information from that area and the local paper is the first place they turn to.

The vast majority of people value local news and believe local newspaper content to be as relevant as ever. Local papers are acknowledged to be the most effective of all media channels, including social media, for generating word of mouth conversations. (IPA Touchpoints Hub 2010)

Lynne Anderson

Local newspapers are the most effective channel for generating word of mouth conversations...

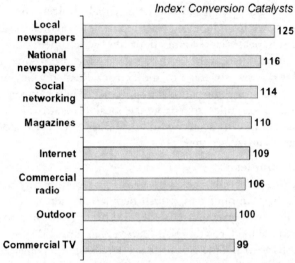

Index: Conversion Catalysts

- Local newspapers: 125
- National newspapers: 116
- Social networking: 114
- Magazines: 110
- Internet: 109
- Commercial radio: 106
- Outdoor: 100
- Commercial TV: 99

(Chart source: IPA Touchpoints Hub)

The local press has more journalists on the ground than any other medium: some ten thousand professionals focused on local news. A study by Ofcom (*Local and Regional Media in the UK*, 2009) pointed out that "*as well as reporting the news, journalists also help to reflect elements that bind local communities together, such as coverage of local sports teams and local events.*"

It concluded:

> "*Local and regional newspapers play a particularly important role in informing, representing, campaigning and interrogating and thus underpinning awareness and participation in the democratic process. Newspaper journalism is also a crucial part of the local and regional media ecology because it supports journalism on other platforms.*"

The importance of the regional and local press in disseminating important local information was demonstrated again during the riots of August 2011, as people turned to their local papers in print and online.

Dominic Ponsford, editor of *Press Gazette*, wrote at the time: "If ever more proof was needed that citizen journalists will never replace professional ones it was provided during the England riots... The vital job those [regional] journalists played in covering the riots and then providing a rallying point for communities showed why the local press still has such a vital and cherished role to play."

A study by TNS-RI (2010) found that 85% of people in the UK believe it is important that their local newspaper keeps them informed about local council issues, while 81% said they would be less informed about council budgets, plans and elections if there wasn't a local newspaper in the area. Local papers are also

255

the first port of call for anyone who wants to raise awareness of a local issue or problem.

The importance of the local press in disseminating vital local information is always highlighted at times of emergency and loss of essential services, such as during flooding or heavy snowfalls. The need to support this pivotal public information work has been repeatedly recognised by the government. Local papers, such as *The Herald* in Plymouth reporting from the front line in Afghanistan or the *Whitehaven News'* coverage of the Derrick Bird shootings in Cumbria, often lead the way on stories of national importance. Their campaigns such as the drive by several local titles to encourage local firms to take on apprentices, and the Newspaper Society's successful Local Business Accelerators initiative, allow communities to grow stronger.

Engaging with local communities

In times of economic hardship, people seek out a sense of community and belonging. The importance of community to British people has increased as a result of the recession, fuelled by a growing sense of local pride, according to a study of nearly five thousand adults (Crowd DNA: *Loving Local*, June 2011).

The research found that 81% of people agreed that the recession has made it more important to support the local community and that local media plays a key role in stimulating pride in their local area.

More people feel they are well integrated into their community than in previous years; 74% of respondents to the study said they felt they were a part of their community – a rise of 11%age points on 2008. People are also more optimistic about issues at a local level – 70% of people believe their local area is improving compared to 32% who believe the country is improving.

Seventy-three per cent of respondents said local media was relevant to having a sense of pride in their area – nearly four times higher than the internet (19%), the next highest medium.

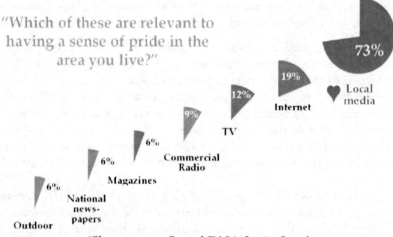

"Which of these are relevant to having a sense of pride in the area you live?"

73%
19% Internet
Local media
12% TV
9% Commercial Radio
6% Magazines
6% National news-papers
6% Outdoor

(Chart source: Crowd DNA *Loving Local*)

Ninety-three per cent of respondents said they liked companies which got involved in the local community and 84% that they were more likely to buy brands that gave something back to the local community.

Local media (73%) was cited as the best medium for making people feel part of their community, followed by the internet (22%), TV (11%), and national newspapers (5%). And local media continues to be the most trusted medium. Forty-five per cent of people said local media contained content they trusted compared to 37% who cited television, the next highest medium.

The findings echo previous research studies which highlighted people's strong and growing attachment to their neighbourhoods (Millward Brown, *Local Matters, 2008*). The study found that the majority of the UK population feel their area is a place where people get on with each other. Nearly twice as many people feel they can influence things at a local level versus nationally.

How local can be positive
One of the main aspects to come out of the research was that people feel a lot happier about matters locally. Perceptions of the local area, public institutions like the NHS, and the local economy are all far more positive at a local level rather than a national one.

People take pride in the area in which they live although this does not appear to be related to the length of time they have been there. People who had lived in an area most of their lives were as likely to agree with this statement as those who had not.

The key factors that appear to determine local pride are: quality of the local economy; quality of public services; institutions; and personal security.

The majority of people are happy with where they live and this is consistent across demographic groups. What came through was the strength of feeling in smaller population centres, with 80% of those in villages and 87% of those in rural areas saying they are happy with the area in which they live while 68% of those in cities and 69% of those in towns saying they are happy with the area.

What are the segments that bind communities?
Community is alive and well, providing individuals across Britain with a sense of identity and culture. The Local Matters study was able to identify six key segments and identify them as making up the fundamental framework of a strong community:

(Chart source: Crowd DNA *Loving Local*)

The level of importance of each segment varies across Britain, life stage and population centre. On the website www.localmattersresearch.co.uk, it is possible to look at each segment and how it varies by regions, life stage and population centre.

The long-established bond of trust between local media and its audience gives a credible and authoritative platform for official messages. This explains why local media is seen as the most relevant platform for delivering messages with information about local institutions, services and facilities.

Family and social interaction
Community means different things to people at different stages in life. The Pre-Family stage can be a relatively selfish time of selective connections with the community. It is surprising therefore that so many people at this stage regarded themselves as connected to their community, although this tended to focus on their interests and passions, most often leisure or sport. Pre-Family respondents to the study have a very positive relationship with their local area, which develops as they get older, jumping when they have young children. Community connection then becomes more functional, revolving around things such as school and healthcare.

Lynne Anderson

ENGAGING FAMILIES IN THE LOCAL COMMUNITY

Which sources are important in feeling part of your local community?

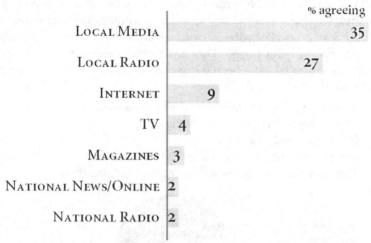

(Chart Source: Millward Brown *Local Matters Research*)

At the Teen Family stage, the focus changes. Although the functional contact points are still in place, the reduced need to keep children entertained allows new activities and social networks to develop.

The Empty Nesters almost revert to the Pre-Family stage in terms of their contact with the community. They have even more spare time and can therefore follow up on interests and activities in their local area.

Geographically, there are some clear differences in perception about where is the best place to bring up children. In the South West, 73% agree that their area is best, compared to 35% in London.

The research showed that local media has a key part to play in engaging people at each stage of their lives.

Sport – passive and active

Passion for sport is well established and its value in engendering pride and recognition locally was highlighted in the research. Across Britain, 21% took part in or attended sporting events regularly but in the North East that figure rose to 26%.

Passion and support for football teams in the area is well known but the level of participation is perhaps not quite as obvious to outsiders. Participation in local sports events in the North East (18%) is 20% higher than the average across Britain (15%). The local media industry has a unique insight into the particular nuances of different communities on issues such as sport.

Participation in sport is still very strong combined with enthusiasm for attending sports events. The cult of the "local hero" instigates a strong sense of pride and local media is the key source of information about this.

Five essential beliefs about local press

While the traditional pillars of community have changed, it is clear that community remains a highly valued concept. It is also clear that people feel far more positively about issues closer to home than they do about similar issues at a national level. Local media is clearly hugely important to all aspects of community life, helping people keep up to date with local news and issues. Research has identified what people regard as the five core reasons for engaging with their local paper:

- It helps them get the best out of where they live
- It helps them feel part of the community
- It is honest and believable
- It is more accurate and reliable than other media
- They can rely on it for news they cannot get elsewhere

(Chart Source: GfK/NOP Media *the wanted ads*)

The content of local papers is relevant to people's engagement with their local community and reflects the real issues that affect people's day-to-day lives.

So just how important is local news and the role of the local paper to the concept of localness and community? Media commentator and former *Guardian* editor Peter Preston summed it up perfectly in his recent article for Local Newspaper Week:

> *"Journalism isn't about sitting in some lofty office thinking great thoughts. It is about knowing the people you're writing for, understanding their concerns, their hopes and fears. And you can only do that if you're out there amongst them, being part of the community you aim to serve."*

Peter learned his trade on Liverpool's big regional daily newspapers.

> *"I did funerals, Rotary Club speeches, dog shows, council rows and rugby matches. And at the end of that stint, when I moved on to cover local politics for the Guardian, I think I'd learned something precious. That politics doesn't exist in some rarefied world at Westminster. That democracy lives, breathes and reacts in the minds and the lives of the people you catch a bus to work with every morning. That the local dimension isn't some remote stepladder on the route to the top. It's where everything begins. It's the foundation stone of society.*
>
> *"And that's as true today as it ever was. Your local paper, in villages, towns and cities up and down the land, is there to reflect you, yourself – your own running commentary on life. In the mazy world of the world-wide web, where nothing seems more than a click away, it is still the place where the people around you put down their roots.*
>
> *"There's been a local press in Britain for as long as there have been newspapers. There will be newspapers – in one form or another – for as long as people care about what happens around them. News is a necessity, your link to your neighbours. Prize it, relish it, support it."*

Note on the author

Lynne Anderson is Communications and Marketing Director at the Newspaper Society, the association representing Britain's local media industry.

The future needs radical action

Long-term management failure has brought the industry to edge of the precipice, argues Neil Fowler. Now it's time not just for innovation – but for radical thinking, economically and politically.

In the time since the end of the last war, the regional newspaper industry was basically held back by a combination of weak management and the intransigence of the print craft unions.

This meant that when three golden eggs were laid in the 1980s – the sale of Reuters shares being the first, which funded the second by buying out the unions and investing in new technology and colour presses, all of which was followed by the third of economic growth in the Thatcher era – managements and owners did not generally have the appropriate skills and vision to exploit them in an imaginative manner.

Until then the main preoccupation had been focused on the print unions and just getting the paper out. Forward thinking had not been not an integral part of day-to-day life.

There had been some innovations – notably the launching of a ring of suburban evening newspapers around London in the 1960s – but there was little else. Research and development, the staple of most other industries, was simply ignored.

Essentially the long-term decline in readership, which began in the early 1960s, and the decline in the sales of regional daily newspapers in particular, that began in the late 1970s, was masked by the massive growth in classified advertising – and especially the situations vacant category.

Newspaper paginations mushroomed, profits grew massively and all was rosy – until the Internet came along and stole those rivers of gold, as Rupert Murdoch named them.

Politically, ownership rules have lain untouched for a generation or more. Misguided views on plurality amongst policy makers have, I believe, held back the industry.

And all the while society and people's lifestyles were changing. The industry knew it but hoped that its superficial responses would allow it to carry on it the same old way. It was wrong.

A failure to innovate

The regional and local newspaper sector did not research the future in the way that almost every other sector of industry does as a matter of course. During the golden years of high profits between 1989 and 2005 it could have looked ahead but failed to do so? It did not research its customer base effectively. It looked at how readers interacted with the newspaper products themselves but did not look at how their lifestyles were changing.

New product development was seen as short-term way of making more money, rather than a long-term way of investigating new routes for the business.

The groups failed to experiment as the changing market place became apparent. Having thirteen or fourteen daily centres meant that different business models could have been tried. They weren't. The sole attempt to be truly radical was by the *Manchester Evening News* in the mid 2000s when it launched it part-paid/part-free distribution system. Few other trials of any other radical note ever took place.

Giving all a newspaper's output away for free on the web has been a disaster. The message that the Internet would be the new rivers of gold was always false.

Dreaming up new brands for newspaper websites has also been and continues to be, with a few exceptions, a disaster too. I can buy a Mars bar in a variety of forms, I can buy Fairy detergent in different styles – but if want to read the *Leicester Mercury* online I have to go to thisisleicestershire.com and then struggle to be sure that it actually is the same brand that has been established for well over 125 years. Politicians have believed that phone hacking on one newspaper out of 1200 is the real issue that bedevils the media. They are wrong and need to begin listening to the industry – and perhaps, to those who read newspapers, too.

The fear of the concentration of ownership and a lack of plurality has been overblown. The editor dancing to the tune of a power-crazed proprietor does not exist in the regions. And never has done.

But the groups allowed distant ownership to become a problem, when careful management could easily have negated it. Senior executives have been viewed by their staffs, both senior and junior, as being too focused on one figure, the bottom line and not taking a more longer-term view. Even now, in this economic climate, there are some (not many I admit) news businesses making 30 per cent margins. No one I spoke to understood how this will help the survival of brands in the future. At one point in the 1980s the CEOs of the big four chains were all graduates of various parts of the Thomson empire – 'Thomson-trained' was seen as a badge of honour thanks to the legacy of a businessman who combined care of the profit figure along with a desire for future security.

As those leaders left the industry they were replaced with those from a different school of business and from outside the industry. That many were to enjoy substantial monetary rewards, and continue to enjoy them in times of businesses shrinking rapidly, has not helped their image at all.

Most worryingly of all is that they did not believe it would end. An end to boom and bust was not just a parliamentary cry. Senior executives did not see the damage that the Internet would bring. They did not see that its arrival would merely conclude what had been happening for decades.

The necessary pain of cost-cutting

But equally I must say what has been done correctly:

The industry has been right to cut costs as much as possible. The mistakes of high operating margins was not in making them, it was not using some of them for genuine research and development. Press sharing should have taken place years ago and back office centralisation is a necessity that every business of whatever sector seeks to achieve. Cost cutting has been painful but has been necessary. Even the family-owned businesses that have seen their circulations perform better have not been protected from this assault.

But managements must ensure that enough resource remains to provide the right kind of service that readers will pay for. I say this because no one I have spoken on all sides of the debate has been able to say what could have been done differently to prevent the advertising model changing so radically with the Internet.

It may be that local newspapers are a victim of a vicious combination of a changed socio-economic environment and advanced technology. Even the most far-sighted of managements may not have proved to be up to the challenge.

There was an attempt by the industry to seek unity of purpose when it developed the Fish4 brand for classified advertising – but no agreement could be reached and that it is why it struggled until it came under one owner in Trinity Mirror.

But to have succeeded it would have had to have done something so counter-intuitive that it would have been almost impossible to sell to its shareholders and to maintain credibility – and that would have been to have included jobs advertising at knock-down prices – and so lose vast amounts of revenue before the power of the Internet really became apparent. They would have had to invent Monster.com or even eBay before they'd been invented themselves.

There have been attempts to diversify – brand extensions into book publishing, events and other activities – but they were never going to replace the core purpose of the business – the collating and the passing on of local information.

They have been right to become more aggressive on cover prices. Small can be beautiful. Sir Ray Tindle has proved that success can come about with careful husbandry and without acquiring huge debt. His papers may be small – but they have retained their markets and look after them. And at the age of eighty two he is not finished. He launched four newspapers in 2011. He also has a pay wall on his websites. Some news is offered – but you pay if you want to read the product in full.

What must happen now?

I hope people are willing to listen. There needs to be a fully-rounded debate.

The current coalition government has said it recognises the difficulties the regional and local press is facing.

It has said that it intends to change ownership regulations to make it easier for groups to buy, sell, and swap titles to enable some greater geographical grouping – well, as we saw with the Kent Messenger Group fiasco, it has failed at the first attempt with what should have been a logical, easy and straightforward decision to allow it to buy seven newspapers in Kent from Northcliffe.

The Kent Messenger Group is not a business that has milked huge profits over the years. Arguably if it had been more ruthless and driven for higher margins in the 1989 to 2007 period, its path through the last four years would have been easier. As its profit margins didn't have so far to fall, once the pincers of structural and economic came it had immediate problems.

The deal, had it been allowed to happen, would have been good for Kent, good for the industry and a sign that the government actually understood what the position of the sector is.

The government, through culture secretary Jeremy Hunt and business secretary Vince Cable, must show that it understands there is a crisis in the funding of general news in this country – specifically for regional dailies as well as the quality end of the national market and that this is the real media issue of our times.

The model of news being subsidised by advertising is broken and cannot be fixed, but more than just platitudes from our policy-makers is now required.

Consolidation and title swapping should be made easier, especially geographically. Plurality is a red herring with the competition for both advertising and comment created by the Internet and should not used to hold up further mergers. These changes will not necessarily produce vast savings – but will help. The industry should press this case as soon as possible – and the government should make the right signals too.

The industry should continue the bold moves instigated by Northcliffe Newspapers at Lincoln, Scunthorpe, Torquay and Exeter (and followed by Trinity Mirror with the Liverpool *Daily Post*) in turning some of its daily titles to weekly production. Over the last year it converted four of its daily titles to weeklies – on the back of a successful change to the *Bath Chronicle* four years ago. These are radical attempts to find solutions for the long-term and should be encouraged.

Readership, rather than sales and impressions should become the new currency to sell to advertisers. In Canada newspapers focus on NadBank, the agency that produces readership figures. ABC sales figures are very much second division.

An orderly default

Moves should be made to help the three PLCs – Johnston Press and Trinity Mirror in this country and Gannet in the US – to have, in the words of the moment, an orderly default on their debts.

This is not to allow them off the hook in any way – or to forge a path for them to continue as they have been operating. But it is an acceptance for both the businesses themselves and those who own their debts that it is almost impossible for that debt ever to be paid off and to have any business of substance remaining.

Ashley Highfield, the new CEO at Johnston, has already said that attempts are being made to restructure its loans, but I can't see that being enough.

All three are stuck in a no-man's land of inertia. Their shares are all very low – the individual parts of their companies are clearly more than the present sums – Johnston has a market capitilisation of around £30m and Trinity Mirror just over £100m. In March 2005, Trinity Mirror was in the FTSE 250 index with its shares at around £7.29. Since then the index has grown by 40% yet Trinity Mirror shares have sunk by 93%.

They are pulling as much cash as possible out of their businesses, by very tight cost control (i.e. job losses) to service their debts, which is in turn causing those businesses long-term damage. The companies may argue that they are still profitable and that they have strategies in place to pay off this debt but, as one analyst said to me, the City has lost interest in them.

A return to local

They have futures as news business brokers, providing print, back office and technology services to the industry – but I believe a way of returning titles to local ownership is required. Here there is a very basic analogy with the 72 football clubs outside the Premiership that, in the main, are supported by groups of local business people. Those business people tend to believe often for vanity purposes, that it is good for their hometown to have a high profile football club.

The case must be made for the return of the locally-owned news business, supported by local enterprises, so that local engagement is maximised. It is good that towns and cities have their own news providers. This recommendation is not at odds with further consolidation. Having news business brokers providing cost effective support services will be a necessity for re-localised enterprises.

And in the case of DMGT it must decide whether it is in or out. Its Northcliffe division has made handsome profits for it for 90 years and propped up its Daily Mail for decades. To be fair Northcliffe is now being highly innovative in it approach to the market – but for DMGT it barely merits a mention in the annual report. DMGT could lead the way and find a home for these titles amongst local businesses.

The government should include the recommendations of the recent Reuters Institute for the Study of Journalism report on the potential of charitable and trust ownership of newspapers in its forthcoming Communications Green Paper. This important piece of work sets out the case for a new way of looking at the funding of news and should become part of the agenda.

In this Green Paper the government should also examine ways in which the tax system can be used to assist local entrepreneurs, business people and individuals to buy back into the ownership of local media.

Start charging for online

University media schools should move from their pre-occupations with the study of journalism to include much more of the study of the business of journalism. They should work more with their sibling business schools to help the industry find real solutions to its woes. I believe there is a gap in the market here ripe for filling.

The industry still has time to experiment, to try new models and be brave. There remains a demand for local and regional news and no one else can provide it with the same level of expertise and independence than the existing news businesses. It should work together more to share risk and results – what will work for one may well work for another.

Start charging for some online content – and hold your nerve. Ditch fancy website names and use your brands – their value is immense.

And it may be the time to restrict mass free distribution of titles. Competition law does not allow rival titles to co-operate but with the cost of newsprint the move towards pick-up must be accelerated as well as the move back to some form of pay wall.

There remains a level of local advertising that is available to traditional businesses. However, much of it is being scooped under the radar by local entrepreneurs and franchises that are developing solid advertising-driven glossy magazines delivered to highly targeted areas.

An intelligent debate

In all this bloggers and members of the public will have their part to play, but the fundamental question remains: who will cover Hartlepool Magistrates' Court on a wet Wednesday afternoon? It will not be a well-meaning amateur and has to be a professional journalist – the question is how will it be paid for?

Finally, let all of us in the industry have an intelligent and realistic debate about the real state of this business and how it got there. And let this debate be soon.

There's an awful lot of scrutiny, human interest and fact about our localities that we risk losing if we don't get this right.

Politicians and bankers have a role to play with the industry in getting this right for the future. This is a genuine societal issue – and society will lose if a route is not found through this current crisis.

Note on the author

Neil Fowler was the 2010/11 Guardian Research Fellow at Nuffield College, Oxford where he investigated the decline of the UK regional and local newspaper sector. This chapter is based on the lecture he gave at the end of his Fellowship. Previously he was editor of four provincial dailies in England and Wales as well as *Which?* magazine. He was also publisher of the *Toronto Sun*. He has just been appointed Director of Creative and Content at Headlines Corporate News Ltd. His full end-of-fellowship report, from which this lecture was taken can be found at www.nuffield.ox.ac.uk